Literary Theory

LITERARY THEORY

A Practical Introduction

Second Edition

Michael Ryan

Blackwell
Publishing

@ 1999, 2007 by Michael Ryan

BLACKWELL PUBLISHING
350 Main Street, Malden, MA 02148-5020, USA
9600 Garsington Road, Oxford OX4 2DQ, UK
550 Swanston Street, Carlton, Victoria 3053, Australia

First edition published 1999
Second edition published 2007 by Blackwell Publishing Ltd

3   2008

Library of Congress Cataloging-in-Publication Data

Ryan, Michael, 1951–
Literary theory : a practical introduction / Michael Ryan.—2nd ed.
        p.   cm.
Includes bibliographical references and index.
ISBN 978-1-4051-0719-8 (hardcover : alk. paper)
ISBN 978-1-4051-0720-4 (pbk. : alk. paper)
1. Literature—Philosophy.   2. Literature—History and criticism—Theory,
etc.   I. Title.
PN45.R93 2007
801—dc22
2006019315

A catalogue record for this title is available from the British Library.

Set in 10 on 12.5 pt Sabon
by SNP Best-set Typesetter Ltd, Hong Kong
Printed and bound in Singapore
by Markono Print Media Pte Ltd

The publisher's policy is to use permanent paper from mills that operate a sustainable
forestry policy, and which has been manufactured from pulp processed using
acid-free and elementary chlorine-free practices. Furthermore, the publisher ensures
that the text paper and cover board used have met acceptable environmental
accreditation standards.

For further information on
Blackwell Publishing, visit our website:
www.blackwellpublishing.com

for E. P. Kuhl and Robert Scholes,
for teaching me how to read

Contents

Contents

Note to Teachers

Literary Theory: A Practical Introduction should be used with the following literary texts:

Elizabeth Bishop, *The Complete Poems*
Elizabeth Bishop, "In the Village"
Joseph Conrad, *Heart of Darkness*
Kiran Desai, *The Inheritance of Loss*
Henry James, *The Aspern Papers*
Toni Morrison, *The Bluest Eye*
Alice Munro, *Friend of My Youth*
William Shakespeare, *King Lear*

I find the 1997 National Theatre production of *King Lear* directed by Richard Eyre and starring Ian Holm to be an especially good way to get students to engage with the play. It is an excellent production, and it is available on DVD.

CHAPTER 1

Formalism

One of the first things one notices about literature is that it consists of language that has been formed and shaped so that it no longer looks like ordinary language. It is easy to tell a novel from a weather report. Usually, such shaping and forming serves the end of telling imaginary stories, or of evoking intense emotions, or of communicating ideas. People who thought about literature in the early twentieth century were called "formalists" because they said literature is unique because of how it is done (form) rather than what it is about (content). A novel may be interesting because it is about the "hypocrisy of the bourgeoisie" or "the dangers of passionate love," but it is worthy of study because it is executed in a way that is innovative, compelling, or significant. Its form makes it unique.

For some formalists, known as the Russian formalists, how literature is written, not what it is about, constitutes the essential component of literature that distinguishes it from other kinds of writing such as history or science. The language of literature is different from ordinary, everyday language because it has been bent away from habitual usage. This bending and shaping constitutes what these theorists called form. Literary study, they felt, should focus on this dimension of literature only.

The Russian formalists took issue with the notion that form is merely a clothing attached to meaning. Rather, they contended, form stands on its own and is what makes literature "literary." Form is not "motivated" by meaning. It has its own autonomous rules and history. The history of tragic drama is not a history of the different ideas expressed in the plays; rather, it is a history of how the form has changed, how its conventions have evolved. Form thus has no "correlation" with content. What matters in literature is not meaning but the literary techniques, devices, and procedures that writers use.

Shakespeare's *King Lear*, in this view, is an important object of literary analysis not for its ideas about human life but for its technical devices. Its themes of family betrayal and personal failure are worthy of discussion, but to study what is literary about the play is not to study ideas. They are rightly the province of sociology or history or psychology. Literary analysis should be concerned with how the play is constructed, how language is used, what imagery is found in it, and the like.

Tolstoy's *Anna Karenina*, for example, is a novel about adultery, but what distinguishes it from a sociological study of the phenomenon is the way it is executed. At one point, Tolstoy recounts a horse race from the perspective of a rider in the race. This unique and novel device could be connected to thematic issues, such as the way stasis and motion are aligned with characters in such a way as to explain Anna's attraction for her future lover, who is the jockey. But for the Russian formalists, the more important quality of the narrative moment is the device itself and the unique point of view on the action it creates for the reader. By placing us in the rider's seat, Tolstoy takes us out of our ordinary universe of experience in much the same way that the officer takes Anna out of her ordinary world of experience. We not only hear an idea about the origins of adultery; we actually enact the reality of a disturbing and exciting new experience.

In another famous example, Tolstoy tells an entire story from the point of view of a horse. In another, flogging is described with a geometrical detachment and a calculated precision that force the reader to see anew – and to feel the shock of – a practice that might otherwise seem routine and acceptable. The device is unsettling, but that, according to Russian formalist Viktor Shklovsky, is precisely the point. Good literature disturbs us and takes us out of our habitual and routine ways of seeing the world. It does so by bending and contorting language so that we cannot use it as we usually might to facilitate the kind of rote understandings of the world that allow us to get through our days. The repetitious nature of life dulls our senses and makes the world overly familiar. We cease to see things vividly. By bending language to new uses and new ways of seeing and understanding, literature reawakens our senses and defamiliarizes the world.

The invention of new formal devices and techniques also, according to the Russian formalists, makes possible new content in literature. Earlier theorists of literature had argued that ideas dictate form, but the formalists turned this around and contended that form gives rise to content.

In the Middle Ages in western Europe, for example, literature was dominated by stories about knights. In the Arthurian romances, knights pursued quests aligned with religious goals. The characters were static and usually embodied virtues such as steadfastness or courage. With the decline of feudalism and of the martial court culture that sustained such literary forms, new forms emerged that embodied the more secular and materialist values and ideals of the new middle class or "bourgeoisie." Shklovsky argues that one of the first modern novels written during this period – Cervantes' *Don Quixote*, a story of a man who imagines himself to be a knight from one of the medieval romances – develops a new form that makes possible an entirely new kind of hero. While the romance hero is static and unchanging, Quixote is pliable because the new narrative form strings together episodes rather than moving in a single plot line. The new episodic narrative form makes it possible to have a hero that can change from situation to situation. Form, in this instance, determines content and not the other way around.

A pure Russian formalist reading of a literary text would attend to form alone without any reference to content. Not all formalists, however, thought the form of a work was the only thing worth studying. Some concerned themselves with the relationship between form and meaning, the essential link between the different ways language is used and the ideas such uses communicate. For the American "New Critics," who dominated American literary discussion in the mid-twentieth century, literary form is welded to content or meaning in an organic unity.

Cleanth Brooks noticed that writers often rely on a particular language shape known as paradox that brings together two contrary qualities or values, such as "the last shall be first." They do so, according to Brooks, because this particular form of expression embodies an essential quality of human experience. There are many versions of such paradoxes in literature and culture. In *King Lear*, for example, a man is blinded, but only then does he truly see what is going on around him. In *The Matrix*, a young man must die in order to be reborn as the person he truly is. In John Keats' poem "Ode on a Grecian Urn," the vivid experience of life is paradoxically captured most truly in the "cold pastoral" scene painted on a vase. According to Brooks, paradox is the only way of expressing or describing the unity of the eternal and the temporal, the universal and the momentary.

The New Critics were concerned with the universal aspects of human experience. Such universals, they believed, are true of everyone everywhere, and "great" literature captures them best. Such universals are general or abstract rather than specific and concrete, but literature makes them concrete. Since the time of the New Critics in the mid-twentieth century, literary scholars have come to question the idea that a writer like Shakespeare can indeed write plays that describe "universals" that apply equally to peasant women in India and wealthy aristocrats in Renaissance England. This is not to say that there are not universal ideas in the world or in literature. It is to note, rather, that the world, with all of its specific differences of wealth and station and status and power, does not allow all universal ideas to be equally applicable everywhere. Even a very abstract universal truth such as "hard work is usually rewarded" is belied by the educational system in the United States, for example, where children with similar test scores from different economic backgrounds fare differently in education. Those from wealthy backgrounds attend and graduate college more often than their poorer counterparts. Similarly intelligent children in rural India might not even have a choice.

Moreover, the works of literature that seem most universal often are the most religious or idealist. The New Critics were able to confirm their hypothesis about literature by choosing examples from eras such as the Renaissance and Romanticism when religious idealism – the belief that there is a spiritual world behind or outside the physical world – was taken seriously. Writers therefore wrote in a way that confirmed the New Critics' essentially religious and idealist view of literature.

Exercise 1.1   William Shakespeare, *King Lear*

The method of "close reading" for which the New Critics are famous seeks to demonstrate how meaning inheres in the form of a work. A New Critic would seek in the play examples of irony and paradox, especially ones that represent a successful reconciliation of the universal and the concrete. In one of the dominant image patterns of the play, for example, two opposing values are joined in a single formulation. What is prized is suddenly despised, what without worth suddenly valued. The powerful and the powerless change places, and the virtuous are branded as vicious. Both the action and the imagery of the play are characterized by such paradoxes and ironic inversions. The pattern is evident in Lear's caution to Cordelia: "Mend your speech a little, lest you mar your fortunes." The two characters are close yet distant at this point in the play, joined by blood yet separated by judgment, and the image evokes phonetic alliteration or proximity (mend, mar) only to draw attention to a more destructive dissonance or disjunction (between repairing something and harming it).

How might such paradoxes be said to fuse a universal idea and a concrete example?

In the same scene, France draws attention to the social inversion that Lear's rashness begets: "Fairest Cordelia, that art most rich, being poor, / Most choice, forsaken, and most loved, despised." These paradoxes underscore Lear's folly, the fact that his actions invert the right order of things. The images embody the sense of social disorder created when valuable things are disvalued and worthless ones elevated.

How do these paradoxes become a way of demonstrating what is truly valuable in the world as well as what, despite its apparent value in a worldly sense, is in fact without value?

In pursuing your own New Critical reading of the play, you might consider other paradoxes associated with sight, clothing, and madness.

A Russian formalist analysis of the play would be less concerned with universal ideas and more concerned with how the actual form of the play – its devices and procedures of dramatic construction – functions.

For example, rather than begin with a direct presentation of Lear, as one might expect from the title of the play, the play begins instead in a mode of indirect presentation. It tells his story initially through the voices of Kent and Gloucester. We learn in their conversation that Lear is both unpredictable and difficult to know: "It did always seem so to us [that Lear favored one duke over another]; but now in the division of the kingdom it appears not which of the Dukes he values most." The device of indirect presentation of the main character thus coheres with the theme of the opening scene. This theme – that people's real intentions are difficult to know – becomes part of one of the major themes of the play – that one cannot trust what people say because real intentions can be different from professed feelings. These themes in turn link to the political argument of the play – that strong monarchs are necessary to maintain control over the unpredictability and treachery to which people are prone.

A small, seemingly inconsequential dramatic device or formal procedure can thus have quite broad ramifications.

In the scene that follows in the play, we learn just how dangerous and harmful language can be. It is a medium without any built-in guarantees of truthfulness. It can be wielded to deceive someone who makes the mistake of taking for granted that words mean what they say. But as a form of verbal representation, an image rather than a thing, language has the potential to create a semblance of truthfulness and of accurate representation where there is none. The procedure of indirect presentation in the opening scene thus evokes themes that will prove central to the play's core concerns. By placing the audience in a position of faulty knowledge (we only partially know Lear at the outset and only hear of him obliquely), the play formally executes one of its principal thematic concerns. It alerts the audience to the opacity of others' motives and inner thoughts, and inscrutability will be a major motivator of plot action throughout the rest of the play.

The procedure of indirect presentation also, of course, decenters and distances Lear as a character. We are instructed by the procedure not to take his speeches in the scene that follows Gloucester and Kent's conversation as seriously as we might had he been presented to us directly, in his own voice, as it were. His words are deprived of some of the authority they might have possessed had not the procedure of indirect presentation framed his entry, and we are positioned to consider him a character to be observed and perhaps even criticized rather than identified with.

A Russian formalist would also notice the bawdy language of the opening dialogue, which is filled with puns and ribald innuendo. The low language of gossip in the initial dialogue between Kent and Gloucester is strikingly at odds with the language of high statecraft in the scene that follows. The more florid speech is associated with Lear's delusions regarding his daughters' affections and with his daughters' false flattery. And as we learn in later scenes, popular speech, in the form of the Fool's instructive taunts and Edgar's mad speeches, has a crucial redemptive effect on Lear. A victim of flattery, with its inflated and false images, he learns from the Fool and from Edgar, both of whose speech is laced with raw, literal, bodily imagery, the truth of what the real state of the world is, without the adornment of rhetorical inflation or of artifice.

The low or bawdy speech of the opening dialogue, therefore, which at first has a defamiliarizing effect that upsets our expectations regarding a tragedy about kings, in fact instantiates a crucial procedure at work throughout the play. The use of low language deflates the pretensions of high language and guides perceptions toward truth and away from falseness. In this initial instance, it prepares us to hear Lear's inflated high speech in the rest of the first scene as being at odds with reality. It is certainly quite different from the more plain style associated with Gloucester's honest acknowledgment of adulterous reality in the opening dialogue, a style that will be linked throughout the play with virtue and innate nobility.

The motif of the sexual pun in the dialogue between Kent and Gloucester ("Do you smell a fault?", "I cannot conceive you") has a similar function. The puns imply that words can have two meanings, one hidden or implicit, the other explicit. Such linguistic duality is at the origin of the political crisis of the play. Goneril and Regan can deceive Lear only because words can have more than one meaning, and the public or explicit meaning may have nothing to do with the private and withheld meaning.

Such duality also bears importantly on the play's theme of true nobility or virtue. The topic of the initial conversation between Kent and Gloucester is the difference between Gloucester's two sons – the illegitimate Edmund and the legitimate Edgar. As the same word can have two meanings, so the same object – a son – can have two different social meanings. Gloucester's refusal to accept the inverse valuation of his sons – one legitimate, the other illegitimate – which feudal society imposes foreshadows a failure to differentiate truly noble from falsely noble in the scene that follows. For Gloucester, Edgar is "no dearer in my account" than Edmund, but for Lear, Cordelia will be much less in his account for not having flattered him. Lear fails to read his daughters' speeches as Kent and Gloucester read each other's in the opening dialogue, which is to say, as puns, as acts of language with dual meanings. Lear fails to read Goneril and Regan's praise as an expression of dislike and Cordelia's silence as an expression of love.

Of the opening dialogue, finally, a formalist might note that the action occurs out of the way of the principal events with which the play is concerned. Compared to the declarations of Lear that follow immediately, it has more the quality of an aside. Moreover, its topics are an event (adultery, illegitimate birth) that occurred behind the scenes of legitimate social action and a hidden intention kept from public view ("it appears not which of the Dukes he values most"). The behind-the-scenes quality of the opening dialogue might thus be said to dramatize the problem of hidden intentions (kept behind the scenes of public statements) that will bring about Lear's downfall. As it is difficult to decipher Lear's thoughts, so also will it be difficult to know Goneril and Regan's real feelings. And as it is difficult to know the difference between the legitimate and the illegitimate son and heir, so also it will be difficult to know where true nobility lies – in the frank Cordelia or in the more rhetorical Regan and Goneril. That the play begins off center stage suggests the position it will advocate in these debates: truth is not a matter of external show and consists not of staged words but of true feelings that are necessarily experienced out of view – "Speak what we feel, not what we ought to say." Legitimate nobility or virtue will also prove to be a matter of internal noble qualities rather than external public display. The fore-stage, the play itself suggests in its opening background dialogue, is a realm of deception. The motif of indirect presentation through an initial aside therefore serves an important function. It frames what follows as a dramatization of the play's lesson regarding truth and value, and its own use of language and staging suggests already what the point of that lesson will be.

A Russian formalist approach would seek out devices or literary procedures that seem important in themselves, without any connection to meaning. Consider the structure of the plot. What are the different "moves" in the plot? By "move" would be meant an event like "betrayal" or "enlightenment." If you draw a map of the moves in each parallel plot, what parallels or differences do you notice?

Exercise 1.2   Elizabeth Bishop, "The Moose" and "At the Fishhouses"

"The Moose" is an elegy, a kind of poem written on the occasion of someone's death that offers a way of understanding or coming to terms with death. Dedicated to Bishop's recently deceased aunt, its point of departure is a bus journey Bishop took back to New England from Nova Scotia after attending her aunt's funeral. The poem required almost two decades to compose, so its apparent simplicity belies a great deal of careful crafting. The union of simple narrative (a bus journey) and grand thematic concern (how to understand death) would appeal to a New Critic interested in the way universal meanings and concrete particulars are welded together in poetry, while a Russian Formalist would be attracted by the high degree of "literariness" evident in Bishop's crafted use of rhythm, rhyme, euphony, repetition, and metaphor.

The poem seems entirely concerned with the careful observation and precise description of ordinary events and objects, from a dog's bark to moonlight in the woods, yet this simple concern can be related to the issue of life and death on which the poem ultimately dwells. Observation and description occur at the surface where human consciousness or subjectivity encounter objective world, and that surface is also the line which distinguishes life from death, the human or subjective from the thingly or objective world. To cross that line is to move from the vivid to the inanimate. The way the poem describes objects, therefore, itself bears on the issue of death, and the form that the contact between mind

and world assumes can be understood as having a thematic consequence. A fearful attitude toward death would posit the world as inanimate object. The mind's contact with the world would from this
perspective be with an entirely alien realm, and the subject's passage
into objectivity in death would be understood as simple extinction.
Subject and object, awareness and world, thus come to have the meaning
of life and death.

But it is possible to imagine the relation between life and death,
subject and object, awareness and things in other ways, and that is what
"The Moose" is about. The task of the elegiac poet is to conceive of
death in such a way that it no longer inspires fear, and addressing that
task takes the form in the poem of a journey of consciousness from an
initial external perspective that observes the world in its separate objectivity to an immersion in human subjectivity that emphasizes such
human powers and capacities as memory, imagination, and naming to,
finally, a vision of an object that is itself a subject and that provokes a
kind of communion across the line dividing subjective awareness from
the world of objects. The very simple recording of observations of
natural things and everyday events in the poem is therefore also about
the very human problem of how to confront one's own naturalness and
objectivity, one's own final belonging to the world.

The "narrative" of the poem has four parts: the first is concerned
with the movement of the bus through the landscape as seen from the
outside; the second records the onset of evening; the third describes the
nighttime events inside the bus from the perspective of the speaker; and
finally, in part four, the moose appears. The first six stanzas of the poem
consist of one lengthy sentence which begins with an unusually long
introductory clause ("From narrow provinces . . .") and whose subject
and verbs are "a bus journeys west" in line 2 of stanza 5 and "waits,
patient" in line 2 of stanza 6. The effect of this form is to emphasize
the predominance of the landscape over the subject, the immersion of
the bus in the world around it. In the unusual form of the sentence, the
centrality human subjectivity usually accords itself is displaced. If the
bus is a figure for humanity or for the "lone traveller" of stanza 6, then
already in this poem it is portrayed as part of a world that in a profound
manner precedes and exceeds it. Even when the bus finally is named as
the subject, it is described in a way that emphasizes its placement within
nature: the windshield reflects the sunlight, the sunlight glances off and
brushes the metal, and the bus's side is called a "flank," an animal simile
that foreshadows the moose and metaphorically implants the human
vehicle in the natural world.

The delayed presentation of the subject also unsettles and defamiliarizes the distinction between human and natural worlds through a confusion of reference. The word "where" occurs three times in the first three stanzas as a modifier of "provinces," but stanza 4 begins with a clause that modifies by anticipation the bus: "on red, gravelly roads." The uninterrupted flow of reading, facilitated by the parallel of "where" clauses and the "on" clause, merges the description of the provinces with the description of the bus and further underscores the inseparability of the human and natural worlds by making the referent of "on" seem the same as that of "where." At first, one seems to be reading about provinces, and only when one reaches the next stanza does one realize that a shift has occurred and that provinces have given way to the bus as the object of the modifier.

The merged inseparability of the human and the natural is made emphatic in the use of rhythm, rhyme, and alliteration in the first four stanzas. From the "fish and bread and tea" of line 2 to "the bay not at home" of line 12, Bishop characterizes nature with metaphors of human domesticity and uses the repetition of sounds to suggest the naturalness of human civilization's constructs. The civilized "roads" of stanza 4, line 1, are echoed in the "rows of sugar maples" in the next line, and the "ap" sound of "maples" carries over into the "clapboard" of the following two lines – the "clapboard farmhouses" which are echoed in "clapboard churches," a repetition that links human subjective concerns such as religion with work on nature. If natural woods can become literal wood for human construction, the rhyme of "churches" and "birches" intimates a more profound congruence between the two worlds.

That congruence also takes the form of a mirroring between realms. The rhythm of such parallel lines as "the bay coming in, / the bay not at home" mimes the movement of the tides coming in and going out, while qualifiers like "veins" suggest that nature's work on itself is akin to a living organism. This crossing assumes a humorous form at the end of this first part where the "collie supervises" and the bus "waits, patient."

Nature itself is characterized by a harmonic mirroring between its parts that makes the bus's journey into it – a metaphor for the passage into death – seem not so much a loss of life and a fall into cold objectivity as a move from one realm of vividness into another. The rhythmic alternation of vowel sounds in the opening stanzas, for example, suggests a nature that breathes in and out while circulating water like blood (the "silted red," "red sea," and "lavender" of stanza 3). The repeated o's of line one ("From narrow provinces") alternate with a's, e's, and i's in line 2 ("of fish and bread and tea"), then with o's again in line 3 ("home of the long tides") and with e's and a's again in lines 4 and 5 ("where the bay leaves the sea / twice a day and takes"), before line 6 harmonically unites the three alternating sounds – "the herrings long rides."

Stanza 2 performs a similar alternation of sounds to match the description of water filling and emptying a bay. Now e and i sounds ("where if the river / enters or retreats") contrast with a's and o's ("in a wall of brown foam") to match the swing of the tides ("the bay coming in, / the bay not at home"). The "er" of "enters" and the "re" of "retreats" ("enters or retreats") enact the same kind of syllabic mirroring. Such mirroring, if it extends to all realms, both human and natural, implies that the harmony of the observed world balances a harmony in the human observer, and indeed the reading experience would suggest that the verbal form of the poem through these first few stanzas posits in the reader/observer a sense of orderly congruence with the world. This would explain why stanzas 5 and 6 are characterized by images of a mesh between human and natural worlds, from the "dented flank" of the bus which flashes sunlight as if it were paint to the family scene that includes the supervisory collie. If nature is domestic, so also the human is natural, and it is so in a way that is itself perfectly domestic. To be in the world is to be at home.

One might by now glean how the poem might be said to allude to the question of death even though it has yet explicitly to do so. Like the opening sentence which implants its subject within its object ("through the landscape the bus journeys" rather than "the bus journeys through the landscape"), the poem places humanity within a natural world characterized predominantly by a rhythmic alternation of movement and counter-movement. The effect of the second possible narrative pattern – the bus journeys through the landscape – would have been to privilege the activity of the subject on the object. The pattern chosen instead emphasizes the passivity of the subject as it encounters an object larger and more powerful than itself. The subject is therefore a part of something whose movements anticipate its own. That those movements consist of an alternation of contrasting elements ("coming in," "not at home") suggests that the death figuratively alluded to in the bus's westward journey will not be conceivable in any way other than as an alternation, rhythmic and necessary, with a counter-movement that forms a complete strophe akin to the poem's alternating vocalic patterns. One effect of the form of the poem, therefore, is to imply without stating a way of understanding death that fulfills elegiac expectations. It will be understood as part of natural life.

If the natural world of part 1 is accommodating, even comforting in its domesticity and vocalic harmony, in part 2, which begins with the line "Goodbye to the elms," that world begins to disappear in the fading light of evening, and its disappearance gives rise to images of instability, the loss of attachment, and solitariness. Warmth ("burning rivulets") gives way to cold ("cold round crystals"), and the primary red of the first part is replaced by gray or displaced into the solitary point of a red light swimming through the dark. Awareness now withdraws from the world of external objects and those objects themselves begin to close in upon themselves, withdrawing from view. If the disembodied perspectiveless voice of part 1 is able to provide a grand vision of nature, of harmonic natural movements, and of the human community with/in nature, the perspective of the traveler in part 2 takes the form of partial impressions of things going past: "On the left, a red light / swims through the dark." The mind's awareness becomes fragmentary ("A pale flickering. Gone."), and the objects in the world become less connected to each other and to humans: "Two rubber boots show, / illuminated, solemn. / A dog gives one bark." The boots indicate the absence of the person who wears them, much as the world itself now seems evacuated of that human or domestic content that had characterized it in part 1. Night is a kind of death, an enactment of the dying out of light and of the world of objects it illuminates that would occur at death. The first part's communion of human and world, indicated by the link of church, farmhouse, and land, comes to a conclusion, a conclusion suggested by the image of the woman shaking a tablecloth "out after supper." In the place of contact with natural things are now the signs or names that humans append to things – "Then the Economies – / Lower, Middle, Upper; / Five Islands, Five Houses."

Images suggestive of death and of the fragility of human contact with the world come to dominate, but Bishop carefully maintains a certain faith in the naturalness of such changes, in an underlying holding together of things that withstands the falling apart that occurs at the level of perception, and in the possibility of finding alternative kinds of sustenance. That the onset of evening is initially characterized in positive natural imagery – "The light / grows richer," "the sweet peas cling / to their wet white string" – places the withdrawal of light and the loss of the world within the framework of the natural rhythms described in part 1, and the continued use of images such as "lupins like apostles," which compares the rows of upright flowers to paintings of rows of apostles, continues the link of nature and religion. Moreover, the instability of perception is balanced by an image of a more profound holding together of things: "An iron bridge trembles / and a loose plank rattles / but doesn't give way."

In the stanza that follows the negative images of the loss of the world and the instability of perception – the lone red light in the dark, the solemn empty books, the dog's single bark – a compensatory image of an elderly woman bearing sustenance in the form of two market bags who gets aboard the bus and announces affirmatively that it is "a grand night. Yes, sir" further balances and rectifies the negativity of the oncoming night. Her request for a ticket "all the way to Boston" is a metaphor of continuity that seems to resolve the discontinuity of the flickering perceptions in the preceding stanzas. The last line – "She regards us amicably" – shifts the focus of the poem away from the lone subject's unstable perceptions of the external object world and toward a more social subjectivity. A first person pronoun – "us" – is used for the first time, and part 3, which begins "Moonlight as we enter," will be concerned with human subjective powers and how they might be used to come to terms with the kind of loss described in the move from the first to the second parts of the poem.

Already one senses in the amicable encounter between the elderly woman and the passengers that those powers and their work will have to do with the ability of speech to make communities between otherwise isolated human subjects and to transform the world through acts of naming like "a grand night." If the woman's greeting creates an "us," a community out of different passengers and "lone travellers," language in the following stanza is shown transforming the negative nighttime world into something more positive through a creation of similitude: "the New Brunswick woods, / hairy, scratchy, splintery; / moonlight and mist / caught in them like lamb's wool / on bushes in a pasture." With the shift from daylight to moonlight, the poem shifts from a concern with the fragile perception of objects to a concern with the internal subjective power of the imagination, its ability to substitute images for things and to posit similitude between different things. Fragile objects can be replaced by more enduring images, just as the loneliness of a world of objects that pass and disappear can be alleviated by the company and benevolence of others. In this instance, the image is particularly important because it embodies the poem's ambivalence (a New Critic might say its irony or paradox) regarding the compensations for loss it proposes. "Lamb's wool" suggests literal physical warmth, but lamb also refers to the Christian tradition of religious symbolism to which Bishop has alluded at least twice already in the poem, since lamb is an image associated with Jesus. Lamb also, of course, suggests fresh life or birth, and that meaning seems more in keeping with the other transformations at work at this point of the poem. Splintery woods, for example, are supplanted by "pasture," something which, like the old woman's two bags of groceries, provides sustenance.

After this transformation of disturbing objects into comforting images, something like rest is possible for the travelers. The troubled instability of the perception of external objects gives way to an "hallucination," a "divagation" or wandering from the awareness of objects. The fragmented temporality of the trip through space is replaced by a different temporality "in Eternity" that allows the past – grandparents' voices overheard in childhood – to enter the present, so that memory and perception mix. Freed from the limitations of perception, the mind can engage different powers – memory and imagination – that allow a healing understanding – "things cleared up finally," "half groan, half acceptance" – of the kinds of losses one experiences as one travels through nature and time. If the bus journey is a metaphor for the inevitability of loss, of the passage of things and of people into the past of the ongoing journey, memory and imagination allow that past to be retrieved so that a conversation heard "back in the bus" can also be "an old conversation," one that recalls other conversations throughout life – "Talking the way they talked / in the old featherbed, / peacefully, / on and on."

Rhythm now returns to the poem, an alternation of sound and phrase in the tallying of life's losses and gains that mirrors the earlier alternating rhythm of nature: "what he said, what she said, / who got pensioned; / deaths deaths and sicknesses; / the year he remarried; / the year (something) happened. / . . . He took to drink. Yes. / She went to the bad." Unlike the use of rhythm in the description of nature in part 1, however, the use of rhythm here seems to struggle against disordered contingency of events and to be at odds with what it names. Life in the conversation does not follow nature's alternating form, entering and retreating, coming in and going out according to a logic that draws forth a matching language. Language must struggle now to meet (or miss) what it names ("the year (something) happened"), and although the elements of the earlier vocalic and syllabic rhythms are there (the i's of "She died in childbirth" alternating with the o's of "That was the son lost / when the schooner foundered"), the two events are disjoined, unmatched, and only contingently related. Life's experiences cannot be like nature and cannot have the same kind of compelling and necessary alternating rhythm. They are strophic in that they alternate good and bad, but all together they comprise a list rather than a living unity, a series of accidents rather than anything with internal coherence. If the coherence of nature's movements evoked religious images, from the churches like birches to the lupins like apostles, now religion is put in question as an option for dealing with the alogical hazards, pains, and losses of life: "When Amos began to pray / even in the store and / finally the family had / to put him away." The deliberately clumsy use of "and" and "had" as end words renders formally the inappropriateness of the events described, but it might also be construed as suggesting that religion itself is nonsynchronic with the events of life.

Life's losses are unamenable to the kind of rhythm used to describe nature, and a different strategy of naming and describing is required, one that relies on poetic repetition to match the sheer redundancy of the events: "what he said, what she said," "deaths deaths," "the year he remarried; / the year (something) happened," "He took ... She went ..." No logic or coherence or rhythmic unity can be found in events that simply repeat without strophic alternation of movement and counter-movement. Instead, repetition functions to emphasize the seeming endlessness of loss: "the year ... the year ..."

But repetition might also make possible affirmative acceptance. This possibility is clear in the line: "'Yes...' that peculiar / affirmative. 'Yes...'" The first step in such acceptance is to recognize and affirm the events, to say "yes" to them rather than to turn away in fear. The kind of religious meaning evoked by the story of Amos (the name is biblical) would arrest the repetitiveness of the events and give them a meaning that would make them cease repeating. With such an alternative discarded, one must instead not only affirm losses, but also greet and affirm them again and again. The pain of the events is not something that happens once and is finished; it is so identical with life – figured again in the bus journey as something in constant ongoing movement – that it occurs repetitively. For there to be life is for there to be such repetitive ongoing losses. Any affirmation, acceptance, and understanding of them must therefore itself assume the form of a repetition. The grandparents' "yes" must therefore be repeated: "'Yes...' that peculiar / affirmative. 'Yes...'"

Repetition in the affirmative understanding of life's losses cannot have the form of the full strophed, alternating rhythm of the description of nature, but the repetition of understanding nevertheless gives rise to a kind of rhythm. By repeatedly affirming loss, the grandparents' act of understanding creates a mirroring and a rhythm akin to that of the opening stanzas: "A sharp, indrawn breath, / half groan, half acceptance." Repetition is endurance, and endurance means learning to accommodate what might be entirely alien to the subject's mode of observation and understanding. It is to repeat it, though in slightly different form, from "half groan" to "half acceptance." By being taken in in this way ("indrawn"), the object loses its cold objectivity and becomes subjective. By moving to the side of animation, loss and death enter awareness and become animate.

The poem's process of simple description now displays its full importance. It is the way (perhaps the only way) of fulfilling the elegiac task of coming to terms with death. Or as Bishop herself puts it with appropriate simplicity: " 'Life's like that. / We know *it* (also death).' " The statement embodies the way affirmative description works by repeating the object in the subject's terms, by finding some familiar and similar term of comparison ("like"). Here, however, the term of comparison is life itself, a different moment of life of which what one is understanding is a repetition. Repetition, life's repetition of itself, thus creates familiarity and similarity: "Life's like that." It is something, to use the terms of part 1, with which one can feel at home because "we" already know it.

The full capacity of repetition to promote a therapeutic understanding is rendered in the repetition of life by death: "We know *it* (also death)." To know life is necessarily, by the poetic logic of the apposition, to know death. But one consequence of the acceptance and affirmation described in this part of the poem is that death is now something appended and made parenthetical in relation to life. If life is a journey of observation and description and, through observation and description, affirmation, then all one can know is observable life. Death is known only as what stands outside life (in parentheses) and as what stands in strophic, rhythmic balance with it. By italicizing "it," Bishop underscores the rhythm and directs the reader not to place the emphasis on "know." The stress therefore falls in the middle of the line, creating a flow upward that then descends downward and back up again into "death": "We know *it* (also death)." Repetition here assumes the form of rhythm. The painful repetitiveness of loss, by being repeated in the mind's own language of observation and affirmation, is transformed into strophic, rhythmically alternating, harmonic form.

The sense that death has been understood and accepted is under-scored by the comparison of the grandparents' talk to "the way they talked / in the old featherbed, / peacefully, / on and on." Such talk is ongoing, itself a repetition that promises more repetition, endurance that takes its model from past acts of endurance. The poem now also returns to (repeats) the earlier image of the dog who accompanies humans on their journey ("down in the kitchen, the dog / tucked in her shawl"). The dog wrapped in a human shawl is a figure of the nonhuman accommodated to human forms of understanding and life. The loss of awareness, of life, that would be death, can now be construed as something other than the becoming blank object of the human subject. It need not have the meaning it seemed about to have in part 2, that of the loss of the world in which one is immersed. The acceptance of loss fittingly now coincides with an acceptance of the loss of awareness: "Now, it's all right now / even to fall asleep / just as on all those nights." Repetition allows one to conceive of the loss of consciousness as some-thing familiar ("just as on all those nights"), and it permits one to understand and accept the departure of any observable moment ("Now") as something which implies a repetition of a similar moment ("now"). Because of the ongoing repetition of nows, one can let go of conscious-ness, of the token of one's subjective life, without fear of loss. As rhythm seemed to hold things together in part 1, here at the end of part 3 repeti-tion has become a mode of assurance, a promise that things will hold together, be repeated. Like the bridge that does not give way, it sustains the subject in the passage through the loss of the awareness which betokens life.

If the loss of awareness in sleep can be construed as a metaphor for death, then the appearance of the moose, which follows immediately, might be understood as itself having something to do with the issue of death. If the bus's journey has been a figure for human life moving through the world, that movement now is arrested, "stops with a jolt." Lights, those tokens of the artificial illumination cast by human civiliza-tion, are turned off, and the road of the human journey is blocked. We are in confrontation, direct and unmediated, with nature – "A moose has come out of / the impenetrable wood / and stands there, looms, rather, / in the middle of the road." The surprise is that nature, which up till now has been a landscape without subjectivity, appears as a subject, an animal which "approaches," itself the agent of the encounter, and "sniffs at / the bus's hot hood" as if it were greeting another animal. The line that divides human from natural, subjective awareness from object, life from death, is crossed in a way that confounds by reversing the distinction.

If the moose is nature understood as the possibility of the death of human life and human awareness, it is an especially harmless version of such nature. Though "Towering" or grand, it is nonetheless "antlerless," "high as a church, / homely as a house / (or, safe as houses)." It is so harmless because it is so familiar. The series of similes compares it to such comforting human institutions as a church and a house, and to the safest commercial investments ("safe as houses"). The similes cross nature and civilization and draw what might have been completely other and alien into the realm of human understanding. Life understood as the possibility of death can be understood, which is to say, taken in to familiar human terms, made comparable to what most assures us we are out of danger. By listing the passengers' reactions to the moose, the following stanza draws attention to the therapeutic power of the vision of nature as fellow subject, and the rhyme of "passengers" and "creatures" underscores the crossing of realms. The rhyme of "childishly, softly" and "It's a she!" evokes the common human and animal processes of maternity and nurturing.

The moose is now described as "Taking her time," like the grandparents speaking "in Eternity," and as looking "the bus over." Of the many continuities between the third and the fourth parts of the poem, one of the most important is the sense of being outside the limits and constraints of time, especially the time of the bus journey which brings as many losses in the passage of things as it brings gains in achieving a destination. The moose returns the passengers to childhood, just as the grandparents' voices returns the speaker of the poem to memories of voices overheard at night in her own childhood. Time loses the form of passage and becomes instead an elastic medium in which one can retrieve the lost past.

Moments of revelation when the ordinary limits of life are lifted and something else becomes possible – a vision of a different order of being – are generally associated with a suspension of ordinary time, and the revelatory, atemporal quality of this experience is suggested by Bishop's choice of the words "grand, otherworldly" to characterize the moose. Throughout the poem, Bishop has anchored the possibility of such otherworldly understanding or revelation within the everyday and the observable. Even as she capitalizes "Eternity," she keeps it tied to the actual voices of grandparents tallying and remembering and trying to understand the "Eternity" or repetitiveness of human pain and loss. She does the same thing here by anchoring the suggestion of otherworldliness, of an understanding of the moose as a symbol of something that transcends human life in perhaps a religious sense, within the passengers' reactions to it: "Why, why do we feel / (we all feel) this sweet / sensation of joy?" If there is revelation, something "otherworldly" that one can glimpse in this world, she seems to suggest, its significance resides in the feelings it generates. That those feelings are ones of joy can be understood both literally and metaphorically, as the pleasure of an encounter with an animal in the middle of the night or the realization that nature is vivid, the world warm and alive rather than cold and alien, a fellow subject rather than an entirely other object that represents the danger of the loss of subjective life.

That the most metaphoric or symbolic meanings seem difficult to extricate from the most mundane and everyday is, of course, part of Bishop's strategy in the poem. The moose is at once "awful plain" and "grand, otherworldly" for good reason. Like death in parentheses that indicate it can't be known, what spiritual or religious meaning that might exist on the other ("otherworldly") side of the moose cannot be known. Life as depicted in the poem is awareness, observation, description, and naming, and any therapeutic understanding that the poem might offer in the vision of the moose must remain within this realm; it is all there is.

Appropriately, it is to the mechanics of description and naming that the speaker now turns: " 'Curious creatures,' / says our quiet driver, / rolling his *r*'s." In the euphonic repetition of c and ur sounds, Bishop draws attention to what she herself has been doing throughout the poem – supplying sound equivalents of objects in the world, describing what is primitive and primal about human life – the endlessness of life and of death – in rhythmic euphonic terms that might allow them to be understood as inspiring patient affirmation, if not occasional joy. In her own way, with the driver, she says: "Look at that, would you." The passage through life need not be one of lonely observation; in euphonic language, it can be brought to an affirmative understanding.

The brevity of such moments is suggested by the succeeding lines: "Then he shifts gears. / For a moment longer, / by craning backward, / the moose can be seen . . ." If the moose is to be understood in a New Critical sense as an incarnated universal, a glimpse of spiritual life within earthly life, Bishop nonetheless underscores its dependence on earthly things – the shifting gears, the macadam, the acrid smell of gasoline that seems if anything to emphasize the worldliness of the experience. Moreover, the work of rhythm and repetition in language – "a dim / smell of moose, an acrid / smell of gasoline" – emphasizes the inextricable mingling of the otherworldly and the worldly, the vision and the eyes that see (or, in a spirit of more emphatic worldliness, the nose that smells). The rhythmic flow and counterflow – a dim smell, an acrid smell – is once again of natural things and human constructs, this time more in insurmountable counterpoint to each other, but it is also of life in its essence glimpsed and everything literal, everyday, and mundane about life that means that such vision will never be pure. All metaphors have a vehicle that, like the bus, bears their meaning, and even at its most metaphoric, its most suggestive of the possible glimpse of otherworldly meaning in life, "The Moose" reminds us of our literal placement in this world. By comparing her rather humdrum and every-day vision of the moose in the road to an older religious interpretive framework ("high as a church"), Bishop notes the kinship between her way of understanding and that older one, but like the bus and the moose, it is a kinship with a difference. Both offer therapeutic consolation for loss, one by positing a spiritual world beyond this one, hers by affirmatively looking at this world and finding in it cause (albeit momentary) for joy.

"At the Fishhouses" begins with a simple description and ends with a meditation on universal concerns. It also evokes religious themes, but it seems to withhold an endorsement of religious ideas.

Bishop uses the alternation and repetition of sounds to create certain effects. Notice in the first twelve lines how she alternates vowel sounds and think about what some of the effects of this alternation might be. Look especially at how the man working his net and the fishhouses are described, and how seemingly ordinary things are assigned value-laden adjectives such as "beautiful herring scales" and "creamy iridescent coats of mail." What is the point of characterizing ordinary things in this way?

Think about these issues in relation to the central story of the Christian religion, the story of Christ's crucifixion and resurrection. There is a direct reference to this story in the image of the "ancient wooden capstan," a cross-shaped device for hauling in cables. It has "melancholy stains, like dried blood." As for images of resurrection and heaven, look at the description of the fishhouses with their "steeply peaked roofs," which resemble churches, and the gangplanks that "slant up / to storerooms in the gables." Later, Bishop refers more explicitly to religion when she sings a Baptist hymn – "A Mighty Fortress Is Our God" – to a seal.

But what are we to make of these religious references? Is Bishop seriously advocating a religious perspective on the world? Does she believe in transcendence, the idea of a spirit world beyond the physical one? Or does she believe the physical world is all we have?

Romantic poets such as Wordsworth did believe there was a spirit in nature. Natural objects were for them symbols of divinity. One could read the world and see there legible signs of eternity and spirituality. Bishop alludes to their style of writing in the poem, but she does an odd thing with it. She interrupts it twice, as if she were deliberately drawing our attention to how wrong it is.

Notice how the third stanza begins: "Cold dark deep and absolutely clear, / element bearable to no mortal, / to fish and to seals . . ." The reference to "no mortal" suggests a possible evocation of religious or spiritual truth. But the ellipsis (. . .) she uses to interrupt this possibility is striking. It is not a standard device of poetry. Why does Bishop interrupt this Wordsworthian poetic line that seems to point the poem in the traditional Romantic direction of revealed spiritual truth in nature?

The first interruption points outward toward the sea and the seal who is assigned a certain subjectivity ("He was curious about me," "his better judgment"). Religion is summoned here as something that defends us ("A Mighty Fortress"). But what might it defend against? The seal is certainly not threatening, although s/he lives in something that could be an image of danger – the ocean. Why does Bishop call herself a believer in "total immersion" here? What might the human equivalent be of living in water, a fluid medium with no clear, fixed boundaries, no center, no holdable substance? Immersed in the ocean, one might be more subject to chance occurrences, the contingencies of existence, because one had no protection of the kind the walls of church-like fish-houses, for example, provide. Notice, by the way, that the brand of cigarette in the previous stanza is a Lucky Strike, an image that suggests contingency, the chance character of life lived without the kind of security that religious belief provides. Religion supplies life's contingencies with meaning, but is that meaning inherent because spirit resides in matter, as the Romantic poets believed, or is it placed on natural objects by humans too afraid to live without the secure meanings religion gives us?

Look now at the second instance of interruption. Again, Bishop takes up the Romantic phrasing of "Cold dark deep and absolutely clear, / the clear gray icy water . . ." This time, she simply loses track of the thought, as if it was not worth pursuing or as if it bored her. Instead, her attention is drawn back toward the land, toward the "dignified tall firs." Notice that she assigns a very positive term – "dignified" – to the trees considered as natural objects. And notice too that they are a little like water in that they lack "absolutely clear" distinctions – "Bluish, associating with their shadows." Why does Bishop characterize them as "a million Christmas trees stand / waiting for Christmas"? She could mean that Christmas, the time of year, has not yet come, but she might also mean that "Christmas" is a human-made institution imposed on natural trees so that they suddenly are transformed into "Christmas trees." The human-made religious meaning is something we place on the world to protect ourselves from its contingencies, and it has yet to be placed on these natural objects. As parts of nature, they are merely "dignified" trees, but once cut down and adorned with ornaments they acquire a different meaning, one that protects us from the possibility that there are no "absolutely clear" boundaries between us and nature, us and the trees, us and the seal. We, like they, are totally immersed in the natural world, and there is no way out, no transcendence, no doorway that leads upward to heaven, where we might be saved from the contingency of natural, material life. Death might simply be a passage into matter, rather than a step up and out of matter.

Bearing these issues in mind, what is the point of what follows in the poem? How would you read the final stanza?

Exercise 1.3   Alice Munro, "Five Points"

One of the first things one notices about "Five Points" is that it is really two stories, or rather, one story embedded within another. In the frame story, Brenda and Neil are having an adulterous affair. Brenda is married to an older man named Cornelius who is now disabled after working in mines underneath a lake, and Neil is a temporary migrant laborer employed on a project to restore a beach on the lake. He lives in a trailer with another man, and Brenda visits him there after parking her van elsewhere.

In the embedded story, which Neil recounts to Brenda while they talk after having made love, he is a young man who hangs out in a section of Victoria called "Five Points." He takes drugs with his male friends and frequents a candy shop overseen by an overweight teenage girl named Maria, who is the daughter of the owners. She pays Neil and his friends to have sex with her, but they begin to blackmail her and to take money from her for nothing. Eventually, she and her parents are ruined financially; her parents find out that she has given away all their money, and she is sent to jail by her mother.

The two stories intersect when Brenda becomes annoyed with Neil for prevaricating when she asks him about his role in the mistreatment of Maria. He offers her drugs; she refuses; they argue and say mean things to each other. She walks out and begins to walk back to her van.

He follows, picks her up, and as they drive, they make up. The relationship will continue, but each has suffered scars in the fight.

While conducting formal analysis, especially analysis shadowed by the New Critical idea that all literary works are characterized by an organic unity of form and content, method and meaning, it is always tempting to seek symmetries between parts. Do you notice any ways in which the two stories, the frame and the embedded story, are similar?

What reasons might there be, either formal or thematic, for embedding one story within another?

The embedded story is darker in tone than the frame story. Brenda is a woman moved by reasonable fears and hopes, and her affair with Neil is characterized by a certain idealization that arises from her own seemingly justifiable yearnings. But Maria's "gross" appearance makes her convert sexual love into a financial transaction devoid of affection or feeling of any kind. The boys' predatory behavior also strays outside what we normally consider to be acceptable "human" values and norms.

Why do you think Munro juxtaposes these two seemingly incommensurate realities – one characterized by hopes, desires, and fears directed at another, the other characterized by numb predation that would seem an offense to the very idea of affectionate feelings for another human being? Is there more in common between Maria's situation and Brenda's than Brenda cares to admit?

Look at how Munro characterizes love-making between Neil and Brenda and Cornelius and Brenda near the end of the story. Then, consider those sections where she describes Brenda's feelings regarding her physical relationship with Neil. What do you think is the significance of the odd phrasing Munro uses to describe Brenda's thoughts about Neil near the end when she compares his love-making to that of Cornelius: "Is she going to feel the same about this one?" Why do you think she uses such an impersonal construction regarding so "personal" a feeling or event?

How are men characterized in the story, and how might that explain Brenda's feelings toward them? In the next to last section of the story, she thinks about both Neil and Cornelius and reflects on their identities as men. How are they similar? How does she react to them? What does it mean that she is walking alone along a road as she thinks and that a man stops in a car in front of her, then drives away when she refuses to approach? Notice that she thinks that "she's not in any real danger." How does that wariness regarding violence and violation carry over into her reflections about Neil and Cornelius?

What do you think Munro thinks of Brenda's feelings for Neil? Does she give any indication that she might think Brenda is falling into a trap laid for women by men? Notice how she describes Brenda as liking the "good-humored authority" of the men at work. Brenda, in lying to Neil about being slapped for using drugs, calls Cornelius her father. How might this be significant?

Munro uses mixed images to characterize Brenda's relations with these men. Her journey to Neil's trailer takes her past "poisonous fruit," but her meetings with him are also characterized by "lapping sweetness" and "cool kindness soaking up all your troubles." He makes the world feel as if it is "her kingdom," and the relationship gives her a feeling of a "ceremony on which your life or salvation depended." Why does she use such religious imagery here? How does this tally with the very different thought that occurs to Brenda when she meditates on her relations with men after hearing Neil's story: "Men wanted you to make a fuss . . . and why was that? So they could have your marshmallow sissy goodness to preen against, with their hard showoff badness? . . . Whatever it was, you got sick of it."

Finally, what is the point of Cornelius' story about working in the darkness of the mine under the lake near the end? Munro writes: "He says he just can't look at the surface of the water without seeing all that underneath, which nobody who hasn't seen it could imagine." How might this image relate to the formal structure of the two stories, one embedded inside the other?

Exercise 1.4 *The Matrix*

The film is surprisingly similar to *King Lear* at least in a formal sense. Like the play, it begins with a device that defamiliarizes the world. *King Lear* begins with a false world that appears true. In the film, the world the characters inhabit is first presented as real then revealed to be false, and the first part of the narrative is organized around the slow revelation to the primary character of the falseness of the world he at the outset took to be real. Anyone seeing the film for the first time would, like the primary character, assume the world on the screen is a real world, not a computer-generated one in which deluded humans only apparently live full lives. The device of defamiliarization functions, as in the play, to disrupt the audience's assumptions about what constitutes normal reality.

The world that *The Matrix* takes for granted is very different from the Renaissance aristocratic world assumed by *King Lear*, and the effect of defamiliarization is also of another order. In the early twenty-first century, western society is overwhelmingly commercial. It is dominated by large corporations that limit the range of behaviors considered appropriate, especially amongst young employees, who must subordinate to the imperatives of the corporate order urges that until recently had been given relatively free rein in their lives. They must show up on time, obey rules regarding dress and speech, and curtail freedom of movement for the sake of performing tasks that benefit others more than they do themselves. In exchange for a steady salary and a predictable life in which one's material needs for shelter and food are met, young people sacrifice freedom, pleasure, and a sense of their own independent dignity and importance. One becomes a person in a cubicle and ceases to be a significantly different individual.

The film creates a metaphor for this "reality" in the computer-generated imaginary world of the matrix. The matrix is not real, but it seems real enough to its human inhabitants, who inhabit it in mind while their bodies remain in pods that generate energy for the computers running the matrix program. The wit of the metaphor resides in the fact that the computer-generated world so closely resembles "normal" life in a corporate-run society. The redundant brown suits and neat hairstyles that make everyone look alike are a young person's nightmare fantasy of what corporate life feels like. Additional force is gained by the metaphor from the fact that one's life is literally sucked out of one by one's corporate employers, much as it is by the electricity-devouring computers that run the matrix in the film.

Young people in the corporate world maintain an antinomian alternate reality organized around the urban club scene, music, drugs, and mildly illegal behaviors such as computer piracy that is in some senses more "real" than the world in which they work. There they can act freely and creatively without having to obey rules imposed from without. The movie grants that alternate universe a more substantial reality than the corporate world by portraying it as the gateway to the outside of the matrix program in which all humans in the movie live their imaginary lives. It defamiliarizes the corporate world not so much by making it seem strange or new as by making it seem almost too familiar and mundane while yet being entirely false and unreal. The conventions, codes, and routines of the everyday corporate world that many in the audience for the film inhabit suddenly come into focus as so many forms of discipline and control that operate in an authoritarian fashion to subordinate independence of thought and action to the greater good of the corporation.

The point of defamiliarization in *The Matrix* is therefore much more insidious than in *King Lear*. Consider the opening scene. Police arrive at a building and send up a team to retrieve a suspect. We as viewers have no idea what is going on or what crime has been committed. By placing us in the point of view of the police, the film aligns us with the fairly unexceptional assumption that laws are worth preserving, that law-enforcers are worthy of respect, and that crime should be punished. We are placed on the side of the disciplinary apparatuses that maintain social order. But that placement assigns to us the assumption that the social order is virtuous and worth preserving. In *The Matrix*, of course, this is not the case. It is a huge machine for cannibalizing humans. As yet, we do not know this, and one important formal feature of narrative is the way it defers knowledge so that one assumes false positions initially that later are revealed as such. At the outset of the film, we are in one such false position. We are, as it were, in the matrix.

As the opening scene evolves, we witness a criminal suspect fight and kill the police team sent to retrieve her. That one of the agents below on the street predicts that the team is "already dead" even though no such news has arrived suggests that the suspect operates outside normal expectations. She inspires awe, perhaps even respect. In the chase scene across rooftops that follows, the point of view of the film subtly shifts until it is lodged in her perspective. We now begin to sympathize with her as she flees the cold-looking and somewhat robotic agents and performs feats that defy normal expectations such as leaping from one building to another. As the scene ends, she magically escapes a huge, very menacing-looking truck that further recodes our initial valuations of criminal and police. The police now are aligned with images of murderous power while the suspect appears vulnerable and worthy of our empathy.

What might be called one's "normal" understanding of what police are is defamiliarized in this scene. As further scenes are added, the entire world the police protect and preserve comes to appear to be menacing. The social order they preserve suddenly seems criminal, harmful, and dangerous. Seemingly harmless young people are mistreated by robotic agents of social order who harm them with impunity and deposit surveillance devices in their bodies. *King Lear* asks for a slight shift in values within a world whose basic premises and founding assumptions are taken by the play to be good and worth preserving. Indeed, one could say that the entire purpose of the play is to advocate the restoration of those assumptions so that they continue in force. *The Matrix* uses defamiliarization to dislocate one's allegiance to the very idea of founding assumptions and basic premises. In the world of the film, they are depicted as malevolently disciplinary apparatuses for securing obedience from participants whose lives are subordinated to the will of the corporate machinery in which they do not so much live as allow themselves to be consumed. A slight shift in values of the kind performed in *King Lear* from obligation to feeling would do no good in such a world. The only alternative is to break the machine.

Yet *The Matrix* could also be seen as drawing on the same well of assumptions and meanings as *King Lear*. The play was written at a time when "humanist" values were coming to the fore in western culture. Those values favor the individual's freedom of thought and action over the imperatives of such institutions as the Catholic Church or the monarchy. Old value systems that dictated that one should obey those with institutional power were giving way to more "liberal" values that advocated freedom or liberty of expression both intellectually and politically. These values joined with the republican assumption that one should choose one's own political leaders and even participate oneself in the government of one's society. The play records a changeover from an older, more authoritarian style of political organization to a more modern, liberal, humanist, and republican style in which everyone is free to participate. Initially, Lear rules in an authoritarian manner, but by the end of the play, the assent and consent of the governed is depicted as important to successful rule. Feeling, a trait associated with liberal humanism, is depicted to be as valuable as obligation and duty, two hallmarks of the older monarchial form of political organization. Monarchy is restored and preserved in the play, but that compromise points toward a compromise with the liberal humanist aspirations that were coming to the fore at the time. By noting the importance of feeling (as opposed to obligation) and by, at least in Cordelia's case, accepting the right to dissent from authority, the play moves toward a more modern, more liberal kind of justification for political organization.

The Matrix draws on a similar set of themes and ideas to criticize a corporate order that in some respects is not that different from the religious and political orders that early humanist, republican liberalism opposed. Liberalism advanced the ideal of individual freedom in all arenas of life, from politics to economics, as an alternative to social systems premised on authority and obedience. The modern corporate order depicted in the film thwarts the individual's freedom and makes him submit to authority. In the alternative world to the matrix, a more republican style of government is in force, and everyone participates equally in running the society. On a personal or individual level, Neo's path to liberation from the world he has left behind is only complete when he learns to rely on his own insights and powers instead of relying on what others tell him. The Oracle tells him he is not "the one," but he himself, exercising his freedom of will and relying on his own abilities, arrives at a different conclusion. He comes to assume control over his own world, his own life, and his own destiny.

That is the ideal of humanist liberalism, and later in this book we will discuss what is wrong with it. But for the moment let's take it for granted as a legitimate theme of a contemporary film whose semantic limits are shaped by the founding assumptions of the capitalist culture in which it is made.

In pursuing a formalist reading of the film, you might test some of the formalists' assumptions by asking if it is indeed possible to do a strictly formal analysis independent of issues of meaning. You might also ask if the New Critical contention that "great" literature is characterized by an organic unity of form and meaning applies to film. Pick a scene from the film and try to determine how it might fit organically into its larger themes. You might also ask if the film contains paradoxes that are especially significant for its meaning.

Another question you might pursue is universality. Does the film contain universals? Does it enunciate ideas that might plausibly be said to apply to everyone everywhere? You've probably noticed already that there are clear religious themes in the film. It is a "Christ story" about someone who is chosen to save the world and who must die and be reborn in order to do so.

Finally, pick out a scene and try to do the kind of close analysis of form that one normally does with a work of literature. The opening scene is especially interesting in the way it uses shots and camera positions to locate the audience in different points of view. Pay attention to the placement of the camera and note how it "sees" the world from different characters' perspectives. You might even look at a film that opens with a similar rooftop chase and that concerns the confusion of image and reality – Alfred Hitchcock's *Vertigo*. Why might the makers of *The Matrix* summon this obvious comparison?

CHAPTER 2

Structuralism

To grasp what is meant by structure in literature, think of a body. Its skeleton is crucial to how it works, but the skeleton is invisible. In a similar manner, a work of literature has a structure that never appears as such but that allows the work to make sense or to function as a work of literature. Another way of thinking about structure is to picture a sports match like tennis or golf. If you did not know the rules of the game – something that happens to anyone who changes countries and encounters new games for the first time – you would not know how to make sense of two men hitting a ball back and forth. And you might not know the point of hitting a small ball down a long field toward a flag. The actions in each game could be senseless, but invisible rules lend them structure. They come to have meaning within the structure of the conventions or agreements that guide play.

Structure in literature can be described in several ways. Each work of literature has a structure unique unto itself. That structure accounts for how its various elements are organized and arranged in relation to one another. A fictional or dramatic plot begins in one point and ends in another; a poem is organized into similar repeating lines. Works written in the same genre (tragedy, epic, novel, etc.) or mode (romance, satire, melodrama, etc.) also share similar structures. They contain common character and plot elements such as "obstacle" in romance, "villain" in melodrama, and "revelation" in the sentimental novel.

The best way to grasp this dual dimension of structure is to spend a weekend seeing every film available at your local movie theater. Some will be serious dramas with realistic characters and relatively fluid and unpredictable plots, but they will be well structured nonetheless so that they make sense to you. Other films will be more "generic" and "conventional" in that they follow familiar rules and have familiar-looking characters and very predictable plot elements. Their structure will be much more visible to you. And if you rent copies of five films from the same genre or mode such as action/adventure, you will find that you are watching the same plot structure over and over. There will be different heroes in different situations facing different challenges, but the same plot motifs (threat-chase-survival) and the same kinds of characters will recur in all the examples.

All works of literature have an internal structure. While reading Henry James' *Washington Square*, for example, you notice that he is carefully balancing two different worldviews, that of Austin Sloper, which is scientific, rationalist, and unsentimental, and that of Lavinia Penniman, which is sentimental, imaginative, and melodramatic. This structure is spatial or schematic. It exists outside the temporal sequence of the narrative. These two characters do not evolve much during the course of the narrative; they have characteristics that remain the same throughout. Their structural opposition is the ground on which one major conflict of the novel is built.

The novel also has a temporal structure organized around visits, proposals, and decisions. An enterprising but poor young man, Morris Townsend, rather unexpectedly wishes to marry Sloper's daughter, Catherine, who is unattractive and not entirely bright. He clearly wants her money, but he has to pretend otherwise. James draws on a traditional melodramatic plot form – the ogrish parent who prevents true romance from occurring – and this form lends structure to the narrative. The parent indeed poses an obstacle, and the lovers seek to circumvent it. But James is an ironic writer; he mocks the melodramatic form because he thinks it unrealistic and untrue to life. So, in this instance, the melodramatic structure does not work out as it usually does. The lovers do not escape to a secret marriage in a dungeon, only to be forgiven and reconciled with the once ogrish, now reformed father. James evokes the melodramatic expectation only to disappoint it in fruitful ways. And that means that the structure of the novel is not melodramatic; it evolves from delusion to recognition, aspiration to disappointment, in a way that gives it a structure more like that found in other realist novels of the era such as *Madame Bovary* and *Anna Karenina*. Morris Townsend flees when it is made clear by Sloper that he will get no money for marrying Catherine. The conventions of romance are overturned in favor of the conventions of realism. The structure of romantic apotheosis succumbs to that of cynical recognition. Catherine sees the light, only it is not a very nice one.

While reading a novel or watching a film one usually is more concerned with character and action, and one usually does not reflect on how well structured the plot elements are. The story may appear to follow the course and rhythm of life events, but in fact the choice of which pieces of life to recount and the arrangement of those pieces in a connected narrative always means that what you read or see is quite deliberately structured. One of the important distinctions the formalists made was between the life events a novel or film ostensibly recounts and the highly selective story about those events that is the novel or film itself. The events of the first half of *Washington Square* occur over the course of two months, but James chooses to narrate or tell only a very small selection of the numerous events that happened during this time. He inserts only events that are significant and that help build his picture of the world he describes. The Russian term for the events is "sujhet" and for the narrative account of those events "fabula."

At one moment, James chooses to have Austin Sloper notice at a party that his daughter, Catherine, is deeply embarrassed because he sees her sitting with Morris Townsend, the man who pretends to love her but who wants her father's fortune. Sloper turns away to spare her further embarrassment. It is a small, seemingly inconsequential moment, a minor piece of characterization, but it functions in the larger structure of the novel as an important piece of evidence in Sloper's favor. It shows him caring for his daughter, and it will help explain and excuse actions he later takes to prevent the marriage.

Not all narratives follow real-world time lines. The film *The Constant Gardener* begins with an event well into the story the film tells – the death by murder of a woman in Africa. The narrative then goes back in time and tells the story of how her death came about. Then, it proceeds forward from her death, and in the latter third of the movie, her husband tries to find the murderer. Such non-traditional films and novels make clear the distinction between narrative and story, between the telling of events and the much larger flow of events from which the pieces included in the telling are taken. And they underscore the importance of structure to narrative. In this instance, the placement of Tessa's death at the beginning puts the audience in a very unusual emotional situation that serves the ends of this very polemical film, which suggests that large drug companies abuse poor Africans for their own enrichment. After having experienced her horrific death, the audience is more likely to feel sympathy for her principled idealism and likely to forgive behavior that falls outside polite norms as she pursues her laudable objectives. Structure in this instance serves a thematic and rhetorical end.

Literary structure is also the shape a work has by virtue of its similarity to other works. Vladimir Propp noted that many folktales, when compared, follow the same basic plot outline. Claude Lévi-Strauss, a French anthropologist, found that very diverse myths display similar themes, characters, and stories. When placed on top of one another, they display almost identical structures, much as human bodies all have the same skeletal form. Their narratives follow the same moves and generate the similar meanings. This accounts for why so many action/ adventure films seem the same. In some respects, they are modern folktales.

In literature, it is more common to speak of generic groupings of works that have similar compositional elements. All tragedies, for example, have structural elements in common such as a moment of recognition or *anagnoresis*, and epic poems tend to trace similar stories and to pose similar challenges to their heroes. Structure in a literary sense also means that works of literature obey conventions that pertain to particular genres. Epic poems are usually uncompromisingly serious in tone and usually deal with the achievement of heroic nationalist goals. You would not expect to encounter a scathing parody of nationalism in such an epic. That would break the rules. If you did encounter such a parody, you would be in another genre, perhaps a mock epic or a modern novel such as James Joyce's *Ulysses*, which borrows epic structure but uses it for satiric or parodic ends. Joyce's modern "Ulysses" is not in the least heroic, not in the Greek sense at least, and Joyce uses him to mock the epic pretensions of Irish nationalists.

Different generic conventions make possible different events and outcomes. In a romance like *The Scarlet Letter*, it is perfectly plausible that an adulterous minister who conceals his sin might end up with a real scarlet "A" on his chest that resembles the embroidered one his lover has had to wear throughout the story. The rules of romance allow for such seemingly supernatural, but perhaps psychologically plausible, plot events. *The Scarlet Letter* has a passionate love affair at the center of its narrative that motivates much of the action and determines how the story and the narrative are organized. In a realist novel such as *Washington Square*, love is treated less romantically and more skeptically. The slow failure of a "love affair" organizes the narrative. Characters are now less likely to embody round virtues; they have faults that impel them in self-destructive directions. The narrative moves toward failure rather than ideal romantic success.

Structure can also be semantic. The various meanings that appear in a work of literature are significant because they refer to or draw on codes. A code is like a dictionary in that it assigns meaning to particular objects, events, words, or signs. For example, in American football, a ball kicked between two upright posts counts as a point, but if it passes on either side, it does not. In itself, the ball passing one way or the other is without meaning or significance. But when coded by the rules of the game to mean "point," this odd little event suddenly acquires meaning. Similarly, in literature, certain events are made significant by the particular codes that govern the work. Those codes can be specific to a writer, but usually even such codes are influenced and shaped by cultural codes.

In James' *Washington Square*, a character who the reader suspects will turn out to be a cynical, gold-digging cad has dinner with the family of the girl whose wealth he hopes to acquire through marriage. He appreciatively drinks a lot of wine, and the father thinks badly of him because of it. The father belongs to an older generation whose values are alluded to as "republican simplicity" and include a strong sense that virtue should be equated with restraint in regard to appetites such as drinking. In order to understand the significance of James' remarks about the number of bottles of wine the young man has drunk, one has to have in mind the prevalent cultural code of the time that equated an absence of virtue with the unrestrained consumption of alcohol. Fast forward to the 1930s and look at any of the *Thin Man* movies, and you will be treated to a different cultural code in which drinking is a sign of "elevation" in more senses than one. The detectives are almost constantly drunk. And having a highball in one's hand becomes a sign of upper-class gentility.

Without the structure of meaning provided by codes, a work of literature would not make sense to its audience. A list of randomly selected events would not function like a work of literature. Add meaning derived from codes the audience recognizes, and the list or sequence of events begins to be a work of literature. For example, *The Matrix* begins by contrasting the mildly anarchistic and anti-authoritarian club scene of a group of young people with the prescriptive and authoritarian culture of a corporation. Each narrative segment draws on different codes to generate meaning. The young people in the club wear clothes (such as black leather) that evoke positive meanings within their cultural code. The clothing suggests a liking for extreme experiences. In striking contrast, the clothing style of the corporation is coded "bland" and "anonymous." All the agents dress alike, and this similarity conveys the meaning "loss of identity" in the code of the young people on whose lives the film focuses. In the code of the corporation, however, the uniform look signifies virtuous efficiency and rationality of operation.

Finally, all works of literature have structure to the extent that they are logical. In a work of literature, events follow each other in sequence in a logical rather than a haphazard fashion. Often, the logic is causal (one event causes another), but the logical relations can also be structured as similitude, contrast, paradox, irony, and the like. Fictional narratives generally follow a logical pattern shaped by the consequences that ensue from the actions of the characters. In Emily Brontë's *Wuthering Heights*, Catherine betrays Heathcliff, who represents a positive and vibrant sense of nature that Emily Brontë endorses. Tragedy results from her betrayal of true feeling for more worldly goods.

In Virginia Woolf's *Mrs. Dalloway*, the narrative is structured through both a spatial contrast and a temporal progression. The narrative progresses from conventionality to madness to restored conventionality. It is also structured as the spatial opposition between conventionality and the rejection of convention. The novel begins with a depiction of the compromises one makes with social convention in order to survive. It then moves on to a depiction of the madness of a young man who steps outside social conventions entirely. And it concludes with a depiction of a woman's decision to remain within conventions even though she understands what drove the young man to kill himself rather than accept conventions.

In Shakespeare's *King Lear*, the logic governing the plot structure is schematic and rhetorical. The plot teaches a lesson organized around an irony. The old king loses his kingdom because he tries to save it in the wrong way. The irony arises when he chooses the appearance of love over genuine affection and rejects genuine affection that eschews shallow appearances. Many narratives are arguments about the world, and the terms of the argument are usually arranged sequentially so that the conclusion arises logically from the sequence. If you read *Washington Square* with care, for example, you will find that James builds a slow argument that indicts Morris Townsend of callowness by the time one reaches the half-way point of the book. Townsend is associated with upward mobility that places cynical ends before real feelings, with melodramatic theatrical forms that falsify reality, and with behavior antithetical to the dominant standards of good taste and good behavior at that time in American culture, at least in James' social class.

A major contribution to the study of structure in literature was made by the intellectual movement called "structuralism." Ferdinand de Saussure's *Course in General Linguistics* (1916) is generally thought to be the founding work of the movement. Saussure argues that language should not be studied as it is practiced in everyday life; rather, linguistics should study the system of rules embedded in language that makes everyday speech possible. That system exists apart from or outside everyday usage and resembles the rules governing how chess pieces can be moved, which exist apart from the game yet make it possible.

Saussure advances several important ideas regarding the structure of the system of language. The first concerns how words work. It is tempting to think of words as names for things, and they indeed do have that function. The word "tree" seems to name an object. But the word itself is a combination of a sound and an idea. The word "tree" evokes an image in the mind that is different from the image evoked by, say, the word "horse."

All words, Saussure notes, have a tangible and audible phonic side and an intangible ideational side. He uses the word "sign" instead of "word" to designate this combination of sound and mental image. And he uses the word "signifier" to name the physical or phonic aspect of the sign, and "signified" to name the conceptual or ideational aspect.

The simple act of naming requires that each sign be distinct from other signs. "Tree" sounds different from "horse," and because of that difference, it can function to name what it names and is not confused with the name for a quadruped. The mental image that "tree" evokes also is different from the mental image evoked by "horse." When you hear "tree," you do not think of a quadruped. What this means is that differentiation allows each individual sign to have an identity apart from all other signs. Differentiation is simultaneously relation, because to differ from something puts each sign in relation to what it differs from. Relations and differences thus make possible the identity of each individual part of a language.

Each linguistic sign has a value that is distinct from the value of other signs. What this means is that each sign performs a different function within the language. Language is like a currency that allows one to trade signs of monetary value for things. Each unit of a currency gains its identity from its relations to all the other units. But it has value because it can be exchanged for something outside the currency. A one-dollar bill is such because it is different from a hundred-dollar bill, and it has a different value or function in relation to what it can purchase.

Similarly, all parts of language have value along two axes. One is the relations a linguistic sign has to other signs ("cat" is similar to but different from "hat" just as a one-dollar bill is similar to but different from a hundred-dollar bill). The other is the value a sign has in our use of language to name things in the world. "Cat" has the value of being able to name what it names, and that is distinct from the value a different word might have, such as "horse."

Another important concept and term in Saussure is "arbitrary." In the old way of thinking, it was believed that each word bore a necessary relation to the thing it named. But if words or linguistic signs come into being through their difference from other parts of the language, this cannot be the case. The relation between word and thing is entirely arbitrary. "Cat" just might be used to name the thing you sometimes place on your head that sounds like it, but the conventions of language lead us to use "cat" instead for the warm furry creature on your lap. And the reason "cat" is "cat" is that it is similar to but different from "hat" both as a sound and as a mental image, not because it is a better name for the furry creature. No part of language, therefore, has an identity in itself.

Each apparent identity ("cat" is "cat" and nothing else) arises from differences and relations. Saussure calls this the "diacritical principle."

There are two dimensions to language, one spatial, the other temporal. Language exists all at once (in space, as it were), but it also exists in time when we speak. Each utterance is a chain or sequence of signs, and the proper sequence allows sense to be made. That dimension of language is "syntagmatic," and it combines individual "syntagms" into meaningful sequences or sentences. But a sentence also makes sense because of the system of language and its rules for selecting which signs you use at any one point in the sequence. This dimension is "paradigmatic," and a "paradigm" consists of a list of possible elements that might fit into any one slot in a sentence sequence.

In German, it makes perfect sense to say "he to the train station gone is," but in English this sentence would break rules for putting signs in the right sequence. When you choose "cat" over "mouse" or over "hat," you are selecting from a paradigm set. In the place of the noun or subject, you can put any number of things. You have a great deal of freedom. But in combining what you select, your possibilities are limited. The English language dictates what sequence you can use as you create strings of signs. The term for the paradigmatic or spatial dimension of language is "synchrony" (or "the synchronic") because the system of language from which you select exists simultaneously as a whole in any utterance. The term for the temporal or sequential dimension is "diachrony" or "the diachronic" ("dia-" means "the channel of an act" or "through" in Greek).

Signs serve all sorts of functions in human life. They communicate thoughts, but they also indicate who we are. How people speak is a sign often of their moral capacities, their social philosophy, or their class location. Words connote dignity or depravity, and certain citations of well-known words can add an important level of meaning to what we say. When Cordelia in *King Lear*, for example, says that it is "her father's business" that she is about, anyone with their ears and their bibles open would recognize a reference in the prevalent Christian cultural religious code of the time to Jesus Christ. Suddenly her actions appear, or are meant to appear, much more important. When, in contrast, Edmund says that he will pursue his ambitions and get whatever he can "fashion fit," the use of the very negative word "fashion" suggests moral depravity. "Fashion," at the time and in the moral code of Christian culture especially, would have suggested an attachment to material, earthly goods rather than to spiritual ones.

We all live in worlds of signs. Stand on a street corner in a busy city, and you will see signs all around you. They enable social life, and they are indices of the various meanings life has. They make up much of what you see in literature or on film because they make up much of what you see in the world around you. On my walk to work through a United States city, I see different kinds of buildings that signify different meanings. The old red-brick buildings on my route contain decorative details that are emblematic of the ideal of gentility in nineteenth-century American culture. Some of the details, such as crosses, also are indices of that culture's religious belief systems. Over the roofs of these buildings, one can see skyscrapers that signify differently. They suggest corporate power rather than gentility, and the way they dominate the skyline is indicative of how the businesses they harbor dominate the American economy. While the old red-brick buildings suggest bourgeois stability and a world of settled values, the skyscrapers signify "modernity" and progress through the elimination of excess detail. Their glassy lines signify a spirit of economic efficiency for the sake of higher profits and greater income for the economic elite that eschews such unnecessary things.

Now look at the people around you. Their clothes indicate different things about them – the kind of work they do for one thing, but also how they think about themselves and about the world. A woman dressed in a crisp black business suit and coat, wearing low-heel shoes and carrying a valise signifies a newly emergent identity that would not have been seen on the same street a hundred years earlier. Her attitude toward the world around her might be signified by how she walks, by how or whether she looks at people around her, and by how much make-up she wears. Whether she wears too much or "just enough" make-up or jewelry will be a sign to other women especially, but also to some men of her work world, that will give them access to her character, her culture (family background, ethnicity, likely educational background), and her class location.

A man passing by in a pick-up truck signifies in different ways. His long, curly black hair is a sign that he is not concerned about appearances as much as she is. His work probably does not demand giving off certain signs of neatness. The sign on the door of his truck is for a masonry company, after all, and the truck is filled with work equipment. He wears a rough brown coat that shows signs of wear, and he wears a Boston Red Sox hat. The man, in a typical sign of male privilege, stares at the woman in black as she walks past. But the woman in black looks away. She is not interested in sports and avoids people who wear sports paraphernalia because they come from a different class and cultural world with which she wishes to avoid contact.

Works of literature often take advantage of such "semiotic" situations. In *The Scarlet Letter*, for example, extremely legible signs of moral infraction (a red letter stitched on a chest) are juxtaposed to signs that are completely illegible, such as the Reverend Dimmesdale's protestations of his own sinfulness. He is the co-adulterer with Hester Prynne, but no one will believe him when he stands up in church and says how sinful he is. Instead, they take it as a sign of his holiness. In *Remains of the Day*, a man-servant, because he is driving his master's expensive car, is mistaken for someone of wealth and power, and he plays along until a more educated doctor with an ability to read social signs catches him in the act.

The study of structure in literature is concerned primarily with the internal features of a text that lend it coherence, but it can also study a work's external links to the culture in which it is made. All works of literature draw on the codes of its culture. Hawthorne's audience, for example, would have recognized in the seventeenth-century Puritans he criticizes in his novel signs of nineteenth-century Whigs who, like the Puritans, wished to unite church and state. In at least the first *Matrix* movie, many young people saw a figure for their own disenchantment with a corporate culture that is overly routinized and authoritarian.

Exercise 2.1   William Shakespeare, *King Lear*

How might we understand what happens in the play as consisting of
signs that draw on codes of meaning that are either specific to the work
or that come from the culture of the era?

The opening scene has several significant elements. A king divides his
kingdom and gives it away. Daughters profess love in return for pieces
of the kingdom. One daughter refuses to play along. The king loses his
temper and banishes her. A loyal courtier objects and is in turn banished. The king offers the rejected daughter, without her dowry, to
suitors, one of whom rejects her, one of whom takes up her cause. In
the end, the banished daughter says to her sisters that she knows what
they are up to. They in turn begin to plot against their father.

Quite a bit happens, and each element is significant both within the
structure of the play and within the cultural codes of the time.

England in 1606 was a monarchy, and the king drew his principal
support from the aristocracy, a group of wealthy land-owners. Land was
the most valuable kind of property the aristocracy of England owned.
So the giving away of land would have represented something like an
act of madness. In a political sense, for a king to divide his kingdom
would have seemed as arbitrary and irrational. What would have been
the significance of these actions to the audience of the time? They might
have made the king seem fairly capricious and impulsive. His judgment
might not have seemed all that trustworthy. In a larger sense, he might
have seemed a danger to all that meant safety to the aristocracy – land,
national integrity, a coherent government.

Now consider the other events. Because England had no modern
police force, social order largely depended on the good behavior of
everyone. Personal virtue was highly valued. It was also a Christian
culture, and such Christian virtues as detachment from greed or avarice
were seen as being praiseworthy. In this light, what do you think audiences were supposed to think of the two sisters who seem to want land
so avidly? It would seem as if the daughter who chose to forgo land was
being more virtuous. Her renunciation of worldly goods would have
been a sign of Christian goodness.

That this daughter sees into her sisters' duplicity and that they, con-
firming her supposition, immediately begin to plot against their father,
also places her higher on the play's and the culture's scale of values.

How are we supposed to read the king's behavior? Is it virtuous?
Or are there indications that audiences at the time would have been

inclined to read his actions and statements as signs of an absence of virtue?

It would be possible to go through the rest of the play in a similar way, reading actions and statements as signs that bear meaning either within the structure of the play or within the culture of the time. The actions of Goneril and Regan are especially interesting, as are those of Edmund. Edgar, by contrast, is a paragon of virtue. How can you tell? What does he do to set himself apart? What word signs are associated with him that almost lend him a religious significance?

You might also consider the structure of the narrative of the play. It is laid out as progress from power to loss of power to restoration. It is a traditional life, death, and rebirth pattern. Why might it have been significant to audiences at the time? And why did it remain so popular for so many years, long after Shakespeare was dead? Given how the characters and their actions are significant, what exactly dies when Lear undergoes madness? What exactly is reborn in Edgar?

Within this internal structure, the characters are also signs. What is Cordelia a sign of? How is she posed against Edmund?

Exercise 2.2   Elizabeth Bishop, "The Map"

A structuralist approach to literature treats words as signs. Signs usually have meaning because they pertain to codes that assign a particular meaning to a particular word.

In "The Map," for example, Bishop thinks about the relationship between the signs we make to represent the world and the actual world itself. Her strategy might be characterized as taking real things to be signs and signs to be real things. The opening line – "Land lies in water; it is shadowed green" – is a description of a map as if it were the real world. A sign becomes a thing in Bishop's rendering. Notice how she personifies land; it "lies" as if it were taking a rest. That it is "shadowed green" takes the coloration of the map literally, as if in the real world the map color green actually exists. In the next line, she makes the playful confusion of literal and semiotic or literal and metaphoric more explicit. Note the rhyme ("shadow," "shallow") that also confuses a map sign (shadows = shallows) with a real thing, and it treats the map itself as if it might not be a cluster of signs but instead the real world it supposedly represents.

Go through the rest of the poem and look for other instances of such deliberate confusion of sign and thing.

Finally, try to answer the following question: why does Bishop draw our attention to this rather playful problem? You might think of various possible attitudes toward the natural world. A mapmaker might be someone who is charged with making as accurate an image of the world as possible. That's one attitude: scientific, objective, cool. Notice places in the poem where that project of objective representation is mocked or called into question.

What are some other attitudes toward the natural world? What alternate way of being in the world does the poem depict? Note Bishop's use of words like "stroke" ("We can stroke these lovely bays"). A mapmaker would not be interested in whether a bay is "lovely," and he certainly would not be interested in stroking it. (Can one stroke a bay?)

What role does emotion play in the poem? Romantic poets thought of nature as something that inspired strong emotions. Bishop is quite anti-Romantic in temperament; her preferred mode is much more ironic. How does she mock the Romantic conception of nature?

A crucial concern in mapmaking, as in any representation of the world, is accuracy. What problems does Bishop note regarding accuracy? What is the point of her playful questions regarding who gets to decide what colors go where? Is all mapmaking inherently authoritarian or can it be democratic?

Some would argue that all representations of the world, regardless of how supposedly accurate or objective, are plagued by values and perspectives. A map is always still the mapmaker's map. His perspective is evident in the choices he makes regarding what signs to use. Objectivity itself is a perspective. And all representation entails a choice of signs (blue or red, large or small, etc.). How does Bishop deal with these issues?

I sometimes ask students to think about how conservatives and liberals think of nature. In the US, at least, conservatives want to give as much of nature to business as possible. It should be exploited economically, not preserved. Liberals usually argue that nature should be preserved and respected. Economics comes second. The first position treats nature as a usable object. The second almost accords it a certain subjectivity. It is like us; we are part of it; to harm it is to harm ourselves. That position is linked to a more fluid sense of the boundary between the human and the natural than one finds in the conservative position. That position sees a firm boundary between human subject of action and natural object to be exploited.

Can you see these two positions in the poem? Which one does Bishop seem to embrace?

Exercise 2.3   Alice Munro, "Hold Me Fast, Don't Let Me Pass"

So much of life consists of reading signs that we easily forget what we are doing. All verbal communication with others is, of course, semiotic, but things we do are also significant, as are the ways we dress, eat, think, and behave. We depend on the legibility of signs in our lives, but signs, as King Lear learns, can also be used to mislead. They can be made to appear legible in a particular code they in fact do not respect. In a converse fashion, signs can also give us away, tell people things about us that we would prefer to keep concealed. Think of moments when you have flushed with embarrassment. You were in fact giving good sign without wanting to.

"Passing," for example, consists of pretending to be something one is not – another gender or ethnicity or another economic class. *The Talented Mr. Ripley* is all about someone who pretends to be wealthy but is not. Eventually, he assumes another's identity in order to really be what he initially only pretends to be. Doing so means manipulating signs in complex ways. Nella Larsen's *Passing* concerns two women who are African American in part but who are so fair-skinned that they can take tea in a whites-only restaurant without being detected for what they "are." One even marries a white man who hates blacks.

Munro's story, "Hold Me Fast," is about a woman on vacation in Scotland. It is an unfamiliar cultural, social, and semiotic world, one she has difficulty interpreting in some instances because she does not know what the signs she encounters mean. She meets a friendly man in the hotel where she is staying whose life she has trouble figuring out, but the woman who runs the hotel is a bundle of signs that prove more easily legible.

Try listing all the ways Hazel deals with signs in the story. Notice that the story begins with Hazel trying to figure out what the appropriate word or sign is for certain things in her writing. She also has difficulty finding the right interpretation for signs she encounters. Hazel describes being excluded from the pub, and she wonders what that means. It is a sign of something, but she doesn't know what.

Yet, in the end, she figures out what is going on around her. Pay attention to signs in the encounter with Judy and Miss Dobie. How do they "tell" Hazel what to think about this little world of intense relations?

Exercise 2.4 *The Searchers*

Consider a well-structured movie of the 1950s, *The Searchers*, in which the core concern of human culture with making order out of heterogeneity and civilization out of nature is an explicit theme. The film is laid out temporally as a series of parallel quests into the wilderness to find a kidnapped white girl, and spatially as the symmetrical opposition between settler civilization and the wilderness, between European American culture and Native American Indian culture.

Three intermediate characters move between these two universes, and their story lies at the heart of the narrative. Ethan and Marty search for Debbie, a young girl kidnapped by Native Americans. Ethan is at first determined to find her, but after years of searching and the realization that she has by now become the wife of a Native American, he decides to kill her. Marty, while initially a loyal follower of Ethan, ultimately stands in Ethan's way, preventing him from killing Debbie once the two men discover she has "gone Native" and become the wife of Chief Scar, her kidnapper. Marty ultimately takes over Ethan's task, kills Scar, and releases the girl. Ethan finds her, but instead of killing her as the audience has been led to expect, takes her up in his arms, says "Let's go home, Debbie," and returns her to the European American community.

How are civilization and the wilderness contrasted? What distinguishes them? Think about social institutions and economic practices, as well as how each relates to property.

How do the different characters such as Ethan, Aaron, and Clayton relate to both civilization and the wilderness? What distinguished Ethan from Clayton?

How are Marty and Ethan made to seem like parallel characters at the outset?

How, despite these parallels, are they different? How does each relate in different ways to the preservation of community in the face of what the wilderness represents? Why is Marty the one whose values prevail in the end over Ethan's? What does this say about what the community can tolerate amongst its members if it is to survive? How is Ethan so anti-communal that he can never quite fit in?

The meaning of the film is shaped by the dynamic set going by the structuring of relationships between places, characters, and possible actions. The wilderness is opposed to community, and Ethan and

Clayton are opposed representatives of the two worlds of value. Marty is an intermediate figure who moves between worlds and who assures the triumph of one over the other.

Another structural feature of the film is the opposition of certain kinds of action such as gift-giving and trading or economic exchange. How are gift-giving and trade made into explicit issues in the film? How is gift-giving privileged over trade in the marketplace? Contrast Futterman with Mose Harper.

If the film is about the imposition of civilization and of structure on the wilderness, then the seemingly marginal concern with sexuality, courtship, and marriage takes on greater significance, and the structural similarities and differences between Ethan and Scar become more important. How is Ethan like Scar at the beginning of the film? How is he as dangerous to the community? In the end, how is Ethan not like Scar? How is Scar associated with a wild sexuality that the whole structuring project of civilization might be said to work against?

If Scar is a projection outside the community of dangers that lie within the community, the danger particularly of natural male sexual urges, women's natural bodies are also coded as part of that danger. They are available to anyone; the patriarchal requirement of a male-dominated culture that property and patrimony pass on to one's own sons is endangered by the potential promiscuousness of women's bodies. In patriarchal culture, women's bodies are also frequently associated with formlessness and matter, that against which the structuring procedures of civilization operate in creating the orderly demarcations of that culture. According to this patricentric ideology, men bring reason, order, logic, and control to bear on the boundaryless material world. Mother Nature thereby becomes Father Time, the right order of succession whereby property, now bounded instead of boundaryless, is passed on through time from father to son, thus preserving father-centered civilization. This may explain why the initial spatial structure of the film (inside community versus outside wilderness) gives way to a temporal structure of repeated quests to restore civilization and reimpose its imperatives on the wild physicality that has momentarily erupted.

The construction of a successor's "masculinity," his alignment with the claim to a right to violence that sustains male rule in civilization, is crucially associated in the film with the question of proximity to or distance from the female body in its guise as unbounded and promiscuous physicality. Marty is the crucial figure in this equation. How does Ethan act toward him in regard to sexual knowledge? How is this behavior part of the film's structure? Where in the narrative does it change and why?

The various quests the men go on describe a structure that can be characterized as a movement away from civilization to a point in physical nature where the rules of civil life no longer hold (Scar's camp, a site of promiscuity) and a counter-movement that takes them back toward a reconciliation with civilization (the marriage ceremony). The quest, it turns out, is as much one whose goal is to find Debbie and rescue her from Native promiscuity as it is one whose goal is to align Marty with Laurie in a community-building marriage. The two parts of that structure are necessary because the repression of wild sexual urges and of the female body associated with them is a prerequisite of a civil community in the film.

What are the roles women are assigned in the community? How does this identity-building relate to the question of wild sexuality and to Debbie? Notice that she is connected to property and to its transfer.

The will scene between Ethan and Marty occurs in a cave, a place of connection to physical nature that is reminiscent of the underground place associated earlier in the film with the mother's body and foreshadowing of the cave out of which Debbie will be retrieved in the end. Such an accumulation of negative meanings in so structured a film makes almost mandatory a succeeding scene in which the problems posed by those negative meanings will be resolved. How do the succeeding scenes address these negative meanings?

How does the relationship between the searchers and the landscape change during the course of the film? How is it a visual sign at the outset of their inability to control the wilderness?

CHAPTER 3

Rhetoric

Every work of culture, be it a novel, a song, or a movie, is a representation of an imaginary world of characters, actions, ideas, and feelings. Every work of culture also acts on its audience to shape its judgments, its responses, and its feelings. Some evoke sympathy or inspire fear; others align the audience with moral positions. All work to make the audience feel a certain way toward events or characters. Tears, laughter, and suspenseful anxiety are some of the most obvious reactions that literary works provoke. Other reactions include the negative judgment an especially vile character or action inspires, or the feeling of identification and idealization that heroic actions and virtuous characters elicit.

The term for this kind of action on the audience is rhetoric. Cultural works are rhetorical simply by being plausible or credible representations (of imaginary characters and events). Securing belief from an audience is the first rhetorical act any cultural work must perform. But all imaginary representations of the world are also acts of valuation that a writer or cultural producer invites the audience to accept and participate in. Every work of literature is an invitation to endorse or reject the worldview the writer proposes, with its values and judgments. Every part of an imaginary representation (and of a cultural work) entails a choice between different possible elements that might be included or excluded, used or not used. Every such choice is an act of valuation because the writer or film-maker decides that a particular element is more suitable than all others for the story he or she is creating or the effect he or she seeks. To make a literary or cultural work is necessarily to engage in value judgments.

A writer who chooses, as James Joyce does in *Ulysses*, to place a humanist and compassionate Jew at the center of his novel, is making such a choice and engaging in such a valuation. Joyce's choice of that representational element was deliberately provocative in the cultural context in which he wrote, one in which anti-semitism was quite common. By doing so, Joyce criticizes aspects of Irish culture that he found unacceptable. Compare his choice and his valuation to that of Edith Wharton in *The House of Mirth*. Wharton's heroine, Lily Bart, is an embodiment of Anglo-Saxon self-idealization. Her lily-like whiteness is an index of a troubled, but ultimately resolute, moral purity that contrasts sharply with the unvirtuous obsession with money and social climbing that Wharton locates in Rosedale, a Jewish businessman whose ethnicity is remarked upon repeatedly in the novel. Rosedale is the money-grubbing foil for Lily's world-renouncing virtue. Wharton could get away with this derogatory representation largely because anti-semitism was pervasive in American culture at the time. For inverse reasons, Joyce could not get away with his effort to break cultural stereotypes, and his book was banned in the United States.

The makers of cultural works do not simply seek to inspire belief in an imaginary world in their audiences. They seek to create a particular kind of belief, one characterized by positive and negative judgments and feelings. Wharton allows that Rosedale might have positive attributes, but her choice of adjectives positions the audience to arrive at an overwhelmingly negative judgment regarding his character. The narrative voice remains external to his consciousness, and we never see the world from his point of view. In contrast, Joyce spends many chapters recounting Leopold Bloom's numerous and wildly entertaining thoughts, perceptions, and feelings. After hearing his eminently practical idea for saving space in crowded cemeteries (bury the dead upright), it is hard to have negative feelings toward him. Joyce positions the audience inside Bloom in such a sympathetic way that the ambient anti-semitism of Irish society seems violent and unjustified in contrast. We witness Bloom performing a very Christian act of charity one moment, and in the next witness him being mocked and vilified in typically anti-semitic terms by his Irish acquaintances as someone incapable of Christian virtue. The effect on an attentive audience that allows itself to be convinced and moved by Joyce's rhetorical strategies is to feel that Bloom, not his Irish interlocutors, is the better embodiment of supposedly Christian virtue.

The field of rhetoric includes not only the choices and valuations that go into the selection of elements that shade audience perceptions and judgments in different ways, but also the way selected elements are arranged logically in a narrative sequence. Rhetoric is often associated with the creation of emotional effects, but initially, in classical Greece and Rome, it had more to do with logic, with the arrangement of elements of language and thought so that they were convincing. This sense of logical argumentation still is essential to literary and dramatic works. They are plausible representations because they are logical. Logic also inheres in the moral shading of events, characters, and ideas and is essential to the ultimate effect the maker of a literary or dramatic work wishes to create, or the point he or she wishes to make. In the film *Mildred Pierce*, a married woman initiates an adulterous affair in one scene, and in the next, her daughter dies – a seemingly logical, cause–effect consequence in this heavy-handedly moralistic film. The film *Crash* more complexly evokes the possibility of several personal disasters – a black man about to be shot by white policemen, a black woman about to die because she refuses help from a racist white cop, a Hispanic girl about to be shot by an angry Iranian immigrant. The movie steps back from disaster in each instance and merely issues a warning. But the logic is clear: behave like this and you will suffer pain or loss. Although not explicitly a didactic film, it nevertheless seeks to make a point through a quite logical linking of cause and effect.

The field of rhetoric also encompasses the procedures and techniques one can use in working with language to produce effects or make points. I have mentioned some of these already, such as contrast and similitude. I made a point about the significance of certain compositional choices by contrasting Joyce with Wharton. I might have said that Wharton was a "glaring" example of anti-semitism, and that would have been a metaphor. I would have substituted a concrete physical image having to do with vision and light for an idea. There is, of course, a large inventory of possible techniques, moves, and procedures in rhetoric, from repetition to personification to symbolism. And it would be impossible to find a literary or cultural work that does not rely on some rhetorical move or device.

When we read a book or watch a movie, we are not only the passive recipients of someone else's rhetorical acts; we are also active readers and watchers. Our minds bring to the experience a capacity to understand that is shaped by the mind's inherent powers, by the assumptions our culture instills in us through education and acculturation, and by our past experiences. Philosophers such as Immanuel Kant, Edmund Husserl, and Alphonso Lingis argue that the mind organizes experience using its own resources. Think of your own political beliefs. If you have strong liberal or conservative beliefs, then a statement by someone of the opposed belief will not reach your mind without encountering filters that process it, often as being acceptable or rejectable. A liberal might be inclined to think George W. Bush as much an idiot as a fool no matter what he says, while a conservative might find his statements acceptable no matter how distant from veracity. (That last sentence, by the way, is what in rhetoric is called a polemic.)

Similarly, when we read a book or watch a movie, we bring to the experience our own innate cognitive capacities. We all belong to "interpretive communities," groups whose members share assumptions and who as a result see the world in the same way. Those groups can be national or ethnic, or generation- or gender-based, or they can be more a matter of culture or profession or education. For example, John Milton, in writing *Paradise Lost*, could assume that his Christian audience would be familiar with his biblical references, and in consequence he could count on an interpretive community that would read his work in the way that he intended. We respond to cues in novels or movies or poems or songs because we share with the maker a cultural heritage and language that allows him or her to assume that certain kinds of images or ideas or fictional events will be understood in particular ways by the audience. When NWA in "The Nigga Ya Love To Hate" refer to *Soul Train*, a television dance show made for an African American audience, they knew they could count on people understanding the reference. Edith Wharton could assume that a derogatory image of a Jew would not offend her core audience, while James Joyce, in a spirit of anarchic perversity, could equally assume that he was insulting large portions of his Irish audience by portraying their anti-semitism in a mocking manner. In twentieth-century American culture, William Faulkner in writing *Light in August* could count on getting away with references to African Americans as being characterized by "vacuous idiocy." Whites have for decades been able to read the novel at a distance that allows them not to be affected by its racism, but African American students of mine find it insulting. White readers, who do not experience the depiction of African Americans in the novel as being insulting because they have no history of being victimized by racism themselves, can more easily accept the offer of complicity in racism that the novel makes.

Consequently, not all audiences can be counted on to react in the same way to the rhetorical offer a literary work makes. When I watched *Crash*, for example, I thought its early scenes to be convincing renditions of plausible racial conflicts. But its easy resolutions of these conflicts in the end were unconvincing. All punches were pulled, and the audience was spared having to experience too much pain and disappointment. When a pebble is dropped into water with an oil film on top, the surface breaks temporarily, and then the oil film seals shut the surface once again. *Crash* seems to perform a similar rhetorical operation with racism in America. It gives us a glimpse beneath the surface of the benign, happy-making and trouble-avoiding cultural platitudes about equality that Americans use as a way of dealing with unacceptable social inequality (the fact, for example, that African Americans have more stressful lives and lower life expectancy than whites). It shows us the ugly racism at the heart of the American Dream. But then it hurries to close off that perception and return us to the treacly platitudes with which we live. For me, in other words, it did not work; its rhetorical labor failed. And that may be because I have seen other films, such as the French film-maker Mathieu Kassovitz's *Hate*, which tell a story of racial hatred more honestly and which do not shy away from exposing the pain inflicted by racial animosity. Having had that experience, my ability to receive less honest cultural messages regarding racism is impaired.

Rhetoric is also an internal feature of works of literature and culture. Characters address each other in active ways that change behavior, mold perception and belief, or challenge assumptions. *Crash* is a textbook example of multiple rhetorical gestures, from insult to apology, mockery to praise. When characters perceive one another through the filters of racial stereotypes, it is difficult for them to see each other and easy for them to insult one another. In the opening scene, a Latino police officer mocks the speech of an Asian American woman, while in a later scene her own ethnic culture is mocked by another officer. He in turn is the victim of intimidating speech from his superior. The point of this chain of language acts is that no one escapes being reducible to a stereotype and having their specific identity denied by a category that makes them the same as everyone else in the category.

We are all, at some point in our lives, victims of language. English philosopher J. L. Austin pointed out that there is a class of statements in language that make things happen in the world. Such "speech acts" include the marriage vow, contracts, and the naming of a child. In each case, a statement modifies the world. Speech acts. Someone becomes "married," someone enters into a binding agreement that places obligations on one, and someone becomes an identity, a person with a particular name. Austin might just as easily have expanded speech acts to include all those moments when people interact in forceful ways, trying to persuade each other of ideas or beliefs or trying to harm or heal or to betray or deceive. As in the world of *King Lear*, for example.

Exercise 3.1   William Shakespeare, *King Lear*

King Lear might be said to be a play about speech acts, that kind of language that makes things happen in the world (such as the minister's pronouncement that makes two people man and wife). The ability to engage in such speech acts is connected intrinsically to social conventions and to social power. A minister can perform the marriage speech act because there exists a convention or agreement that gives him the power to do so. That convention creates an identity, "minister," and it allows "pronounce" to have a legally binding meaning it otherwise does not have. As a result of the convention, the minister possesses powers, especially the power to say things such as the marriage pronouncement ("I now declare you man and wife"), that will be understood by all to be a change in social reality rather than merely words. The physical world is not changed by the pronouncement that two people are now man and wife, but their legal status is changed. They can now behave differently toward one another, cohabit without raising eyebrows in certain quarters or in certain parts of the country, and have certain expectations about their spouse and about their future that they did not have before the speech act was performed. Their social identity and their behavior change even if their physical composition does not.

How is *King Lear* organized around speech acts? How does it depict the changes that occur in one's identity when social conventions of the kind that license speech acts change? A king can say things that others cannot, for example. What are some of the things that Lear says in the first act that might be considered to be speech acts? How is it clear that his conventional identity as "king" provides a license for saying things that make changes in the world? Take note of what happens when others, such as Kent and Cordelia, whose conventional social identity is different, say things to him that try to effect changes in his world. How do they fare?

The first act of the play contains numerous examples of rhetoric, from hyperbole (or exaggeration) to chiasmus (or crossing of terms) to apostrophe (or address). Go through the act and try to locate as many examples of rhetoric as you can.

Richard Lanham in "Tacit Persuasion Patters" contends that certain forms of language, such as chiasmus ("The first shall be last, and the last shall be first"), imitate logic and so are tacitly persuasive even if they are not entirely logical. How is chiasmus used in the first act? What do the particular uses of chiasmus imply regarding Cordelia especially?

Why would Shakespeare wish to associate a particularly paradoxical rhetorical form with her?

Paradox is like chiasmus in that it equates or associates things that logically are far apart such as "the last" and "the first." How might Cordelia's position in regard to her father's demands and her sisters' flattery of him be best represented by paradox? Think about how logical it is to make every attempt to obtain worldly goods when they are offered, even if it means abasing oneself through flattering professions of affection. Why might the play want you to embrace instead the anti-logical position that it is better to sacrifice the possibility of worldly goods in order to attain a higher virtue? How else does it make that alogical argument?

How are Goneril and Regan on the one hand and Edmund on the other made to seem similar or parallel in the opening act? He says at one point that "all's with me meet that I can fashion fit." What does he mean by that? How does it equate him with Goneril and Regan? What implications does it have for his use of rhetoric?

How would you characterize the Fool's rhetorical function or role in this opening act? What is the nature of his "lessons" to Lear? Notice the different kinds of puns that he uses. Corbett (in "Classical Rhetoric") lists several varieties, from syllepsis to zeugma. How many different kinds can you find? What is the point of them? Like the rhetoric of chiasmus and paradox in regard to Cordelia, they work by evoking illogicality ("since thou mad'st thy daughters thy mothers"). Why is it an important feature of the Fool's critique of Lear to evoke illogicality or alogicality? How might they be linked to irrationality?

The use of rhetoric in a literary or dramatic work often depends on its audience. *King Lear* was first presented to King James' court on St. Stephen's night 1606. King James was homosexual, and his court was known as a safe meeting-place for "catamites" or gay people. The London stage was also known for its homosexual subculture, and actors were also apparently court regulars. It is quite possible then that a certain degree of open homosexuality was tolerated in the court. The only surviving account of the court seems to corroborate that hypothesis.

Does the play make jokes or references that might have been intended for a gay audience? Pay attention to the Fool's taunting of Lear in Act 1. Try to find references to homosexual acts. How does the Fool suggest that Lear's foolish actions may have made him symbolically vulnerable to sodomy?

A gay subculture in the early seventeenth century would conceivably have been one in which heterosexuality – and especially that dimension of heterosexuality that entailed physical contact with women's bodies – might have been a subject of derision. Once Goneril enters in Act 1, scene 4, how does a new rhetoric emerge regarding women's bodies? How would you characterize it? How might it be explained by the particular kind of audience address that Shakespeare may have been engaging in?

One of the more interesting rhetorical moments in the play occurs in Act 2, scene 2. The play privileges "plain" speech and associates ornate, contrived, hyperbolic speech with a lack of virtue. Once again, this position may have to do with audience. King James, when he assumed the English throne in 1603, brought with him from Scotland a strong allergy toward the verbally ornate style of Elizabeth's court. He fought immediately with one of the leading representatives of that court, Sir Walter Raleigh, and eventually arranged for his execution. James himself was famous both for his plain speech and for his highly polemical statements, especially to Parliament. In the character of Lear, one senses something of James himself. But it is in the character of Kent that one finds the plain speech with which James was linked.

What are the different verbal styles in this scene (Act 2, scene 2)? How does Kent's plain speech become a matter of debate? What is Kent's attitude toward the ornate speech used in court? How does he imitate it and to what end? The way language is used in the play by different characters is linked to moral qualities. With what moral qualities is Kent's plain speech in this scene linked?

When Lear's world starts to fall apart later in the play, the change is rendered in part through changes in his ability to perform speech acts that he was used to performing before the collapse of his world. Locate some moments of change where conventions seem to shift and in so doing to change his identity. Why is a change in the ability to perform speech acts connected so intrinsically to his identity? Think about how speech acts only work if people are willing to credit one with the power to perform them. Because they rely on conventions (which is to say, on the agreement of other people), speech acts are inherently unstable as a rhetorical form.

In locating moments of instability in the performance of speech acts, you might begin with Act 2, scene 4, where Lear arrives at the home of Cornwall and Regan.

It is the breach of agreements that leads to Lear's madness, of course. Notice how his sense of his identity changes in Act 3, scene 4. He is no longer a king but a "despised old man." To be "despised" is to be the object of others' verbal violence, their spite. One is no longer a competent and respected agent of verbal action. Notice the emphasis in Edgar's speech in this scene on agreements as remedies for the ills that bedevil Lear: "Obey thy parents; keep thy word's justice; swear not; commit not with man's sworn spouse."

How is the final resolution of the play enacted as a restoration of the power to perform speech acts? Look at Act 4, scene 6. How do the soldiers behave when they find Lear?

Edgar plays a crucial role in the restoration of an order the play obviously considers to be right. How is he associated with speech acts and with the power they give a person who is able to perform them? Notice as well that he is associated with a power of speech that is not only "performative" in Austin's sense of that term. It is also quasi-religious: "Methought thy very gait did prophesy / A royal nobleness." Prophecy is a mode of speech that so controls the world that there is no chance that it will be betrayed by broken agreements. What does this imply for the kind of political power that will be restored at the end of the play? Look at Albany's speech in Act 5, scene 3, lines 301–6.

Once again, audience is a significant factor in understanding the play's argument. James favored an absolutist interpretation of monarchial power, and he clashed with the parliamentarians, who favored a more tempered kind of power for the king. He should not rise above the law.

Many works of literature are argumentative in that they try to position the audience in a perspective that entails a belief in the values or ideals the work promotes. How is Shakespeare's play argumentative? How does it position you to adopt certain beliefs and to have certain emotional reactions? And how do those beliefs and reactions link up with the play's political argument in favor of James' absolutist sense of monarchial power?

Exercise 3.2   Elizabeth Bishop, "Anaphora"

Another dimension of rhetoric is the shaping procedures and forms that we use when we speak and write. We are all familiar with metaphor: "The ship of state will not change course," where "ship" is a concrete image that substitutes for the institutions of government. Or "Ripeness is all," a famous line from *King Lear*, which substitutes for life the idea of ripe fruit. There are numerous other such shaping procedures. They allow us to speak more efficiently and with greater effectiveness and power. "All hands on deck" telescopes a list of names of sailors into an image that uses a part of their body ("hands") for them. That form is called synecdoche. Politicians like to use repetition, a rhetorical form called anaphora, to make points more emphatically. The most famous is Caesar's "I came, I saw, I conquered." When conservative Pat Buchanan wanted to emphasize his dismay with the Republican Party, he resorted to anaphora: "It is soft on globalism. It is soft on big government. It is soft on the 2nd amendment. It is soft on life."

A poem named after a rhetorical trope would seem to be an attempt to draw some consequential meaning or effect from the use of language the trope names. Read Bishop's poem "Anaphora" and note its use of repetition. Some repetitions are of words such as "mortal" in the last two lines of the first stanza: "assuming memory and mortal / mortal fatigue." Others are of sounds, as "begins, with birds, with bells."

Why does Bishop name her poem "Anaphora" or "repetition"? How is the poem about repetition? What are some of the kinds of repetition she describes?

She begins by describing a sunrise, and that of course might be counted one of the more repetitive events in human life on earth. But notice how Bishop uses images and metaphors that suggest that something quite significant and unique is taking place. She refers to it as a "ceremony," and she seems to contradict the sense of dullness that repetition can be associated with by using deliberately idealizing images: "brilliant walls." The sun, rather than being the light source we see every day (day in, day out, one might say), becomes an "ineffable creature." What does "ineffable" mean? Why characterize the sun in this way? Why call a simple sunrise a "ceremony"? And how does this contrast with the end of the stanza: "assuming memory and mortal / mortal fatigue"?

In the second stanza, the sun is described as "falling" and moving toward sunset. But notice now that it seems to interact with or in human life. It showers light on "stippled faces." What does "stippled" mean and why might Bishop use this image for the effect of sunlight on the faces of people? How is the sun now characterized? It seems almost personified by a line like "suffers our uses and abuses." What might be our uses and abuses? Life is characterized as something unanchored in any firm foundation. Human "dreaming" is "squandered upon him," and as the sun sinks it passes through a "drift" of bodies and of classes. Why drift? What does that imply about human life? Note that it is an example of the very repetition the poem's title indicates is Bishop's primary concern. Why repeat "drift"?

The final image of the beggar in the park is almost oxymoronic or self-contradictory. He lacks the wherewithal to read books, yet he is preparing "stupendous studies." Why? How can that be the case?

There is another potential oxymoron here at the end: "the fiery event, / of every day." How is that self-contradictory?

"Fiery event" is reminiscent of the way early Greek philosophers such as Heraclitus described life. What does it imply to characterize life as a fire? And think about the significance of calling something an "event." How is that at odds with the notion of repetitiveness in life?

Finally, why conclude by evoking the possibility of "endless / endless assent"? The word "assent" means something like "agree to" in ordinary usage (as in "to give one's assent to something"), but it also has a different meaning in nineteenth-century Protestant theology. Bishop is not a religious poet by any means; she keeps the Protestantism of her childhood at arm's distance and even mocks it occasionally in poems such as "At the Fishhouses" and "A Complete Concordance." But here she seems to use a theological idea more affirmatively. Indeed, the theological meaning of "assent" is "to express belief in" or even "to have faith." How does that help clarify the apparent oxymoron in the last lines?

Exercise 3.3   Alice Munro, "Goodness and Mercy"

Language acts in ways that can heal or hurt. We act on others by blaming or praising, cajoling or cursing, deflecting or demeaning, and so on. We can use language on others to deceive and insult or to pacify and condole. Similarly, with ourselves, we can use words to exculpate or to blame. By simply telling ourselves a story about how we are living, by representing it in language in certain ways, we can, for example, gain for ourselves a sense of being quite worthy, perhaps more worthy than we really are. We can also, of course, do harm to ourselves by blaming ourselves overly much for things that may be beyond our control or not as bad as we think.

Language is in some respects a licensing procedure that makes questionable actions acceptable or that so transforms our perceptions of others that we permit ourselves to act on them in unacceptable ways. Latin American torturers used to say "Eres mierda" ("You are shit") to those they abused. Language allowed them to place their victims outside humanity, and that made doing violence to them more justifiable. The film *V for Vendetta* makes the point that words like "terrorist" or "deviant" allow those with political and economic power to do violence to those who oppose them or who depart from their standards of what constitutes proper behavior.

This meditation may seem distant from the concerns of Alice Munro's story "Goodness and Mercy," but notice how language is used in the story. Naming or characterizing others through language is an important element in the women's lives. June is called Bugs, for example, and she talks about how unladylike her language is at one point. Her real name should evoke reactions in her fellow Canadian passengers because she is a famous singer, but it does not. What is the significance of the switch from June to Bugs? How does it change who she is or how she is perceived?

Tone in language can be quite significant as we address others. A harsh tone can be off-putting, and a cajoling tone can be winning. How would you characterize the tone of Bugs' speech? Notice that she is described as saying "So long" to Canada as the ship leaves Canadian waters. In what way is it important that she says that rather than something more portentous and less informal? She is dying, after all, and she casually talks about not making it to England alive. But another character, Jeanine, says that people can use charming speech to manipulate others, and insinuates that Bugs is manipulative. Is that true of Bugs?

The other characters characterize themselves in their ways of speaking. The university professor is especially funny. How does Munro position you to dislike him simply by reporting his self-description? What's wrong with him?

What does Averill discover about the speech of her fellow passengers? Notice how she summons a linguistic stereotype about ocean voyages and then challenges it with what her fellows are really doing.

What is the significance of Bugs' naming the artist Toulouse Lautrec? She also says of the Captain that he is a "canny Scot." What do you think a "canny Scot" is and why does she say it of the Captain? How is he characterized in comparison to the other passengers' rhetorical, conversational, and social efforts?

The Captain tells a story about a death on board ship. Why does Averill feel it is her story? And why is there more than one version of the story the Captain tells?

Language can either push people away or bring them closer. That is one meaning of "charm." Language is magical in that regard. Consider the burial of Bugs by the Captain and Averill in terms of the use of language. Then note how the Captain remains with Averill through life; she seems in the end to still think of him. What has he done to merit such attachment? Note how he seems contrasted with one husband whose tone puts people off: "He either charmed people or aroused their considerable dislike." How does the Captain contrast with this character?

Exercise 3.4 *Apocalypse Now*

Apocalypse Now argues for a forceful resolution to the Vietnam War. Written and directed by America's leading rightwing film-makers, Francis Ford Coppola and John Milius, the film links the military argument to the conservative economic individualism that came to prominence in the US in the late 1970s and 1980s, immediately after the unsuccessful conclusion of the war. Conservatives during the post-World War II era molded a convincing cultural and political ideology that successfully substituted "freedom" for "inequality." The struggle against egalitarian national liberation movements or against egalitarian economies in general was presented to the public as a "defense of freedom" rather than as a defense of an inegalitarian economic system in which the wealth of a few depended on the comparative structural impoverishment of the many. Freedom was valued as a concept by conservatives because it both named and enabled the activities of individual economic agents unrestrained by any government power or sense of community responsibility. Attempts by democratic egalitarian governments to establish alternative economic forms in which everyone might benefit equally from economic activity were portrayed as dangerously "bureaucratic" or "totalitarian." In many conservative films of the era, therefore, the idealization of the use of military force against national liberation movements is frequently accompanied by the glorification of individual "freedom." Individualist heroes are frequently portrayed doing battle with not only enemy military forces but also governmental or military bureaucracies, which are metaphors for liberal or socialist governments that attempt to foster economic egalitarianism. They are portrayed as obstacles to the triumph of the heroic individualist's free will.

Coppola and Milius frame their individualist and militarist argument in religious and racialist terms. Asia is portrayed as a haven of primitive barbarism, its Buddhist religion linked to blood sacrifice and mindless violence, while the "mission" of the heroic American soldier, Willard, is framed as a quest narrative with resonances in the medieval fisher king story and the Christ story. The white and the fair-haired are good and civilized, while the dark and the short are faceless, voiceless incarnations of brutal, primeval, savage urges. Most remarkable about the film is the degree to which it integrates the conservative critique of liberalism to the war story. Heroism consists of withstanding liberal bureaucracy, effeminacy, and military inefficiency in favor of an individualist warrior-leader ideal that favors force over negotiation.

How is the film's narrative laid out so as to reinforce these arguments? One would expect it to begin with a negative state and then work toward a positive state that is made possible by an embrace of the conservative ideals for which the film argues. How does the film's narrative map a trajectory from weakness to strength? And how does Willard change as the film progresses? How would you contrast how he behaves at the beginning with how he is portrayed at the end? How are terms like "shit" and "clean" used in this mapping?

Notice how Kurtz is portrayed when you first hear of him in a scene in an army general's camp. How is that camp portrayed? How does it suggest luxury and ease? Why might the military brass or bureaucracy be portrayed in this way?

Now, how is Kurtz portrayed in the file Willard is given, and how does that portrait contrast with the image of the general? Almost immediately, as he studies the file, Willard begins to see Kurtz in a positive light. What is positive about Kurtz for Willard? How, in conservative thinking, might breaking rules, solving problems using one's own insights and intuitions, and breaking away from governmental regulation be seen as virtue?

Note that when Willard is given his assignment, Kurtz is linked to Christ. It begins to become clear that his individualism, visionary leadership, and warrior abilities are unacceptable to an army bureaucracy that dines well while the enemy gets by on rat meat and will accept nothing short of victory or death. America needs to adopt a similar attitude in order to be "saved," according to the film-makers, mistaking a difference between colonial invaders with no motive for winning and liberation forces with a strong motive for fighting hard to free their homeland from foreign intervention for a difference between races. Much of the narrative between the assignment and the killing consists of episodes meant to portray the war as being lost by liberal, bureaucratic pussy-footing. What is needed, the film-makers argue in a traditional conservative way, is strong visionary leadership that transcends bureaucratic procedures, legal rules, civilian democratic protest, and the restraints of moral conscience.

How do the various episodes up to the entry into Kurtz's world portray the regular army? How is it inappropriate for fighting the war?

How is liberalism tainted as preventing the war from being won properly?

How do the points made in each of these episodes contribute to the larger argument of the film?

As he travels on, how does Willard come increasingly to identify with Kurtz? What does he come to think of his extra-judicial methods and his decision to adopt the enemy's guerrilla tactics? How does he come to see him as a heroic, warrior individualist who is a seer-leader capable of winning the war on his own?

In conservative eyes, such leaders should be obeyed because they possess superior abilities and innate authority. Democracy is wrong because it places too much importance on the will of the people. Liberal bureaucracy and rules are worse because they curtail the individual leader's will. Can you link these points to how Kurtz is portrayed?

Willard seems to endorse Kurtz's way of fighting the war, yet at Kurtz's camp, Willard completes his mission by murdering Kurtz. Why does he do so?

Think about the books the camera pans over in Kurtz's room. One of them, *From Ritual to Romance*, recounts the medieval fisher king legend whereby the king dies so that a new king can be born. In a sense, for the king to survive, he must die. Are there elements of the final scenes that might link this argument to the film? In what sense is it about sacrifice?

Kurtz recounts a tale in which US special forces are portrayed as humanitarian saviors while the Vietnamese are portrayed as doing violence to their own people. If I had ten divisions of those men, he says, all our problems here would be over in no time. The argumentative strategy is twofold. First, assign to national liberation fighters the ideal of military brutality that animates the colonialists, while suggesting that the liberals who oppose that conservative military ideal are the ones responsible for the war's being "lost." Second, suggest that, in order to win the war properly against such adversaries, the US needs to adopt the ways of the enemy, which in fact are projections of the conservative ideal.

How does Kurtz's summary of the ideal way of killing "cleanly" and "awake" get transferred onto Willard? How might it be seen to justify his killing of Kurtz? How is Willard portrayed as being reborn? Go back to the beginning of the film and note how images of his later strength are superimposed on images of his initial weakness.

The film is political to the extent that its meaning and its argument are situated within a context of discussion regarding the Vietnam War that pitted conservatives against liberals. It should be paired with the documentary *Hearts and Minds* (1975) that tells the story of the war from the point of view of the Vietnamese. A very different picture of the war emerges once you cross the line dividing "us" from "the enemy" and begin listening to their account of the war. Instead of an allegorical conflict between weak western principles of legal warfare and strong, ruthless, and efficient eastern principles of warfare that we would do well to emulate, what one encounters in this film is a complex sense of the historical reality of the war. The link back to French colonialism is presented not as the continuation of a heroic struggle against restless natives but as the brutal, exploitative suppression of an indigenous population for the sake of access to raw materials for the western economy. Moreover, the racist equation established in *Apocalypse Now* between eastern Buddhist religion and military ruthlessness is contradicted by the voices of Buddhist monks in the documentary, who speak intelligently and reasonably about their opposition to colonialism and to the imposition of a military government on the South Vietnamese by the US. While the opponents of the US are presented in *Apocalypse Now* as the practitioners of ruthless violence, in the documentary what emerges, especially from the testimony of victims of torture, is a sense that the US and its South Vietnamese allies were in fact the greater wrongdoers in this regard.

CHAPTER 4

Post-Structuralism, Deconstruction, Post-Modernism

There have always been two traditions in philosophy. One asserts that there are truths that are universal and eternal. They stand outside history and the physical world; therefore, they are transcendental or ideal in nature. The other school claims that the world is physical and historical and that any truth we arrive at about it is equally historical, equally located within the physical universe. There is no transcendental realm of spirit or ideality. Our knowledge therefore is limited and fallible. The world is not founded on absolutes that exist outside time and space. You may arrive at a universal law, but it will be about the complexity of physical life, not derived from a transcendental or ideal realm of absolute truth that is the foundation of the world and of our knowledge of it. Like religion, which also claims a foundation for truth in an ideal or spiritual realm, the first tradition provides a strong claim of authority for those interested in using philosophy to anchor ideals of social order. The second is closer to science than to religion, and it promotes the ideal of progressive change.

Disputes between these two positions occasionally break out, and one such war erupted after 1967, when a French philosopher named Jacques Derrida strongly reasserted the claims of the second position in three books – *Writing and Difference*, *Of Grammatology*, and *Speech and Phenomenon*, all published in 1967. He argued that the most recent attempt to assert the first or absolutist and foundationalist position in the work of Edmund Husserl was mistaken. Husserl argued that all truth was like geometry: one could in one's mind picture an ideal triangle. It exists outside time and place in an ideal or transcendental realm. Such truth, Husserl argued, qualifies as universal and absolute.

To understand that, you have to think about how your own mind works. In your everyday life, you experience things in something like a flow, an ongoing stream of awareness that is situated in time and space. It is limited in many ways. You can only experience a single mind or consciousness, and you only experience or are conscious of a single historical moment and a very circumscribed amount of space. You cannot attain anything like universality, knowing everything everywhere for all time. But think again. Your mind possesses an ability to abstract. Before you is a society you might be inclined to think of as something of a slave society. People do nothing but work most of the time, and most of the work produces value and wealth for a very small sliver of the population – investors, large property-owners, corporate executives, etc. – who reap the benefits of others' labors. Society might seem like a huge pyramid with a small group at the top and everyone else arranged beneath them in a descending order of increasingly contemptible and distasteful labors. The pyramid is an abstraction like a geometric triangle. As you may recall from geometry class, there are no perfect triangles in the actual world, but you can think of one, abstractly, in your mind, in that ideational place we call consciousness or mind. So also, you have constructed a mental abstraction from what you see before you, and that abstract model can be applied to societies all over the globe. You now are getting closer to a truth that might be universal. All societies are pyramids. You have your universal.

But still, there are all these sticky and contentious differences between places and people, or between moments in time. The pyramid was different two hundred years ago, and no doubt will be different two hundred years down the road. New groups will rise to the top, even if the basic rules that get them there will remain roughly the same. The composition of pyramids around the world will change, even if the basic model will endure. So you are not quite there yet. The universal and absolute truth you thought you had reached is complicated by differences between the various concrete examples of it. And if you start to study those, to get them into your consciousness so that you can process them and abstract from them to make a better universal model, you will find yourself getting sucked into increasingly differentiated detail. You will have to choose between the universalist model of truth and the differentiated model, the one that takes your specific location in time and space as its starting point. If you choose the universalist position, you lose the differentiated detail; if you go for the differentiated detail, you lose sight of your perfect abstraction, the ideal, universally applicable model that accounts for everything everywhere. You come to see that it can only do so by being more or less empty of any specific content. It has to be almost purely abstract, a kind of form or model with nothing specific or worldly or historical or concrete about it whatsoever. The social pyramid you came up with as a model for everything is different in China than it is in the United States, and it is more different still in Finland.

Husserl thought he had solved this problem. He argued that you can start with your consciousness of the world – which is called phenomenology because it deals with phenomena or things that appear as images in your conscious mind. You then abstract from this by distilling what is purest about the experience as it occurs in consciousness. He compared this to geometry, and argued that you can find something akin to the perfect triangle in a part of your mind that is transcendental. By transcendental, he meant that it stands outside everyday experience, the flow of awareness in historical time and actual space through your consciousness. Your ordinary awareness of something in the world depends on what comes before in time and what comes after, and it depends on the differences or relations between what is immediately before your mind and everything else around it. You know this not that, or you know this moment not the one before it. Yet those other moments in time and those other locations in space stick to what you are seeking to know. Your consciousness of it is shadowed by them. You may recall that this is what Saussure said of language – that every part is differential and relational. Its identity depends on what it is not.

But, according to Husserl, if you use your powers of abstraction to transcend or step outside that flow of experience, you attain a transcendental realm of cognition where the thing you wish to grasp with your mind exists in a purely ideal form purged of all connection to the world. You preserve the sense of concrete experience, but you gain a truth that can be called universal and absolute.

Derrida took issue with all of this. He argued that the transcendental place outside time and space where universal knowledge seemed possible is itself merely one more place among other places and one more moment of consciousness that is shadowed by other moments. You can never get outside time and space. There is no transcendence.

This was a very strong claim for the second position, the one that emphasizes the flow of conscious experience in historical time and actual physical space. Essentially, Derrida inverted Husserl. If Husserl claimed the flow can always be converted into an absolutely ideal truth, one that exists in a pure mental space, Derrida said that all absolute truths and all supposedly pure mental states are merely part of the flow.

Needless to say, this argument annoyed those who held to the first position, the one that emphasizes the possibility of absolute, universal truth, and a culture war ensued. In libraries, you will find a record of it filed under "post-modernism."

Derrida's most interesting intellectual move was to suggest that difference characterized not only language but also all reality, from our thought processes to the world itself. You may recall that Saussure argued that difference is the principle that allows language to function. The difference between sounds allows words to be different from one another. A "rat" will not be confused with a "hat" because of a phonological difference. Neither word has an identity in itself apart from that difference. Another way of wording this is to say that each word's identity is contingent rather than absolute. If all other words disappeared, "rat" would no longer be rat because it depends on its difference from and relations to all other words to be what it is. Its identity is contingent on those others. It is not something absolute in itself, an identity pure and simple. If the same is true of the world and of our awareness of it, then absolute truth becomes a little harder to come by. Husserl's idea that you can stabilize a thing or an idea in your conscious awareness and abstract from it is more difficult to perform if the object in your mind is a relation of difference rather than an identity.

In reviewing the western philosophic tradition, Derrida found many instances of thinkers who either were aware of the way difference undermined identity or were committed to a suppression of difference in order to lay claim to absolute truth. With this latter group of thinkers, he developed a method called "deconstruction" that consisted of unearthing evidence of difference within their claims to absolute truth. Such truth usually proved to be founded on an ideal of pure identity, an essence in things that made them unique in comparison to other things. Such ideals of identity were presented either as an ultimate goal of philosophic inquiry or as the foundation from which philosophic inquiry springs. The word for goal in Greek is *telos*, so the term "teleology" characterizes this kind of goal-oriented philosophy. The word in Greek for foundation is *arche*, so the word "archeology" is used for a way of thinking that derives absolute truth from some foundation or origin from which everything else derives (such as the concept of "God," for example). Because the belief in a transcendental truth outside time and space resembles religious belief, Derrida uses the term "theology" for philosophies that ignore the fact that all knowledge is historical and spatially located and therefore differential. To be temporally and spatially located is to be immersed in connections or relations to other things from which the identity of the thing differs. He also uses the term "metaphysics" for philosophy that seeks absolute truth in transcendence, in a realm of quasi-spiritual ideation that is supposedly above or outside ("meta") the physical universe.

He contends that metaphysics usually consists of declaring some principle, such as nature or the ideal world, to be axiomatic. The next step in metaphysics, according to Derrida, is to arrange the rest of the world so that all alternatives to the foundation are characterized as a deviation, a falling away, from a norm, or a pollution of a pure ideal. The narrative inevitably is one of decline. Plato, for example, felt that all worldly examples of his ideal forms were corrupt and limited. None was ideal. The actual world was false; only the ideal world was true. Much religion believes the same thing, and you can see why Derrida might compare metaphysics to theology. According to him, metaphysics seeks absolute foundations and imposes them on a world that in fact has no such foundations because it is characterized by difference and contingency. There is no absolute identity to anything. The attempt to locate such a thing is akin to trying to find the "center" of the ocean. As soon as you have it, the watery point you designated flows away.

One of the more interesting ways of mapping philosophy that Derrida encountered in his investigations concerned the opposition of speech and writing, or of mind and the external techniques of graphic representation upon which knowledge depends. Metaphysicians consistently, according to Derrida, consider writing to be an addition or supplement to conscious thought, which is considered to be purely ideal. Consequently, it is supposedly closer to truth defined as a pure mental image or thought. Metaphysics predictably denigrates writing because writing is in some respects the perfect metaphor for difference and for the absence of identity. In speech, according to metaphysics, the mind is immediately present as a living substance. But in writing, the voice is absent; writing is an empty, lifeless sign made up of formal elements that have no living substance. By definition, writing is a sign of mental speech. But such mental speech is itself a sign of an idea. Writing therefore is a sign of a sign, something doubly removed from truths or from the immediate presence of mind. As such, it resembles the way difference in time and space works against the metaphysical ideal of identity, converting what seems self-sufficient into something relational and contingent. If the apparent identity of something present to your mind is made possible by its difference from other things in space and from other moments in time, past and future, then that thing before your mind is like a sign. It is what it is by referring to something else. But the something else it refers to is in the same position. It too is a sign by virtue of referring to something else from which it differs in order to be what it is. So the first thing ends up having to be characterized as a sign of a sign. It resembles writing. Derrida uses the metaphor of writing in his early work to characterize the world as a field of difference without identity.

Because he finds the word "supplement" used by Jean-Jacques Rousseau to characterize writing, he borrows it as a term for the way difference in time and space breaks up identity and presence. Any idea and any thing has an identity only as it is related by difference to other things, only as it is supplemented by the addition of those other things, one might say. But each supplement in turn requires supplementation. The process is endless. To add one supplement is necessarily to add many. This "logic of the supplement" thus undermines the metaphysical belief that truth consists of a simple presence of ideas in the mind or of self-identical things we might observe in the world. Truth, according to this way of thinking, is complex. It requires that one attend to structure and context, to the way in which things that appear before our eyes in fact arise out of complex webs of relations and invisible determinants. Some would look at America, for example, and see "freedom." That is what appears before one's eyes – people moving about freely, making choices between consumer goods freely, going to work freely, being "themselves" freely, etc. But an invisible web of determinants shapes any one of those moments of "freedom." Those determinants tell us what gender to be, oblige us to work against our will in order not to starve, educate us into being good citizens who are obliged, on pain of great violence against our bodies, to acquiesce in dubious behavior on the part of political leaders, etc. Where some see "freedom," others, using a more complex, deconstructive optic, might see slavery.

The prejudice against graphic representation turns up in many places in western culture and especially in literature. Usually, it occurs in writers who are committed to a metaphysical conception of the world. Derrida contends that writing represents a threat to metaphysics because at bottom metaphysics cherishes an ideal of a living plenitude, an uninterrupted organic fullness often lodged in an ideal of nature or of some transcendental ideal of divinity. Such ideals provide a sense of security in a world characterized by contingency, alteration, and endlessness. If the world in truth has no absolute foundation or end, no absolute truth that makes it all meaningful, then it will be very tempting to seek security in ideals of absolute truth.

A graphic representation such as writing is also conventional: it depends on agreements that allow images to mean certain things. Such conventionality flies in the face of the authoritative standard or measure of truthfulness that philosophic foundations supposedly provide. Such foundations are supposed to be unquestionably true; no conventional agreement is necessary. God is never democratic; he requires obedience. Moreover, in conventions, one thing has meaning because of something that lies outside it, something other. Foundational truth is supposed to be true in and of itself; nothing outside, nothing other, is needed. Yet, Derrida notes in a classic deconstructive move, the very act of designating a foundation as something interior, self-contained, not dependent on other-relations to be what it supposedly is in and of itself requires a prior distinction between inside and outside. One must already be able to make such distinctions, yet if such a distinction is prior to the foundation, the foundation is no longer the first thing, the unique origin, the inside that depends only on itself to be what it is. It requires a more originary act of differentiation.

You can see why Derrida might insist that difference is a primary instance in philosophy, yet it is also not primary because a difference is two things at once in a non-axiological or non-hierarchical relation to one another. Neither is prior because each could not be without the other. Difference can never assume the form of a thing, of a presence, or of something our mind can grasp as a knowable entity.

A school of literary criticism called "deconstructionism" sprang up in America as a result of Derrida's influence. Critics such as Paul de Man argued that literary texts are inherently incoherent. They cannot be read or interpreted to deliver up a meaning or truth that is not vexed by a differential shuttling of reference that destabilizes and ultimately renders impossible any clear determination of meaning.

Derrida's contention that the world is itself differential led many thinkers to apply his ideas to such social issues as feminism. The two most noteworthy practitioners of deconstructive feminism were Hélène Cixous and Luce Irigaray. Irigaray argues, in *Speculum of the Other Woman* (1974) and *This Sex Which Is Not One* (1979), that in western philosophy woman have been portrayed as matter, body, fluidity, boundarylessness, irrationality, artificiality, and the like. Women are the opposite or mirror image (hence speculum) of men, who are assigned reason, truth, authority, and authenticity. Male philosophic speculation abstracts from concrete particularity and bodily materiality when it resorts to metaphysical concepts and categories such as "being," "universality," "truth," and "infinity." In pursuing such speculative philosophy, men have sought to separate themselves from matter and from *mater*, that is, from their own links through their mothers to physical life.

Derrida's work helped inspire a movement called post-structuralism which sought to learn from Saussure and the other structuralists while moving beyond them to other concerns such as social power.

Jean-François Lyotard pursues the post-structuralist argument in books such as *The Post-Modern Condition* (1979) and *The Differend* (1984). Lyotard argues that knowledge and discourse are inseparable. The traditional stories or narratives about the world have been transformed in what he calls the post-modern era. The classic narratives of the Enlightenment such as liberal humanism and Marxism no longer provide a convincing or accurate account of the world. They have been replaced by a proliferation of micro-narratives. In a world dominated by corporations especially, what counts as true is increasingly determined by the financial and technical requirements of those with economic power. Lyotard sees society as consisting of contending stories about the world, no one of which is in itself more true than another. Each person or group must work rhetorically to convince others of the truth of their own particular discourse. Social life is an ongoing discussion in which people seek to make their perspective and their story plausible and convincing. Totalitarianism consists of abolishing this free play of discussion by establishing a consensus which silences further discussion.

One of the most innovative French post-structuralists, Jean Baudrillard, began as a structuralist sociologist interested in the way the semiotic regimes of advertising shape and categorize reality. Baudrillard has since been preoccupied with the power of cultural representations to become lived reality. He argues that the media have become so powerful that simulated realities have now replaced actual reality. This hyperreality is a perfect imitation of reality, much as Disneyland aspires to be a totally enclosed universe of its own created through the manipulation of signs. At his most provocative, Baudrillard argues that something like the first Gulf War "did not take place." Its "reality" was so mediated and constructed by images that in effect it occurred in hyperreality. The real, in other words, can be shaped to be whatever those with economic, political, and cultural power want it to be. If the US lies and claims that weapons of mass destruction exist in Iraq and then acts as if they were there (while knowing full well they are not), they might as well have been there. The lie becomes reality.

In this section I will concentrate on Derrida's deconstruction. Derrida's argument might be summed up in this way. Metaphysics claims that difference arises from identity, but in fact difference generates identity. One thing one might do with deconstruction, therefore, is to figure out how texts committed to metaphysical values work by suppressing difference and making it appear a derivative of identity.

Another deconstructive move would be to examine texts for ideals of truth that seem aloof from representation or signification, but which can be proven to be dependent themselves on the very traits that define representation. One such trait is conventionality. All sign systems are social conventions, agreements that allow signs to mean true things. The deconstructive move consists of showing that metaphysical truth is not transcendental. It does not exist in a spirit realm outside signification and the conventions that make signification work. Instead, it is a product or effect of signification.

Because metaphysics is always associated with conservative social and political ideals, deconstruction inevitably has a political component. Metaphysics underwrites authority and authoritarian political forms. Truth in the metaphysical tradition is invariably paternal; like the father in the traditional conservative family, truth rules unquestioningly. To it, women and children are traditionally subordinated. If metaphysics is true, then certain men deserve to possess social authority for inherent or essential reasons. It is in their nature, a nature that transcends mere social conventions. When Shakespeare wrote, the aristocracy laid claim to such a conception of nature. More recently, the wealthy have claimed to be more deserving than others, more naturally talented at being magnets for money. To deconstruct is therefore to question the bases of authority and hierarchy in society. Derrida calls the metaphysical assumption that underwrites such authority and hierarchy logocentrism. By that he means the centrality given the mind or *logos* in metaphysics. Metaphysicians from Plato to Husserl conceive of truth in terms of the presence to the mind of ideas. That assumption creates a hierarchy of an ideal realm over the physical realm and of an ideal conception of truth over representation. The task of deconstruction is to undo such hierarchies and to show that all truth is differential and physical. What metaphysics imagines is ideality is in fact merely an effect of signification, something physical and historical, rather than metaphysical and eternal.

Exercise 4.1   William Shakespeare, *King Lear*

King Lear enacts a philosophic tragedy as much as a personal one. The crisis of madness in the play is also a crisis of the metaphysical conceptual regime upon which the play's values depend, a regime that privileges identity over difference and truth over representation. The social order of the play depends on an order of truth and representation. The moral ideals of virtue, fidelity, honesty, gratitude, and the like are inseparable from a notion of truth as an internal essence or ideal identity that exists apart from external representation in language. When Cordelia says that she is "so young, my lord, and true," she designates herself as the emblem of the ideal of truth the play defends, an ideal whose pre-linguistic quality she expresses when she refuses to "heave [her] heart into [her] mouth." Because moral virtue transcends language, moral illegitimacy will be inseparable from representation. To behave badly in the play will be to speak falsely. The restoration of moral and philo-sophic order will thus be described by Edgar as a triumph of true speech over false: "Speak what we mean, not what we ought to say."

In addition to a certain metaphysical concept of truth, the play argues for a notion of identity as internal essence. Identity gives rise to char-acter differences, but those character differences are presented in the play as secondary manifestations of internal traits. The crisis the play contends with in this regard is the usurpation of a particular social identity by an illegitimate pretender who refuses to accept his difference (and his derogation) within the aristocratic order of rank. The restora-tion of identity as the source of legitimate social power consists of the re-establishing of a system of differences that distinguishes absolutely the authentic from the imitative or artificial.

Derrida would consider the crisis of representation in the play, which allows truth to be denied, falseness to be taken for truth, and significa-tion to triumph over meaning, to be a crisis of western rationalism or logocentrism. Like logocentrism, the play portrays truth as interior to the mind or logos; it stands outside signification and can do without its external assistance. Signification is an addition to truth, a substitute whose power of imitation, substitution, and repetition represents the danger that signification might do without truth or meaning altogether, take its place, and kill it off. In the dowry scene, Cordelia, of whom Lear says "Thy truth then be thy dower," is the emblem of a truth that stands outside signification: "What shall Cordelia speak? Love and be silent. / . . . my love's / More ponderous than my tongue." She and others describe her relation to signification as one of appropriate delay or defer-ment: ". . . since what I well intend / I'll do't before I speak" and "A tardiness in nature / Which often leaves the history unspoken / That it intends to do." Truth is always described in this way in the logocentric tradition, as an essence outside signification that could exist on its own and that only secondarily and accidentally (after a delay that leaves true presence behind) enters signification, which is characterized as a realm of empty markers devoid of life or of any essential connection to meaning. Whereas truth is living, certain, possessed by the mind or reason, authoritative, and absolutely present, signification consists of mere imitation, empty technique, and repetitive substitutes that usurp the place and value of truth, simulating it without being it.

Goneril and Regan are the emblems of such signification. As signification is an excess or addition added on to truth that is supposedly sufficient in itself, Goneril's speech to Lear suggests her love is "more than words can wield the matter." Indeed, twice she uses "beyond" to describe the limitlessness of her affection, and she implies that reason is powerless to restrain the significations of her love: "Beyond what can be valued . . . / A love that makes breath poor and speech unable." If speech is the representational mode most proximate to truth in the mind, a living pneumatic embodiment of truth which is untouched by passage into the empty monuments of writing and signification in general, Goneril's excessive rhetoric, like writing, depletes the breath of speech. Writing is of less value than speech because the breath of truth from the internal voice of consciousness that guarantees the truthfulness of representation diminishes as it assumes external graphic form. The *graphie* of external signification is breathless, a mere mark on the page, the death of reason unless it is bound and constrained to represent speech accurately and only. Goneril and Regan, in their deceitfulness, their use of signs without meaning, represent precisely the danger that such external signification might not perform this duty. If Goneril's address to Lear suggests the emptiness and excess of external representation added on to a supposedly self-sufficient inner speech, Regan's intimates the emptiness of imitation: "In my true heart / I find she names my very deed of love." Like writing, Regan is a signifier of a signifier, someone whose act of signification derives meaning from its reference to another act of signification. She is repetition, the repetition of truth that, like writing which imitates speech or signification which imitates ideas in the mind, depletes and empties truth, killing it off by taking its breath away.

That the play reproduces certain western prejudices regarding truth and representation as well as speech and writing is borne out in subsequent scenes in which letters play an important role in helping to undermine truth and paternal authority. If truth is linked to the power of the father and signification to the danger of the nomadic and wayward son who threatens parricide against father truth, it is important that

Edmund's subversion of his father and of his legitimate rival Edgar is carried out through letters that betray truth. Indeed, in discussing the false letter with his father, Edmund indicates the cleavage of ideal meaning or truth and representation that constitutes the danger of writing: "It is his hand, my lord, but I hope his heart is not in the contents." Later, Kent, whose ideal of plain speech, of a signification that would not betray meaning intent or truth, provides Lear with an alternative to rhetorical bombast, is posed against Oswald, whom he accuses of bearing "letters against the king," that is, against the father. Oswald is the emblem of a writing that bears no truth, and it is fitting he also be a servant who betrays his mistress. He writes a letter for Goneril to Regan, and Goneril licenses him to "add such reasons of your own / As may compact it more." Signification serves a purpose, and it need not be loyal to intent or meaning. Juxtaposed in the following scene is Lear's discussion with Kent regarding a letter Lear sends via Kent to Gloucester, a letter that appropriately will signify nothing more than is intended: "Acquaint my daughter no further with anything you know than comes from her demand out of the letter."

The treachery of the servant and the treachery of writing intersect most forcefully in Oswald's handing over to Goneril of Regan's letter to Edmund. And it is the discovery of Oswald's letters by Edgar that ultimately betrays the traitors to Albany and allows Edgar to regain the throne. Writing betrays truth, but is also betrays those who depart from truth. Like Plato's *pharmakon*, letters in *Lear* act both ways, as dangers to truth and as cures or agents of restitution. The deception associated with such letters and with rhetoric in general also is two-sided. As Edgar's "conceit," his deception of both Lear and Gloucester, it offers a cure for the madness, the loss of the power and authority of reason, brought on by Goneril, Regan, and Edmund's use of signification to deceive. The play thus acknowledges the negative power of signification, but it seeks to restrain it. Kent represents the ideal of restrained signification, someone whose plain speech is meant to convey only what is intended or meant. Truth requires loyal servants who speak plainly, and do not digress or go astray.

At stake in the play is not merely a debate between modes of signification but rather the idea that there is such a thing as a transcendental signified, a truth or meaning that stands outside signification in an ideal ideational realm. In order for the values and oppositional hierarchies of the play (truth v. falseness, speech v. writing, loyalty v. betrayal, inner virtue v. external show, etc.) to exist, a prior fundamental distinction must be operative, one that licenses all the others. That distinction is between spirit and matter. For this reason, Cordelia, who is truth in the play, is called a spirit by Lear and remains absent, like truth from the mechanics of external signification, throughout much of the action of the play that portrays treachery against the father. That initial hierarchy permits one to distinguish those who are essentially noble and virtuous from those who are not, those whose signs express inner states and those whose signs contrive or concoct an external semblance of such states. The issue is not only a particular relationship between truth and signification that the play aspires to safeguard, but also more dangerously and subversively the power of signs to make realities, to conjure into being things that might not be true in the sense that they would not exist apart from signification.

Edmund is the arch-contriver in the play, and it is important that he is the one least convinced of the ideal of the transcendental signified. He scoffs at his father's belief that the world somehow embodies meaning: "[W]e make guilty of our disasters the sun, the moon, and stars, as if we were villains on necessity . . ." And he meditates on the way signs create realities, separate identities, out of an indifferent matter: "Why bastard? Wherefore base? / When my dimensions are as well compact, / My mind as generous, and my shape as true, / As honest madam's issue? Why brand they us / With base? . . . Fine word, 'legitimate'!" He uses letters and representation to confound identities of good and evil, and in the opening dialogue he is associated with material indifference, the fact that Gloucester cannot tell the difference between him and Edgar except by "order of law." That the indifference of material nature poses a threat to the rational order of Lear's world is indicated by the fact that madness in the play consists of a descent into such material nature. Madness is the taking away of all the differentiating emblems or signs of civilized life. The "marks of sovereignty, reason, and of state" consequently lose their meaning and cease to embody anything.

Without a transcendental signified, which guarantees a differentiation between ideal and material, spirit and matter, truth and sign, inside and outside, all the orders of law that kept things apart ("I'll teach you differences," Kent says to Oswald) in discrete identities and hierarchical oppositions between the virtuous and the nonvirtuous, everything becomes mixed. Children supplant fathers, the nonvirtuous overcome the virtuous, the sign is taken for truth. And signifiers conjure realities instead of expressing or representing them. The right order of truth and signification is overturned. If there is no difference between truth and sign, the real and the signifier of the real, then one might as well have signs as truths, signifiers as realities. The "tragedy" of the play is that this occurs, that this is allowed to occur, and it begins with the abdication of the father, of the transcendental signified from his position of transcendence. Lear says that from now on he will be part with all the other parts rather than being in a position of mastery and command that transcends all parts, restraining their movement and controlling their potential for uncontrolled signification or dissemination.

Edgar restores not only the state but also the proper order of truth and signification as western metaphysics conceives it. If the negative characters use false representation to lure truth away from itself, Edgar uses false representation to restore truth. Fittingly, he is associated with an ideal of the direct expression of meaning in signs: "In wisdom I should ask thy name, / But since thy outside looks so fair and warlike, / And that thy tongue some say of breeding breathes . . ." Edgar, like Cordelia, does not need external signs ("thy name") in order to be truly what he is. The pneumatic metaphor ("breathes") suggests an association with inner speech and therefore with a more true truth than is found in external signification. All his physical signs directly express his internal essence ("breeding"). As Cordelia is linked to the Christian story of incarnation ("O dear Father, / It is thy business that I go about"), which is one model for the western theory that signs embody spiritual meaning and that there is a distinction between ideation and matter, so also Edgar is associated with Christian prophecy, with a mode of signification that immediately embodies truth as presence: "Methought thy very gait did prophesy / A royal nobleness." Here again, Edgar's signs are directly expressive of truth conceived as an inner essence. Edgar's conclusion to the play, which is presented as a prescription for ensuring that such tragedies do not indeed occur, is as prescriptive as the relation between truth and sign itself: "Speak what we feel, not what we ought to say." Signs, in other words, should embody internal essences rather than be fashioned fit to external constraints, conventions, or necessities. They should be speech, not writing.

A deconstructive critic would argue that this oppositional value system conceals its own constitution in the very thing it subordinates and declares secondary, which is to say, in difference. According to the play's metaphysics, internal essences like virtue are identities that then give rise to differences (between an Edgar and an Edmund, for example, or more tellingly, between a Kent and an Oswald). Cordelia's truth is something silent which she keeps to herself in her own mind, not betraying it in external shows of signification. Such signification is nonidentical and is constructed through differentiations between terms. Goneril and Regan's protestations of love are comparative rather than singular. These essentialist ideals and the oppositions to which they give rise depend on a distinction between the ideal, the essential, and the true on the one hand and the material, the nonessential, and the false on the other. All signifying matter is merely a repetition, a substitution, and an imitation in relation to truth. It is defined by constraining conventions, articulations between parts, and the citation of codes, all of which deprive it of a voice, a purely expressive delivery of truth in its living essence or presence. What is articulated and conventional is a machine, a technique, an external contrivance with spaces between its parts, like the spaces between letters in writing. They oblige a pause, a deferment, and a difference that can never be compatible with the shining or breathing forth of truth in its unarticulated and unmediated purity. Nor is such fashioning fit compatible with virtue conceived as inner nobility, as Edmund demonstrates.

Yet strive as it will to expel the qualities of signification and writing from truth and speech, the play nevertheless suggests that its ideals are essentially and originally contaminated and compromised by what they seek to expel. Spirit never sheds matter, in fact is matter, and truth never sheds signification, in fact is signification. Not that truth enters signification according to some necessity of being incarnated or embodied and is thereby fulfilled. Rather, there never was any truth as the play and metaphysics conceive it as something outside signification; there always only was signification and nothing else.

In this regard, the most important distinction in the play is the one that places convention, the conventions especially that make the marks of writing capable of signifying, outside truth. Goneril and Regan's rhetorical protestations of love are conventional because they cite external codes, imitate models of affectionate statements, repeat previous discourses, and substitute such articulations of models, codes, and discourses for the direct expression, immediate and palpable, of internal truth. Yet when Cordelia speaks to Lear, it is to state her true love as a conventional relationship: "I love your Majesty / According to my bond, no more nor less. / . . . You have begot me, bred me, loved me. I / Return those duties back as are right fit . . ." Her love, in other words, cites a code or a model, albeit a different one from those informing her sisters' speeches. Similarly, when the loyal Kent speaks plainly to Oswald, Regan, and Cornwall and teaches them "differences," which is to say, the need to respect internal identities and essences, the authority that he sees in Lear and that he believes they should also see, he discovers that internal essence is meaningless without the support, originally and constitutively, of external convention. The king should be directly embodied in his representatives or messengers according to the metaphysical theory of truth, but that is only the case if others feel obliged to recognize this convention. When Kent is put in the stocks, Gloucester warns: "The King must take it ill / That he, so slightly valued in his messenger, / Should have him thus restrained." Cornwall's response is "I'll answer that," which means, of course, that he will not answer in accordance with the dictates of the code supposedly at work in Kent's representation of Lear. For the king's truth to go so astray, it must be originally contaminated by the weakness to which it falls prey, must already contain the potential to be unrecognized. And that is because the "Authority" which Kent thinks he sees in Lear's face and which he mistakes for an internal essence or truth is in fact externally supplied by and derived from the convention that allows someone to possess authority, with authority here meaning the power to have one's representations or one's messengers recognized and obeyed. There is no authority without a subsequent confirmation on the level of signification, which is to say, there is no authority as metaphysics (and Kent) conceives it. The author of authority always comes after the fact of authority, as that necessary representation and confirmation without which there would be no authority.

Lear himself discovers this internal fissure and danger – that power, authority, and truth might be conventions, mere repetitions of codes, rather than essences whose expression compels recognition – in his encounters with Goneril and Regan, encounters which provoke him to lose his sense of an internal identity. He does so because his identity comes from without, is supplied by signifiers, "the marks of sovereignty, knowledge, and reason." That his identity is so dependent on marks or on writing suggests that the essences the play seeks to safeguard suffer from an original defect which consists of the need for external supplementation in order to be what they supposedly are in themselves. If at the origin or in the essence of Lear's authority is a mark of sovereignty that comes from outside (which of course makes it a re-mark, an original doubling without which its supposed present identity could not exist), then his origin is secondary in relation to that which signifies it, is given or supplied by what supposedly is added on to it.

The ideal of the direct expression of truth conceived as an internal essence of the mind is realized most forcefully in Lear's performatives, his curses and commands particularly ("Into her womb convey sterility," "The King . . . commands, tends service"). In a converse version of the metaphysical ideal of truth, he uses language to directly bring into being, to make present, the thing he names. He banishes Kent and Cordelia and denounces Goneril. Yet when he reaches Regan and "commands, tends service," he receives no appropriate reply. He himself names the problem when, a few lines later, he accuses Goneril of scanting the "offices of nature" and the "dues of gratitude," images that suggest the complicity of convention and essence, the nonidentical articulation of external models ("offices," "dues") and supposedly internal identities ("nature," "gratitude"). The play would like us to read the difference between Lear and his daughters Goneril and Regan as an opposition between truth and falsity, virtue and vice, nobility and treachery, good and evil, essence and errant signification, but it also points to the possibility that all of these oppositions can be deciphered as versions of the same, so that the ideals of nobility might be understood as treachery toward other possible social ideals, the play's virtue understood as a very parochial, class-based brand of viciousness, its good understood as a species of evil, and so on. Lear mistakes the "additions to a king" (his following of knights, etc.) for supplements to a royal essence, but in fact, as Goneril and Regan rightly point out, the additions are what make the king originally a king. Without an external exercise of force, after all, virtue would not triumph in the play.

Finally, at the end of the play, Edmund is portrayed negatively for having contracted with both Regan and Goneril, while others, Edgar especially, act in accordance with more virtuous inner motives that stand aloof from the play of articulation and signification in such contracting. Whereas Edmund falsely adopts the external mark of nobility by taking the name Gloucester, thereby hoping to use inessential conventions to generate a semblance of an internal reality or truth, Edgar puts aside all the external marks of nobility yet acts more nobly. Of him even Edmund is obliged to say "Th'hast spoken right. 'Tis true." If Edgar restores the priority of truth over signification, he reconnects that truth with authority: "The weight of this sad time we must obey; / Speak what we feel, not what we ought to say." Yet just as he resorts to a different contract from Edmund's, that of the martial code for testing truthfulness and virtue, so also while apparently voicing the play's ideal of an inner truth that stands apart from determination by external conventions or linguistic contracts, from, in other words, writing, he portrays truth as an imperative and as a citation (with all that this implies of imitation, substitution, and repetition, all the qualities of writing that place it outside inner truth and speech). What he essentially says is "we ought to, nay must, say what we feel." The "not what we ought to say" that follows refers to external conventions of the kind that Goneril and Regan obeyed and that the truthful Cordelia did not. Yet the fact that truth ("what we feel") is itself the effect of a prior ought, an imperative that it cites ("we must obey," "[we must] speak what we feel") suggests the complicity of convention and expression, truth and signification, inner essence and external articulation that I have noted already.

In order for feeling to be spoken, signification must be at work, and if signification is at work, so is convention, an "ought" or a set of rules that govern the expression of content in form, of meaning in signification. No doctrine of truth can elude this necessity by claiming to be exempt from its compulsion. For feeling to speak or be spoken, it must enter repetition and substitution, and speech must imitate feeling. That is the rule of representation that the metaphysical ideal of a transcendental signified, of a truth that can stand outside signification and do without it altogether, refuses to acknowledge. And it refuses because the dangers attendant upon writing and external signification in general, the dangers of unpredictable effects, of uncertain knowledge, and of meanings going astray, can never be fully and completely exiled from truth as metaphysical philosophy (and *King Lear*) conceives it.

"I cannot conceive you," Kent says to Gloucester, when Gloucester cannot tell the difference between his two sons. Conception or knowledge requires the differentiation of separate identities, but in order for this to occur, the origin of identity in difference, in an act of differentiation, must be forgotten. Forgotten as well must be the essential indifference of things, the fact that without a concept or a custom of law, Edgar and Edmund would be the same. No identity could be established, no cut made in the continuum of matter that assigns the one virtue and authentic nobility, the other vice and pretense. Differentiation and sameness must be forgotten because they could never be accounted for in a mode of knowledge based on identities. That would already be to turn difference into identity, to begin with one's conclusion. For what differentiation and sameness imply is that prior to knowledge conceived as the establishing of identities is a state of things in which things have no identities. In order to argue for metaphysical oppositions between the clear-cut identities of truth and falsity, noble virtue and ignoble vice, speech and writing, etc., *Lear* must ignore the origin of all of its concepts in acts of differentiation. For what such differentiations consist of is the imposition of a model or a code so that form can be made from what is undifferentiated and formless.

The original and foundational values of the play, therefore, such as truth and virtue, are the effects and the products of a fashioning fit, a forming according to a model or a convention. The terms the play wishes to expel and subordinate as the opposed others of its most valued values – difference, fashioning fit, signification conceived as a maker of realities rather than as a representation of them – come back to haunt it as its most original condition of possibility. The play wishes identity (the internal essence of noble truth in Cordelia and Edgar, for example) to appear to give rise to differences (between them, Goneril, Regan, and Edmund), but the play also demonstrates that these figures could not appear to have identities if a prior act of differentiation were not from the outset at work, shaping their identities and determining them as the products of differences, as the effects of conventions, codes, and external constraints. This mixture, this difference which suggests a lack of difference, this complicity of essence and convention, is what the play demonstrates in Edgar's final speech. Internal truth (what we feel) is as much an ought (we must obey) as convention (what we ought to say). They may be different, but they are not identities that form an opposition. Truth (as metaphysics conceives it) is constrained to speak as if it were outside such imperatives, but that of course is itself an imperative, a form or a convention that must be obeyed.

The play is a reflection on what it means to allow someone like Edmund to rise above his proper place in society, but linked to that is the problem of what it means to allow language to have other functions than to convey true ideas. The same is the case with Goneril and Regan. They stray from their assigned roles in society, and they engage in a language practice at odds with what must be the case if the social order to which they belong is to sustain itself. If fathers are to continue to rule, the proper relation of language to truth must be maintained.

Edgar is the character most charged with curing the madness brought about by the overturning of the right order of truth and signification. Truth should precede and determine signification in language, but in the play that relation is inverted. Signification creates apparent truths where none exist. If signification is both cure and poison for ideals of absolute truth (in which truth is a transcendental signified that stands outside differentiation), how is the false signification that Edgar engages in curative?

Edgar is associated with a spiritualist ideal of absolute truth. Notice how he is characterized when he challenges Edmund. How is he assigned religious meaning? And, in the end, how is this associated with the restoration of an absolute conception of political power?

In the end, the ideal of restored absolute power in a social and political sense depends on the elimination of those associated with signs, rhetoric, and the inversion of the proper relation between truth and signification. When Edgar concludes that we should "Speak what we feel, not what we ought to say," he restores the right order of truth and sign. Signs should embody internal essences or truth rather than be fashioned fit to external conventions. They should be speech, not writing, a direct expression of nature rather than an artificial contrivance or technique for creating effects.

Yet pay attention to what happens when Lear arrives at Cornwall's castle to find Kent in the stocks. He orders his daughter to attend him, but she does not come. Lear's madness begins. It is such moments that a deconstructive reading would focus on. They show that convention, signification, and difference (or the relation to the other that constitutes identity) are more essential to metaphysical ideals of truth than metaphysics cares to let on.

Exercise 4.2   Elizabeth Bishop, "Over 2,000 Illustrations and a Complete Concordance"

"Over 2,000 Illustrations and a Complete Concordance" is about an illustrated Bible which contains modern photographs of Middle Eastern scenes. The Bible, as a story about God and humanity, contends that the real world is actually just a metaphor or symbol whose meaning is spiritual. Behind the physical universe is a spiritual one. The literal physical world itself is just an illusion, or even an illustration.

What does Bishop's attitude toward this idea seem to be?

If the poem is about the two contending philosophic positions described above – with one favoring absolute foundational truth and the other emphasizing the flow of experience through space and time without any transcendental foundation – which one do you think Bishop favors in the poem?

Notice how Bishop begins with a reference to things that might be as ponderous as foundational truth – the Seven Wonders of the World. She mentions travels she has taken, and she says they should have been like the Bible, "serious, engravable." Yet despite the fact that her ordinary travels do not attain the stature of biblical seriousness, she notes that the images of the Seven Wonders in the illustrated Bible are a "touch familiar." That would seem to imply that they have lost some of their original meaning or significance. One might expect the same to be true of the other illustrations.

Note too that the idea of a spiritual world depends still on something physical – being engraved. What are some of the implications of this? Engraving is a kind of writing, and we have noticed that Derrida associates writing with the principle of difference – that all things spiritual or self-identical or transcendental are in the end lodged in physical reality. They are contingent and historical, rather than eternal and extra-worldly. They exist and have identity as a result of relations to other things. They are stretched out relationally in time. How might engraving work in a similar way here? It seems to ensure the enduring permanence of the ideas of the Bible, but does it also undermine them?

Her tone is mocking at times. The Arabs in one photograph, she suggests, might be plotting against "our Christian Empire." She might be referring to an actual empire, but she might also have in mind a broader sense of "empire." How might Christianity be imperial in other ways than simply military? Crusaders did of course literally return to the Middle East to convert it from an Arab homeland into a "Holy Land." Think about how there are two kinds of imperialism at work there. One is military and physical – the taking of someone else's land by force. The other has to do with language and meaning, even with capital letters. How might it be imperial to convert someone's pasture or backyard into "the Tomb, the Pit, the Sepulcher"? How is a change of meaning imperial? How might transforming a backyard or a pasture into a "Tomb" lead to the first kind of imperialism?

Think about what I said above about hierarchy and authority in metaphysics. How might a regime of metaphysical truth be imperial?

The Tomb, the Pit, and the Sepulcher seem to refer to biblical stories, and the capitalization seems to suggest that each thing has spiritual meaning or at least some large significance within the Bible. But notice now that she turns to a description of the actual physical world – the courtyard, the dry Well (why is it still capitalized?), and the brickwork conduits. Why does she engage in this contrast between the supposedly very significant thing and the ordinary world? And notice that she characterizes the physical world as a kind of writing – "diagram." That would seem, in the metaphysical tradition of which the Bible is a part, to suggest something alien to the ideal of a living spiritual meaning.

She suggests that time has eroded something: the "human figure," which seems to be a figure in one of the illustrations, is "gone in history or theology." What different meanings do the words "history" and "theology" imply? And how does Bishop direct your interpretation toward a preference for history by mentioning, somewhat mockingly again, the figure's "faithful horse"? It is worth noting that "figure" is another term for writing or rhetoric, forms of representation that supposedly lie outside metaphysical truth.

Writing, according to Derrida, is a form of representation from which spiritual meaning would seem to be absent because it is not living, not the voice of consciousness, and more images of writing immediately follow in the poem: silence, gesture, thread, page, grim lunette, "the toils of an initial letter." Why does Bishop insert these references to graphic script, the physical side of the world of meaning and truth? The Bible supposedly conveys spiritual truth; why not concentrate on that? Why not look through the illustrations to the spiritual meanings they supposedly convey? What is gained by emphasizing the literal rather than the metaphoric or figural sense of the images?

Bishop now seems to look closer at the writing of the Bible itself, so that the lines made by the burin or writing instrument "move apart." The literal graphic image, however, seems to become the thing it represents – "ripples above sand, / dispersing storms." But then she evokes what the image is supposed to be: "God's spreading fingerprint," some sign of his having once been present enough to leave behind a graphic or written indication of his presence.

Notice, however, that her encounter with the literal lines of the letters also gives rise to imagery usually associated with mystical encounters, with spirituality. Such encounters are often figured as fire, and here she uses the image "ignite," but it is "watery" rather than fiery. What do you think she is doing here by mixing images of fire and water?

The second stanza is so completely different from the first that you wonder if you have not in that final image of the first stanza passed through a doorway of some kind. Now, she talks about those travels she mentions in the first line of stanza 1. As you read through the brief accounts of her travels, pay attention to the references to the Christian religion – Easter, Mary Magdalene, flocks that might have a shepherd, death and rebirth, the Annunciation, etc. What follows is a curious account of a visit to a "holy grave." How is it characterized? If the travels are literal in contrast to the metaphoric or illustrative images in the Bible from stanza 1, how is the account of the grave also literal? What is the point of emphasizing the literal physicality of it? And why the final remark about Khadour, probably their guide, looking on "amused"? Why might he be amused?

The first line of the third stanza is in keeping with the second philo-sophic position described above, the one that emphasizes the endless flow of experience and life through space and time, a flow that never can be converted into a transcendental meaning or truth that stands outside the flow. Everything in such a world would be "connected by 'and' and 'and.'" It would also be a world that could not be considered to be an "illustration" of a spirit world that stands behind it or of a transcendental truth. With these ideas in mind, how would you interpret this stanza?

Exercise 4.3   Alice Munro, "Differently"

Let's think about what some of the implications of the foundationalist position are. It helps to bear in mind that foundationalist sounds like fundamentalist. Foundationalists, like fundamentalists, believe that truth is absolute and is authoritative. But are they like fundamentalists in believing that women should honor traditional "female" roles in society? *King Lear* would lead one to think so. Cordelia ensures that truth wins out in the end (or at least Shakespeare's version of truth), but she herself is just a helper. The men occupy center stage, and in the end it is Edgar and Albany who manage the allocation of power and blame. Cordelia, no longer needed, dies.

Because men have ruled society for all of human history and have managed the invention of philosophies to make this rule seem necessary and unavoidable, the difference between the absolutist position and the deconstructive one is often calibrated as a difference between men and women. Women writers are sometimes quite good at mocking the abso-lutist position and at drawing attention to its shortcomings. Virginia Woolf, for example, has great fun picking on male philosophers in *To the Lighthouse*. They aspire to attain complete and absolute knowledge, but they miss most of what passes under their noses, the thick detail of life. To Woolf, that detail seems more true than their complete diction-ary, even if it is the kind of knowledge that does not fit in a dictionary. Another woman writer who likes to mock male pretensions is Alice Munro.

"Differently" is something of a love story between women, although its plot concerns a sexual affair between Georgia, the central female figure, and a man named Miles. Miles also sleeps with Georgia's best friend, Maya, and that ruins their friendship. One senses in the end that Georgia, as she leaves the home of Maya's former husband (Maya in the mean time has died), wishes she had done things differently and not cut off her friendship with Maya because Maya slept with Miles. But now it is too late. Her friend is dead. "We never behave as if we believed we were going to die," Georgia remarks to Raymond, Maya's husband. "How should we behave?" he asks. "Differently," she answers.

If truth were available for knowing in the way that both foundationalists and fundamentalists believe is possible, such regret would not be possible. Georgia would have known absolutely what the right way to act is and would have done it. She might simply have looked up the right way to behave in the Bible (ignoring all the stuff about mass slaughter in God's name), and that would have been that. No questions asked, no regrets, no debate. The right way, which of course, given foundationalism's equation of absolute truth with a clear set of rules for what is absolutely right or good, is also the moral way, would have been clear. Because it is so clear and so derived from the authority of truth, one cannot doubt it in retrospect. There would be no sense that things could or should have been done "differently."

But this is a story by a woman, and that sense of absoluteness that in the past so assisted men in managing their world with such authority and certainty is missing. We instead as readers find ourselves in a world of missed chances, missteps, problematic motives for action, and complex feelings of anger and obligation toward others. Truth in these complex matters is not available in some ideal sphere outside life to be drawn on to show one the right way and to allow one to feel righteous about pursuing it (the purpose of such metaphysical authorities as the Bible). Instead, what there is of clear knowledge and the right action that it supposedly makes possible is fragile, tentative, prone to mistakes, and far from clear. It emerges in part from our negotiations with one another. It is more differential or relational than absolute and certain.

The story begins with what seems like a contrast between the two contending philosophic positions. On the one hand are "too many things going on at the same time," which sounds very much like life as proponents of the second, non-absolutist philosophic position see it. On the other hand is the question Georgia's writing instructor asks: "What is the important thing?" And that sounds like how a foundationalist or absolutist would think. Of course, for Georgia there is no one important thing that transcends all the other possible things one could write about or think about or even live through. When she visits the husband of her dead friend, Maya, Georgia's project is still characterized by uncertainty rather than clarity. She notes that "she has already been taken over some fairly shaky ground." That's an amusing image for this philosophic debate because "ground" is another word in the debate for "foundation." To be on shaky ground is a bit like not having a Bible or a Dictionary of Complete and Absolute Knowledge in one's pocket to help one know in advance what the truth of a situation should be. Instead, on shaky ground, one has to make one's own way, tentatively.

Given that Munro specializes in mucking around with male power and male pretension, how would you expect her to portray men? How is Raymond portrayed? What do you make of his relation with his new wife? How might he be said to embody a traditional sense of male power and privilege, especially in regard to women? How is that associated with knowledge, with knowing in advance what is or should be the case, for example? And how is that power linked to violence against women for men's convenience?

How are the other men in the story portrayed? Why does Munro say of Ben, Georgia's husband, that he has "the look of someone who longed, bravely, to be given orders"? Why does she choose to portray the world of men in terms of the military and of obedience?

How we identify things is crucial for how we know the world and for what the meaning of things in the world is. Why does the narrator say, for example, "Maya's house – Raymond's house"? There is an empirical reason, of course. But what else is Munro getting at here? Why point out that things can be identified in different ways?

How is Georgia's former husband Ben characterized? She remembers him reading a story from James Joyce's *Dubliners* about a poet with a "mean pretty wife." Joyce's stories are quite acerbically realist; no fairy tales at all. Notice now that in wandering through the old neighborhood where she and Ben lived, Georgia thinks of fairy stories. What is the tension in the passage as she walks? What does "what-for" mean? How might it connect with the tension between the reference to fairy stories and the recollection of Ben reading the story about a family in which one is poetic and the other mean?

Link all of this to what follows regarding Maya's final garden project. What is the connection?

A story within a story now begins, and we hear more about Maya. Note that she is described as "gifted and brittle" and "the most vulnerable person of all." You need to bear this description in mind in order to understand Georgia's feelings at the end of the story.

What is the story within a story about? How are the women and the men characterized differently?

What is Georgia and Maya's friendship like? How are they different together in comparison to how they are with their husbands? What do they do together, and how is it significant for what the story has been about so far?

In terms of the philosophic issue we are attending to here, you might bear in mind that, from a foundationalist perspective, there is only one truth to reality, not multiple truths. And reality cannot be modified by human knowledge or human imagination. It is what it is. The Bible says so. Plato says so. You cannot mess with the fathers or with their version of truth.

We learn that Maya and Harvey are having an affair that she characterizes, humorously, as "exercise." We are clearly in a world of fuzzy moral lines here. How is Maya's behavior justified by what you have seen or heard about her life so far?

Georgia's life in the bookstore evokes the possibility of absolute knowledge. That would be one way of understanding what books do. They give us a clear line to truth. Instead, Georgia sees "plausible promises," and notice that the first book she mentions is *In Praise of Folly*. Why? And how does that relate to her activities in the bookstore?

Since Munro is so different in regard to metaphysics from Shakespeare, it might be fun to compare her humorous conception of madness or "folly" and his tragic one.

Notice that, in her account of her affair with Miles, she crosses pronouns so that she could be talking about Maya. This occurs at the moment when she says "How many, she asked Maya." What do you make of this confusion of Miles and Maya? How might they be indices of the same thing for or in Georgia, the same proneness to folly?

How do things change with Miles once they proclaim love for one another? How does Miles seem to interpret her statement? What rights does he now assume? How does it change power relations between them? How is this a comment on men and marriage in general?

What do you make of Georgia's actions toward Miles and Maya once she finds out they slept together? How does she feel, and how does that justify what she does? How does the event broaden in significance for her?

What does it mean to say that her marriage seemed "a world of ceremony, of safety, of gestures, concealment"? Think back to the descriptions of the married couples earlier in the story. Does this passage in retrospect characterize their lives?

The narrator begins the final section of the story with what might appear to be a conundrum. She says that the change she made in her life by leaving Ben was "real and dishonest." Why does she say it was real despite the fact that her remorse is dishonest? And what do you think she means when she implies that she would have behaved "differently" in regard to Maya? How does Raymond's parody of a passionate kiss drive home the point that she somehow betrayed her friend? And then why, given all this, does she think about her bookstore experience in the end? What does it seem to offer her?

Given how the story is about missteps and mistakes, about not seeing clearly and yet acting on the basis of unclear knowledge, how does Maya's vision in the end offer a kind of protective security against the contingency of things and of human relations?

Why do you think Munro ends the story with the phrase "The accidental clarity"?

Exercise 4.4   *The Birds* and *Run, Lola, Run*

As you noticed in regard to *King Lear*, works of culture that are committed to the idea that there is a foundation of absolute truth to the world and that this foundation is of a spiritual or ideal nature also argue for gender and class hierarchies. Women are supposed to be virtuous seconds to men; servants are supposed to obey their betters. One gets the sense that the philosophic model of a transcendental foundation or a final absolute truth is linked to male privilege and to an authoritarian model of social relations. It guarantees a male right to rule, since men, traditionally, are the ones who are privileged with knowledge of absolute truth. They are the keepers of the keys to the temples and to the foundations in the traditional societies in which ideals of philosophic or religious transcendence arose and still prevail. To maintain their positions of domination in such societies, men exercise control over and impose discipline on others. Such control is often physical, but it can also be ideational or cultural. People are trained to think subordination is virtuous. And if the dominant school of thought in the society – be it religious or philosophic – teaches them that their male rulers deserve to rule by virtue of some law or principle in the world that is incontrovertible and beyond debate, then control and domination are likely to be easier. The idea of transcendental meaning and foundational truth has always served a social purpose.

It also would appear to serve a psychological purpose for ruling men. When Lear collapses psychologically, the event is characterized by images that suggest a dissolution of psychological and personal boundaries. Women in western culture are associated with fluidity, a breaking down of boundaries. They initially nourish babies in a watery milieu, then nurse them in close proximity to their own bodies. Male children, after initially feeling in a mother's control and feeling they have no identity apart from her, separate and develop boundaries, but one senses, especially in those committed to the model of absolute foundational truth, that those boundaries are always fragile, always threatened with the possibility of dissolving. The firm boundaries such men manufacture for themselves assure personal and psychological identity; they are ways of controlling experience so that it can be regulated.

There appears to be a link between that personal exercise of control to assure one's identity and the kinds of control one sees being exercised in societies committed to philosophic foundationalism. Workers are controlled by owners; women are controlled by men. In *Lear*, one witnesses the enactment of a fantasy of disruption in which women and those assigned secondary status rise up against ruling men. In consequence, the ruling male loses his identity, his sense of impermeable boundaries. He dissolves. But in the end power is restored, as is absolute truth. The "justices" above side with Albany against his wife. And absolute "authority" returns to the rightful male rulers. These issues are not antique; they are with us today. Fundamentalists insist that women have a secondary role to play in the world; and they seek to impose discipline on wayward subjects.

It is instructive to compare two films that take quite different positions regarding these issues by focusing, in quite contrasting ways, on the lives of women. *The Birds*, directed by Alfred Hitchcock in 1963, portrays a woman, Melanie Daniels, who initially is quite independent, an anomaly for women before feminism came along in the 1960s. In the 1950s, housekeeping was idealized as the proper role for women. Needless to say, the 1950s were also a time when the claims of foundationalism – in the form of a resurgence of Christianity – were reasserted in US culture. The opening sequence even has a reference to a possible religious understanding of the world. A boy whistles in a gesture of sexual attraction at Melanie; she smiles, seeming to enjoy the sexual teasing despite the age difference; and then she hears birds squawking and looks up at the sky. Looking up could suggest looking at divinity or at his emissaries. The birds, who resemble a biblical plague, evoke another type of foundationalism as well, the idea that a fate that resides in nature shapes human life in a law-like manner. We can as a result do nothing about our individual destinies. Men are destined to rule, women to be subservient care-givers, as Melanie learns in the course of the film.

Melanie's interaction with the boy suggests the possibility of an infraction of basic social rules, especially the rule against sex between an older woman and a young boy. How does she continue to break rules or disturb the social order in the sequence in the pet store that follows?

The interaction between her and Mitch Brenner is in some respects a summary of how the whole movie proceeds. Notice how he is portrayed visually as Melanie and the shopkeeper try to capture the bird Melanie has released. Pandora is another woman who assumed too much power for herself and released bad things on the world. Notice how the women seem out of control. How is Mitch portrayed in contrast?

Melanie assumes a man's role of sexual pursuer in the scenes that follow. Notice how Hitchcock, in the way he composes images, suggests she is getting in over her head. She drives a boat away from a dock and seems completely in control in a medium shot, but then the camera pulls back to show the boat in a much larger natural environment. It appears small and vulnerable. Nature is another foundation, an absolute truth that is often evoked as a source of laws that are incontrovertible. They must be obeyed, or bad things will happen.

Bad things do start to happen to Melanie almost immediately after her assumption of a man's role and her inversion of "proper" gender roles. She is attacked by a bird. Notice how she looks at Mitch just before the attack.

And what about Mitch? How does he represent an inversion of gender roles assigned humanity by nature? Notice how he is portrayed in the dinner sequence.

The Brenner family is outside the law of patriarchy. The father is dead; the mother, Lydia, has assumed the father's role that rightly, in the patriarchal scheme, should have gone to Mitch. If you pay attention to the composition of the images before and after the first bird attack against the Brenner house, you will see that Hitchcock is portraying a world in which women have assumed centrality and prominence to the detriment of men. Lydia literally stands between Mitch and Melanie and symbolically prevents him from forming the kind of heterosexual bond with a woman that would be his license to be a patriarch in his own right. Lydia and Melanie are therefore parallel characters, and, of course, they look alike.

The rest of the film will straighten out this bad situation by making it increasingly necessary for Mitch to assume control. If women are associated with water, hysteria, and an overwhelming of boundaries, the male will be busy repairing permeable boundaries by boarding up the house.

The most important sequence in this process is the "Pandora's box" scene, in which Melanie goes upstairs, only to be assaulted by a flock of birds who have broken into the attic. What does the attack do to her? Notice how Mitch leans over her when she wakes up. What is the significance of this image? How does it equate the bird attack with his power over her, even his sexual power?

The birds remain at the end, a sign of the permanent – foundational, one might say – threat that nature poses to those who breach its rules.

The Birds seems like the elaboration of a truth that cannot be contested. Nature is like this; you must obey. That, of course, is the purpose of foundationalism. It ensures that people obey their rulers.

Run, Lola, Run is a very different movie. Rather than assume a foundation of absolute, natural truth in the world that sustains human institutions, it begins with the assumption that the world is contingent. What is true or what counts as reality changes depending on one's perspective or on the multiplicity of possible encounters one might have as one moves through life. This film explicitly embraces the second philosophic position, the one that emphasizes fallibility and malleability, the non-absolute flow of experience.

How does the film question the idea that human life expresses a foundational truth that is absolute and uncontestable? Pay attention to the different ways Lola's father is portrayed. As one might expect in a film that questions foundationalism, the role of the patriarch becomes a central issue.

How does the film draw attention to what Derrida calls difference – the idea that things exist in relation to other things or to other moments in time? How too does it embody the idea that there is no ultimate anchor for the world, no point of transcendence outside it where its truth is revealed?

The film thrives on what might be called "versionality," the possibility that life could or might assume different forms or versions depending on simple chance. How does it make a theme of versionality? And chance?

To be anti-foundational is also to break rules, since foundations sanction rules that maintain social order. How does the film deal with the issue of rule-breaking?

And finally, why does Lola's scream play such an important role in the film? Think about Cordelia. She is silent yet loving in *King Lear*, a foundationalist play that is all about how one should respect and obey fathers. Why is it appropriate in this anti-foundationalist movie that just the opposite occurs?

CHAPTER 5

Psychoanalysis

Sigmund Freud invented psychoanalysis with the publication of *The Interpretation of Dreams* in 1901. The book was revolutionary because it broke with the tradition in psychology that assumed that what goes on in the mind is limited to what happens in consciousness. The "I" is only one part of the mind, according to Freud. If we pay attention to such things as dreams, we come to realize that there is another dimension to the mind that is outside the "I" but that plays a role in shaping what happens in conscious thought. The "unconscious" consists of several things. It is a record of all of our significant experiences. It is the repository of feelings and urges that get pushed out of consciousness. And it is the place in the mind where instinctual urges are at work. The experiences of every day remain in the unconscious part of our minds and reappear often in dreams. In a similar way, significant experiences from childhood remain filed away in the mind and exert an influence on our thoughts and behavior as adults. It is easy to see how these ideas might be useful in the study of literature. Fictions, like dreams, are fantasies, and they can be expected to contain a large amount of unconscious material.

The unconscious material that Freud found in dreams had overwhelmingly to do with the most powerful feelings we as humans experience. Those include primarily but not exclusively our relations to our parents and the sexual-romantic relations we form with others. Those relations inspire strong emotions such as attachment, identification, and fear, and those feelings often clash with what society deems acceptable. In the most famous instance of this dilemma, Freud posited the existence of yearnings for sexual contact with parents on the part of children. Those yearnings, when they confront the social injunction against incest that prevails in all human civilization, must be pushed out of the mind or repressed. Yet, according to Freud, it is natural for all children to experience attachment, necessarily tinged with a sexual-pleasurable component, to their parents. Children can either learn to accept the curtailment of those natural urges or hang on to the urges in some other form.

The mind, according to Freud, often finds alternate ways of expressing urges, desires, and yearnings that are deemed unacceptable by society or that for some other more local reason have to be repressed. It does so because the instinctual urge to seek pleasure is so powerful that it tends inevitably toward expression. Such urges seek ways to elude the displeasure that the ego censor, internalizing injunctions from its environment, imposes on feelings or desires deemed unacceptable. It is possible, in other words, to find indirect expressions of unacceptable urges toward pleasure in seemingly acceptable personal behavior or in forms of cultural expression that seem on the surface perfectly appropriate. The mind figures out ways to elude the inner ego censor that enforces repression by finding indirect modes of expression or by inventing substitute forms of expression. It displaces unconscious feelings onto something that does not resemble the feeling that was repressed or it conceals the feeling in another substitute guise. Shakespeare in *Macbeth*, for example, depicts feelings of guilt as hand-washing, a symbolic substitute form of expression that represents the guilty feelings through their opposite, a cleansing of guilt.

Freud divided the mind initially into the conscious part and the unconscious. Later, he proposed a new topography of ego (or conscious mind), superego (or conscience), and id (or unconscious). He coined the word "libido" for the pleasure-seeking instinctual urges that propel us through life and that account for some of our most basic physical urges such as sexual desire. Moving beyond his initial hypothesis of two processes – displacement and substitution – for moving unconscious material into consciousness, he also developed a detailed account of the ways in which the mind reworks repressed urges into acceptable forms. He described the different forms that unresolved conflicts between the unconscious and consciousness can assume. These taxonomies often coincided with different forms of neurosis or mental illness, such as compulsive obsessive disorder and paranoia.

An important concept in this regard is "compromise formation." The mind often seeks compromises, or ways of allowing repressed material to attain expression, but in such a way that it compromises with the repression the ego exerts against it. Symptoms in neurosis are good examples of such compromises. They allow us to exercise the pleasure-seeking urges of the libido while nevertheless honoring the injunctions of that part of the mind that makes us respect restrictions imposed on our behavior from outside (either from parents or from the moral culture in which we live). Such repression works by making our feelings unpleasurable, so that we learn not to exercise them. A man might repeatedly terminate romantic relations when they become too intense because a parent exercised too much control over his behavior as a child by, for example, forbidding him to venture out to play in his neighborhood. His repetitive symptomatic behavior as an adult allows him to seek pleasure but simultaneously to respect the parent's injunction that he not venture too far beyond the house (or beyond himself in his relationships). He experiences the pleasure of romantic adventure for a while but then compromises with the internal derivative of his childhood parent by withdrawing, terminating relationships, and accepting unpleasure. Nevertheless, the man is trapped in a repetition compulsion; he repeatedly replays the same personal scenario because he has failed to come to terms – through therapy – with the core conflict in his personality.

Freud found that the conscious mind often performed significant transformations on unconscious material that meant that its final expressed form little resembled the unconscious urge or conflict that inspired it. He called these the "defenses" the ego mobilizes against unacceptable libidinal or unconscious material. The mind can invert a feeling into its opposite, so that a yearning for contact can become a desire to do violence. Conscious behavior can also be a negation or denial of the real urges that inspire it. A man who insists on "clean" relations with women may in fact be negating his real but feared desire to have "dirty" relations with them. The ego can also be split by conflicts between urges and repression so that one part of the mind indulges the urges while the other retains a strict sense of rectitude. Literature is full of examples of such "hypocrisy," especially in religious characters.

Other defenses include intellectualization, projection, rationalization, reaction formation, regression, sublimation, and suppression. In intellectualization, we avoid potentially overwhelming feelings by focusing our attention on things that allow us to exercise that part of our mind devoted to reasoning rather than emotion. At a funeral, rather than experience grief, we might focus on the details of the service or the burial. In projection, we assign to others feelings or thoughts in ourselves that are unacceptable. Having lost an argument, we might accuse someone of being stupid. In rationalization, we avoid feelings of displeasure by explaining our own losses or failures as someone else's fault. We blame others and thereby refuse to accept an unpleasurable sense of our own limitations. In reaction formation, we move from one extreme to another as a way of dealing with strong emotions that either threaten to overwhelm the balance the ego seeks to maintain in the mind or are unacceptable in the culture in which we live. In regression, we retreat to emotional stages or emotional reactions more appropriate to an earlier time of life. Rather than deal with disappointment rationally and maturely, we might resort to temper tantrums to get our way. In sublimation, we act out unacceptable impulses in an acceptable way or we redirect libidinal energy into non-libidinal outlets. Someone with strong sexual impulses might as a result become an artist. In suppression, we deny access to expression of unacceptable unconscious material.

Freud did not limit his study of mental processes to the dynamic of desire and repression. He studied how people relate to the world around them, and this interest became the basis for later developments in psychology that are usually referred to as "object relations theory." Freud was interested in the way children idealize parents and then internalize versions of those ideals as part of their own psychological make-up. Such internal ideals then become models for regulating one's libidinal impulses. He also focused on the strong feelings that parental departure can produce, feelings of rage at abandonment that can only be regulated and controlled when the child develops an independent capacity for play. In one instance, Freud noticed that a child learned to control his rage at the loss of his mother by devising a game in which he controlled her departure and return. Feelings of lack of control were thus turned into their opposite.

Later theorists such as Melanie Klein, Margaret Mahler, and Bernard Winnicott took these ideas much further. They studied the way a child learns to separate from primary care-givers and to become an independent being. Their work is called "object relations theory" because an "object" is anything that the self relates to, from a person to a professional goal to something in the physical world. The physical and social world around the self is its "object world." As the child emerges from its primary, close relation to its parents, it must develop a separate sense of self, and it does that by learning to distinguish between self and other, self and objects. By learning that the primary care-giver is a separate being and not part of the self, by seeing the care-giver as object rather than part of the child's subjective universe, the child begins to acquire autonomy, the ability to exist and survive on its own. If the care-giver provides the child with a sense that his or her object world is constant and stable, the child will mature successfully as a separate person with a strong sense of its own independent identity.

A crucial issue in this process is boundaries and how they are formed. The initial boundary between child and parent is fluid; the child thinks of the parent as an extension of his or her self. The child must learn to give up the initial object – often the mother – and move to a separate sense of self by forming a boundary between self and care-giver as well as self and object world. The child must move from the primary object to new objects, and that taking of new objects is itself a way of bringing about separation from the primary care-giver. That possibility is premised on the provision of stable care by the primary care-giver. That permits the development in the child of internal mechanisms for taking over that parent's role. One learns to provide oneself with comfort and not to need it from outside. And this usually means that there is neither too much yearning for fusion with the parent nor too much of a sense of dangerous, anxiety-provoking separation.

Interestingly for the study of literature and culture, an important component of this process has to do with representation, with the ability to make images of the world. Full separation from the care-giver is made possible when the child acquires the ability to make mental images or representations of its initial care-giving object. Instead of living in a shadowy symbiosis with care-givers, it learns to see (to mentally represent) the care-giver as a separate person, an object or other that is not part of the self. The mental image of objects is itself an instrument of separation because it assumes that what is represented is other than the mind doing the representing. Such mental representations can either be complex and differentiated, or simple and undifferentiated.

Separation is fraught with anxiety, and it can inspire neurotic behavior. Unsatisfactory early relations with primary care-givers might provoke feelings of terror around separation or anxieties about fusion with others. Consistent care is required to provide a sense of object constancy that assures the child that separation is not loss of oneself because one confuses the other with oneself. But if separation fails, the child might experience a narcissistic wound, a sense of a basic fault in existence that prevents the development of healthy relations to objects (other people) in one's world. To lose the other is to lose oneself because one has not learned to distinguish other from self. As a result, as an adult, one's relations might be characterized by feelings of rage regarding the independence of one's partner that are abreactive in that they hark back to much earlier experiences of frustration with one's early care-givers. What can result is neurotic behavior such as the splitting of the world into good and bad objects, into people who satisfy one's yearning for fusion and people whose independence produces rage. Another outcome is ambivalence, the inability to decide whether one's primary affectionate object is good or bad, just right or deficient. One can also experience fantasies of abandonment or persecution, a sense that the world is against one or that certain people "have it in" for one. People can also experience yearnings for the reparation of wounds or for the restoration of lost objects by constantly seeking out romantic partners who resemble parents or who perform reparative functions that heal very old wounds.

Melanie Klein focused on the dynamic of introjection and projection. A child might take inside itself, or introject, a part of the parent to which it is attached. External objects become internal fantasy objects. Similarly and inversely, a child might project internal fantasies that are derivatives of instincts out of itself into the world and assign them to objects. We live in fantasies, and our emotional life is characterized by instability. Fearing disintegration, we split our objects, project inner impulses onto them, and treat others as part-objects.

One of the more influential psychoanalytic approaches was developed by Jacques Lacan in France in the mid-twentieth century. Lacan drew on the structuralist theories of Ferdinand de Saussure as well as the existentialist philosophy of Jean-Paul Sartre. From Sartre, Lacan took the term "imaginary," which he applied to all the operations of the ego. The ego is narcissistic; it makes us feel good about ourselves; but the cost is that it works by denying the reality of our unconscious, perhaps the most important determining force, according to Lacan, in our lives. What we are in the deepest wells of our being does not match up with what we appear to be as conscious selves. Yet the ego allows us to imagine we are whole and unified. It provides us with an imaginary sense of being fully identified with our conscious self.

Using Saussure, Lacan constructed a linguistic account of the mind. The relation between the ego and the unconscious resembles the way language works in several ways. The mechanisms for dealing with unconscious material – displacement and substitution – for example resemble two key ways in which language works. All language is metaphoric in that it substitutes a word for a thing, but all language is also metonymic in that it involves a displacement from one word to the next in an endless chain of differences.

Lacan could be justifiably accused of absorbing the sexist assumptions of his era. The imaginary, a negative psychic register in his theory, is associated with the mother and with her role in a child's life. The mother gives him or her a false sense of wholeness that must be superseded if maturation and individuation are to occur. The father, on the other hand, plays a positive role of intervening (in the form of the Law of the Father) between mother and child as the rule against incest that imposes castration, the denial of one's initial longing for one's mother, on all children. Lacan describes this process as the accession by the child into the Symbolic Order, the realm of cultural rules and symbols. It makes our identities in as much as we are members of societies that impose restrictions on our desires, and assigns us identities as members of families, classes, nations, and the like.

A rather different concept of the place of the mother in psychic development and in civilization was developed by Julia Kristeva. Kristeva noticed that women's bodies are often the objects of intense negative affect in certain works of culture. The mother especially is feared as a source of engulfment that threatens male psychic and corporeal boundaries. As a result, one encounters images of what Kristeva calls "abjection," a placing of the mother outside the symbolic discourse of culture. She is figured as the matter against which cultural symbol formation works. Cultural symbols distance us from the world by putting a sign in the place of a thing, a symbol in place of a material object. In this way, the mind, especially the male mind, can abstract from and protect itself from what threatens it. By distancing or "abjecting" matter, the power of the mother over male children that is a prerequisite of all human development is undone and reversed.

Klaus Theweleit develops a similar argument in his psychoanalytic study of the fantasies associated with radical rightwing thinking, *Male Fantasies*. Using object relations ideas, Theweleit argues that Nazi writers share a sense of loathing and fear directed at maternal women, who resemble communists in these men's fantasies because they threaten to overwhelm boundaries. These males react by creating excessively rigid body armor in the form of Nazi uniforms, ideology, and ritual. Theweleit detects signs of the routine abuse of children in pre-World War I German culture in these writers. There is at their psychic core a sense of missing substance, of identities that never formed in a healthy manner. In consequence, these men became excessively dependent on outside sources for their adult identity. A failure of initial care created yearnings that later in life were satisfied by violent fantasies directed

against women and communists, and feelings of strong attachment to
rigid authority figures such as the Führer.

Developments in feminist object relations psychology have also
attracted the attention of literary scholars in recent decades, and the
work of Nancy Chodorow (*The Reproduction of Mothering*) has been
especially influential. Chodorow notices that boys and girls experience
psychic maturation differently for a mixture of social and psychological
reasons. The fact that much early care-giving is still in the hands of
mothers has implications for both genders. Chodorow accepts the Freud-
ian idea that boys form their identities by identifying with their fathers,
while girls form theirs by identifying with their mothers. Girls have less
distance to go in finding an object of identification. The proximity of
their mother during the intense care-giving phase of childhood means
that the model on which girls form their selves is easily accessible. The
close, boundary-fluid relations between mother and child are not a
source of anxiety. As a result, girls and women have less difficulty with
questions of boundaries and are less anxious when they seem to be
threatened. Boys, in contrast, have a greater distance to travel in locating an object with which to identify in forming their gender identity.
Their initial proximity to their mother can be experienced as a danger
to their emerging identity, which must seek out the more distant figure
of the father for identification. Moreover, they experience their connection to their mother as something that must be overcome. Because
boundary fluidity is associated with contact with their mother, their
tendency is to seek more rigid boundaries in constructing their
identities.

Literary scholars have also taken note of work being done on the
theory of trauma in recent years. Psychiatrists who study trauma point
out that its symptoms include the denial of experiences that then continue to shape later behavior. Victims of trauma suffer a flattening of
affect that derives from the mind's attempt to deal with trauma by dis-
sociation, by refusing to integrate the reality of an experience, so that
one seems to experience it in the third person, as if it were happening
to someone else. The result is that they never deal successfully with the
traumatic experience. They replay it over and over again and are essentially "stuck" in the experience. Victims of trauma suffer intense feelings of shame that they deny or dissociate because they are linked to
feelings of humiliation. They can engage in "revictimization" because
a diminished sense of shame allows them to abuse others.

There are thus two different strands of thinking regarding human
psychology. The psychoanalytic emphasizes the intra-psychic dynamic

of the ego and the id, the conscious mind and the unconscious. The object relations strand emphasizes the inter-psychic dynamic between the self and its objects (physical world, other people, culture, etc.). In the psychoanalytic approach, what is interesting to study is the symptomatic expression of conflict between the conscious and the unconscious parts of the self. For the object relations approach, what is interesting is the range of problems that arise when an imbalance between self and object world occurs. Those consist of strong yearnings for separation on one end and strong desires for fusion with one's objects on the other. Both extremes are types of psychopathology.

Several reading strategies emerge from these psychoanalytic theories. A text might be read for the way unconscious material manifests itself through indirect symbolic or metaphoric means. The relations between characters can be studied for what they disclose about well-observed human psychological dynamics. A psychoanalytic reading might attend to such themes as loss and separation, anxieties about boundaries or fusion with others, and the struggle to form a coherent self out of a traumatic personal history. Finally, language itself can be studied as a means of instantiating unconscious processes.

Exercise 5.1   William Shakespeare, *King Lear*

If *Lear* is a psychologically symbolic story, then it is noteworthy that it begins with a discussion of male children in relation to a mother who is characterized in sexual terms. Freud noted that male children fantasize that their mother is sexually available, that no cultural restrictions or injunctions apply to her, and that her sexual body is therefore accessible to the male child. These incest fantasies portray the mother's sexuality as wild and outside paternal rule. Notice how the mother of Edmund is described. How might she be seen as a male fantasy?

If the implicit maternal fantasy in the play is of a sexually available body that evokes the possibility of incest, then one might expect the play to breach cultural restrictions on sexuality in other ways. How might the rest of the first scene of Act 1 be read in this light? Are Lear's demands on his daughters tinged by desires that might be characterized as incestuous? The fantasy of a perfectly available mother's body might be associated in a male child with feelings of omnipotence, as if he, not the father, were the sole object of the mother's affection. How might this idea help characterize Lear's behavior or what happens between

Lear and his daughters? If his demands transgress restrictions normally imposed on fathers in patriarchal societies, how might Kent and his objections to Lear's actions be understood? Is he a version of the role of the father in culture?

Children who fear separation from the mother and who as a result yearn for fusion with her suffer from an inability to regulate their own emotions and to monitor and control their self boundaries. They feel threatened with dissolution and with being overwhelmed because their own emotions are so powerful and seemingly uncontrollable. They project their own unregulated affect onto the surrounding world. Rage at being abandoned is an especially strong component of a personality that cannot tolerate separation and loss. How might Lear and Cordelia's interaction be interpreted using these ideas? Notice Lear's reference to "her kind nursery" in 1.1.124.

Let's now consider the relation of language to psychic and physical processes. Highly symbolic language seems to distance material life by requiring a complex act of ideation or cognition in order to be understood. The mother's body, on the other hand, certain theorists argue, is associated with raw literal matter that is outside symbolization. It is the physical thing male psychology must distance, even flee, as it seeks a separate identity. You will need to decide whether Lear's mental collapse suggests problems associated with a failed relation to the mother such that she has not been properly symbolized and integrated into a successfully developed self. Anxiety over engulfment of one's boundaries by a mother perceived to be overly proximate might take the form of images of her body as something that resists symbolization.

Now, consider the end of Act 1, scene 1. What kind of language forms are associated with Cordelia? How might these be said to require a more complex form of cognition than a simple name? How do these complex language forms idealize her, lift her out of material physicality? Pay attention to how this idealization, this distancing of her from physical life, continues throughout the play. As you might expect, Regan and Goneril, who might be said to represent the bad mother in the fantasies the play mobilizes, merit a very different use of language. How is it less symbolic, more anchored in physical and material imagery? Recall that the opening discussion between Kent and Gloucester touches on a woman associated almost exclusively with sexuality. The pun used there – "fault" for vagina – returns at the end of Act 1, scene 1, and is associated with Goneril and Regan. Cordelia says to them: "I know you what you are, / And like a sister am most loath to call / Your faults as they are named." How does Cordelia link literality – a use of language that has no symbolic or metaphoric distance between word and thing – with her sisters?

Throughout, Goneril and Regan will be associated with an almost frightening image of the female body, one that evokes violent fantasies from Lear as well as provoking strong anxiety about disintegration and loss of self-identity. Symbolic language forms are like defensive devices that protect one against such a threatening physical reality. Symbolic language forms distance the physical as they distance the literal. Lear's language is initially filled with symbolic allusions, but notice how it breaks down as the play progresses and as he loses power.

The Fool's taunts are full of sexual innuendo. How does he further the idea that Lear's relations to his daughters resemble a male child's relations to its mother? What are the psycho-sexual implications of the Fool's taunts in this framework?

A powerful "bad" mother would be one who would overwhelm the child. How are Goneril and Regan portrayed in this regard? How is Lear's sense of identity, of possessing a separate autonomous self, affected by their behavior? What feelings do they inspire in him, and how are they significant? Consider how one appears in the eyes of others and how much one's sense of self can depend on how others see one. Notice too that when pronounced rapidly together, Goneril/Regan sounds like "gonorrhea."

The Fool ends the first act with a rather obvious allusion to castration. How might Lear be said to be "castrated" in this act? A psychoanalytic critic would say that he yearns for inappropriate sexual contact with his mother and must suffer the pain of not being able to attain it. That pain is metaphorized as castration. An object relations theorist would say that he yearns for a maternal care that is impossible because what he really wants is fusion with another, an impossible state of blissful unity in which his own autonomous existence ceases. Which interpretation seems more justified?

How would you interpret the rest of the play using these ideas? Pay attention to the way women's bodies are characterized. The mad scene on the heath is especially important in this regard.

Exercise 5.2   Elizabeth Bishop, "Sestina" and "In the Village"

In reading "In the Village," which can be found as an appendix to this book, you realize rather quickly that Bishop is describing events that might justifiably be called traumatic. Her mother suffered from mental illness and was confined to a sanatorium. Bishop was raised by relatives in Nova Scotia and lived with other family members until she was an adult. In this prose recollection, she describes a return visit by her mother to Bishop's grandmother's house. The visit fails, and her mother is returned to the sanatorium. "Sestina" is a poem that deals with the same events. In it, a child tries to come to terms with some traumatic experience that is associated with great sorrow. A central question for this exercise, then, would be: how does Bishop deal with trauma in the poem and in the prose piece?

Let's begin with "In the Village." Victims of trauma might be expected to distance the event, to try to move away from it and to put other things between it and themselves. Study the opening paragraph and notice how Bishop uses displacement and substitution throughout. What indications are there that the "scream" is indeed traumatic? How does she use changes of register (from object to vision, from literal to figural, etc.) to displace the scream? Freud suggests that play and repetition are means of dealing with trauma by controlling it. How does Bishop use playful repetition here? And how at the end of the paragraph does she arrive at an image of gaining control over the trauma?

Why does Bishop refer to herself as "the child"? How might that be a strategy for dealing with trauma?

What role does Nate the blacksmith play at this point? How is his hammer sound significant for the child?

The sentence "The child vanishes" might have two meanings. What are they? How is the vanishing related to the scream?

The unpacking of her mother's boxes exposes objects that inspire fanciful thoughts in the child. Pay attention especially to the postcards. One issue in trauma is how a trauma victim represents the world in his or her own mind. Trauma can lead to disturbances in mental representation that can be dangerous but that can also be exploited to attain control over traumatic experiences. Both the prose piece and "Sestina" are about representation. What significance do the cards have for the child? Why does she make such a point of comparing them to the ordinary ones in the town store that do not resemble the actual world outside the picture ("full-size, and in color")? Think of how mental representations work to help establish a self and self boundaries. One boundary would be between the world of actual objects and one's fantasies about them. Bishop has trouble keeping the distinction straight. Often images are taken for things and things melt into images. But this disturbance can be used constructively to rebuild a damaged sense of self. Mental representation is crucial to that process. A postcard is like a mental representation, and it is interesting that she seems to test them against the real world of objects.

How do you interpret the child's theft of the sharp ivory stick? It is a potential source of pain associated with the mother, and notice that she buries it under a "bleeding heart." Why is it important to her to declare that "it is never found again"?

If the prose piece itself is a symbolic process designed to deal with and distance traumatic experience, then its layout or narrative structure should be significant. Notice that, after reporting the burying of the sharp object, Bishop turns to an account of Nate, the blacksmith. Study the description of the shop. What things do you notice? What metaphors especially stand out? Why might Nate be associated with metaphors? Bear in mind that metaphors substitute one thing for another; they are a representational strategy for keeping a world of potentially threatening objects at bay. They transform matter into idea, physical object into mental representation, one thing magically into another. They are a way of controlling the world. How might this mental ability be associated with Nate, the blacksmith?

Bear in mind that a blacksmith at his forge is a traditional emblem for the artist reshaping nature and that metaphor is essential to the art of poetry.

At the end of the next section, which deals with the purple dress, Bishop gives examples of a metaphoric confusion of the real and the figural. How might such confusion be at once a symptom and a source of empowerment?

The next section (about the grandmother) is interesting because it echoes "Sestina," especially in the image of tears. Notice how the "grandmother's tears" are described.

The next section juxtaposes the grandmother and the mother and links them both to Nelly, the cow. What is the difference between the grandmother and the mother in how they address the child? What is the significance of the juxtaposition of the mother's gesture toward the child and the escape to walk Nelly?

We can expect Nelly to be a displacement as well as a protective substitute. How does she function in this way? What kinds of things are associated with her? What do you make of the child's treatment of Nelly? What might it say about the kind of psychological disposition the traumatic experience has induced in her? Why is she fascinated with the "cow flops"?

In the next episode, the second dress fitting, what are the significant elements that are juxtaposed to the mother or used as displaced compensations for her absence of care?

The fire would seem to be an ordinary recollection, but how does it become linked to the trauma and to the child's attempts to deal with it?

The loss of the mother's care can provoke boundary problems and disturbances in the child's ability to represent the world in a way that provides object constancy. It can also lead to compensatory strategies that transmute pain into pleasure. How might the final two sections of the piece be read with these ideas in mind?

In "In the Village," Bishop mentions being in the kitchen with her grandmother, and in "Sestina" she centers a poem on the relation between child and grandmother. The poem seems also to deal with an unnamed traumatic episode.

Why is the poem called "Sestina"? It is a poetic form. What are its characteristics? Why would Bishop choose to write about trauma in such a poetic form?

Study the poem and note the transformations that the key repeated words undergo. How do "tears" especially change? The boundary between inside and outside is important as a measure of one's ability to regulate one's own internal affective states. Victims of trauma have trouble with such regulation. How does the poem record disturbances in that boundary?

What does the grandmother represent? What does she try to provide the child?

An almanac is a book farmers used to predict weather among other things. How is its predictive ability important as a metaphor of healing in the poem?

How does the child's art act to repair the wound caused by trauma? How might it be seen as a way of gaining control over her emotion? How is it also a way of internalizing the care the grandmother seeks to provide?

Stanza 6 has an interesting image in it that is like an act of internalization. Something outside is moved inside. The moons from the almanac enter the child's art. Why is it important that they are moons and that they come from the almanac? And why are they "like tears"? What is their relation to the child's suffering?

What is the significance of the line "time to plant tears"? And why is it said by the almanac?

One power that both art and poetry have is to transform literal things into metaphors. Notice the metaphors in the last stanza. How might they be connected to the therapeutic action of art?

Exercise 5.3   Alice Munro, "Meneseteung"

Stories with frames (stories within which other stories are told) would seem to invite reflections on psychological interiority, the way the mind exists apart from the world, or the way the mind harbors within it unconscious feelings, thoughts, and urges. How might this story, which begins with a narrative frame and then tells the story of a woman poet's life in a small Ontario town in the late nineteenth century, be read as a reflection on both kinds of interiority?

First, what kind of person is Almeda Roth? How does Munro characterize her?

From a psychoanalytic perspective, it is noteworthy that she is described in one of the first details given of her as having eyes that "seem ready to roll down her cheeks like giant tears"? What do you make of this detail? How might it be explained by Almeda's own account of her life?

What is unusual about Almeda? How does she not quite fit in to the culture in which she lives? Munro suggests that the linkage of poetry writing and femininity might be "predictable," but notice as well that Almeda says she is incapable of the embroidery that was a favorite activity of other women at the time. Is there any significance to the fact that the narrator sees her as resembling "a young nobleman of another century"?

The description of Almeda's house is suggestive of the theme of interiority. Notice that the "lace-curtained windows look like white eyes," as if the house itself were a figure for the self. How might it be significant that the enormous shade trees are gone so that there is now a "great exposure"? How was the world of the late nineteenth century different, more shaded?

If Munro is instructing us to think about Almeda and her world in psychological terms, what is significant about her description of the town?

In a culture such as the one she is describing, great stress was placed on respectability and propriety. Wild urges were usually restrained; emotions were not freely expressed; passions were indulged at the peril of one's reputation. What role does the local newspaper, the *Vidette* (a word whose root – *videre* – suggests watchfulness), play in maintaining this regime of self-discipline?

How in the town, as Munro describes it, are propriety and all that it represses and that threaten it juxtaposed? Notice how the women must "hitch up their skirts" to avoid "horse buns, cow pats, dog turds" in plain view on the street. What other signs are there of things against which you must be "on your guard"?

What about the children's treatment of Queen Aggie, the drunken old woman? What does it suggest is being kept in check by the town's self-censoring? And why is a woman's loss of propriety, her descent into self-indulgence, the occasion for what appears to be a mistreatment licensed by the town?

Notice that heat brings on accidents, one of which is the outbreak of what might be insanity. How is this significant? How does it character-ize the "considerable respectability" of at least certain people in the town?

The area of respectability in which Almeda lives is juxtaposed to the Pearl Street Swamp in which the "unrespectable and undeserving poor" live, including Queen Aggie. It has connotations of moral indecency ("No decent woman ever would" go there). This indecency is an impor-tant idea in a psychoanalytic reading because it suggests the emergence of repressed unconscious urges that public morality might consider unacceptable or unclean (one meaning of "proper" and of "decent" is clean). But we've already begun to sense that Almeda is different. Notice how section II concludes. Why is it important that she sleeps in the back of the house toward the swamp? What does it say about her? About her relation to what the swamp symbolizes in a psychological sense?

Section III of the story opens with a direct evocation of a connection between "the river" for which the story is named and "the inland sea." Later, we will encounter a parallel between the swamp and Almeda's own bodily fluids, especially menstrual blood. That Queen Aggie comes from the swamp and turns up, apparently dead and covered with blood, at Almeda's fence opens the possibility of a reading that sees some link between the two characters.

But first we must contend with the figure of Jarvis Poulter. How is he characterized? How does he relate to the difference between decorous restraint and everything the swamp might connote as a metaphor for bodily processes that decorum, decency, and respectability require remain concealed?

The *Vidette* and the references to respectability associate the town culture with repression. The swamp seems to connote the release or expression of natural urges that might warrant repression in the "respectable" moral scheme. Munro humorously evokes the conflict between culturally sanctioned restraint or repression and natural urges when she describes the early relations between Jarvis and Almeda. She teasingly mocks the surrounding society's moral assumptions about men and women's behavior when alone. Her description of what actually happens suggests much greater complexity of feeling and fantasy. How does Almeda think of Jarvis? Why does she think of him in relation to her father?

We are clearly meant to see him as very different from Almeda. How are they contrasted? How is salt a good metaphor for their difference?

How does he become a figure for obstruction, especially the obstruction of her creative talent? Once again, Munro evokes manure piles and boggy fields. Why does she do that here?

What do you make of Munro's funny, playfully sexual reference to wildflowers and horned cows at the end of this section?

Almeda thinks that it takes a good deal of labor to see the land properly while she is out riding with Jarvis. The next section begins with another image of obstructed vision. Her "eyeballs felt dry" because of sleeplessness. Notice that the section begins with a poem of Almeda's in which she speaks of the departure of the Gypsies and expresses a longing to have them back. How might this relate to her emerging relationship with Jarvis? How might he be said to have a blinding effect that is akin to losing what the Gypsies represent? Her father is associated early in this section with trained vision (with, one might say, the ability to form mental representations of the world as a prerequisite to attaining an identity). She sees a constellation her father has taught her to recognize. What might Pegasus hanging over the swamp represent?

The section has at its heart a quotation from Freud – "A child is being beaten." In the story, this becomes "a woman is being beaten." In Freud, the sentence refers to the way people avoid disturbing experiences or memories by projecting them onto someone else. In trauma, the victim of beating often assigns his or her feelings to another who seems to be being beaten instead. How might the "woman being beaten" be Almeda?

The fracas outside that wakes her up could be construed as a figure for the eruption into consciousness of unconscious material. How is the incident described in such a way as to justify this conclusion? Notice for one thing that what the people are doing is something they feel "powerless to stop."

Why does Almeda associate the words she hears with "danger and depravity and foul smells and disgusting sights"? Notice how this other world of experience is associated with a relinquishing of the self-discipline associated with repression – "self-abasement, self-abandonment."

Such a move away from socially sanctioned repression toward the release of unconscious feelings, memories, and urges would be associated with a move away from the mind and toward the body, away from the instrument of censorship and toward the source of those uncontrolled urges. This shift might also explain the metaphors of impaired vision, as if the *Vidette* and all that it represents in regard to self-censorship were being turned off for once. Notice that Almeda decides that she "must go downstairs" toward the sound of a woman being, she thinks, murdered. Going downstairs in a house, according to Freud, is like descending into the body or into the unconscious from the conscious mind.

She has been thinking of her father, and Jarvis is certainly a father-like figure. Is this descent a move, then, away from them and toward a figure that would be maternal? If so, how is the figural mother's body characterized? How might it be seen as being, in Kristeva's sense of the term, "abject"?

Almeda summons Jarvis, whose behavior toward the drunken woman is less than kind: "Gwan home, where you belong." What are the different ways in which this remark is significant? What did it imply to say to a woman back then that she should go "home" and that home was where she "belonged"? Think of the fact that Almeda has sought herself to enter the world of public accomplishment associated with men by aspiring to be a writer.

Is there any way in which Almeda is identified with the drunken woman? What do you make of the fact that Jarvis turns to her and says, "There goes your dead body." What might be implied by that "your"? How might the drunken woman's body be Almeda's?

Notice that immediately she wants Jarvis to depart so that she can attend to her bodily urges. She wants to go to the privy but he lingers. His own bodily urges now come to the fore, and for the first time he sees her sexually. But what do you make of his response to this – his order, command really, that he will come fetch her and take her to church the next morning? What does it signify for him to take her to church?

The poem with which the final section begins situates Almeda at the bottom of the ocean. Why? If Jarvis is salt and the swamp that is home to the drunken woman water, what does it signify that Almeda has chosen the latter?

How is Jarvis' world associated now with death?

Almeda's experience is carefully characterized as an ambivalent mixture of sanity and insanity. At times, Munro seems to suggest a withdrawal into madness – "So much is going on in this room that there is no need to leave it." But Munro also emphasizes that "she knows that she is sane." Given the earlier association of the house with the psyche or with psychological interiority, this sentence might also be a way of saying that so much is going on in Almeda's mind that she does not need the external stimulation someone like Jarvis might provide. It is an image of female autonomy. How is Munro using the metaphor of sanity here to characterize a world that seems to do routine violence to women and to assume the subordination of women as part of its normal operations?

Notice that Jarvis' economic rationalism is characterized negatively here, while Almeda's act of looking "deep into the river of her mind" is given a much more positive resonance. For the first time, Almeda's poetic activities are linked to her mother's art, her "crocheted roses" that do not "look like real flowers." But Munro doesn't seem to think much of the realist accuracy, the "money-making intent," of someone like Jarvis. Notice that she uses a much more positive vocabulary to describe the labor of the women: "They look bunchy and foolish, her mother's crocheted roses – they don't look much like real flowers. But their effort, their floating independence, their pleasure in their silly selves do seem to her so admirable. A hopeful sign. *Meneseteung.*" You are being given a very explicit equation here: river, art, mother. How is it significant, then, that Almeda allows the grape juice to overflow and that she seems not to care about the effects when she tracks grape footprints all over the house?

Given all this, why does Almeda's manner of death seem perfectly appropriate?

And given the juxtaposition of a realist, practical epistemology with Jarvis and a very different kind of seeing and knowing with Almeda, why is it also appropriate that Munro should end on a note of doubt regarding the status of her own discourse, her own knowledge?

Exercise 5.4 *Blue Velvet*

"Family Trouble" might be a good title for a book about the films of David Lynch. The action in most of his films is framed by family relations and dynamics, from the dysfunctional family of *Eraserhead* to the pathological marriages of later films such as *Lost Highway*. *Blue Velvet* explores similarly troubled psychological territory. One way to approach it is to treat it as a fantasy that enacts a young boy's yearnings and desires as well as fears and anxieties. It is as if a young boy were projecting into a dream story his deepest feelings about himself, his parents, his possible mate, and his sexuality.

How might Frank and Dorothy be read as symbolic parents to Jeffrey? A young man trying to figure out what sexuality is all about might be tempted to fantasize about his parents' sexual relations. If he does not know much about sex, he might even get it wrong and assume that a father who plays the traditional family role of disciplinarian might also behave in the same manner in the bedroom. In such a fantasy scenario, the young man might also think of his mother as a victim who requires saving. In what other ways are Dorothy and Frank fantasy projections of a mother and a father?

Freud argued that all children undergo a moment of passage in which they first experience sexual desire for their mother or father, then learn to relinquish the parental object. For boys, it is the father who represents the cultural interdiction against incest. Boys accept separation from the mother and then pass on to more suitable, extra-familial objects. How might this scenario be applied to *Blue Velvet*? Is Jeffrey acting out in fantasy form incestuous desires that evolve into more suitable forms as the film progresses?

How is the mother's body represented in the film? Dorothy at one point appears naked, and one character asks Jeffrey if she is his mother. How does the film combine fascination with and fear of the mother's body?

Like Alfred Hitchcock, Lynch is pessimistic regarding human nature and the liberal dream that we can all temper our animal urges, make civil institutions that allow us to live together peacefully, and achieve a community of mutually respectful equals. Such pessimists are more likely to think that the violent urges in human nature are immutable; they can only be controlled by discipline and policing. The liberal dream is just that – a vacuous and sentimental fantasy that has nothing to do with this hard reality. How might evidence of this attitude be found in how Lynch portrays the town of Lumberton or in how he portrays the final "romance" between Jeffrey and Sandy?

The film makes reference to an essay by Freud called "The Uncanny," in which Freud discusses a short story called "The Sandman." Freud argues that things that feel close to home or familiar can also be things that are the most strange and unfamiliar. They are evidence of the unconscious, which is close to us and therefore quite familiar, yet outside our awareness and hence strange and unfamiliar. The strange way that things repeat mysteriously, so that we keep having the same experience over and over again, is a version of this "uncanniness" in our lives. We do things repeatedly without realizing it because we are driven by unconscious urges. Freud accounts for it by arguing that our unconscious is like a stranger within ourselves. The unconscious propels us to act in repetitive ways. We repeat behavior because we have not succeeded in dispelling the unconscious feelings or urges or traces of past experiences that cause the behavior. This might account for why adults continue to act out problems that are specific to a much earlier period in life. And that might account for why an adult film-maker like Lynch continues to meditate on and fantasize about a problem-filled and unresolved adolescent sexuality. Moreover, traumas leave their mark on the psyche, and abused children recall and continue to act out the feelings that accompany trauma even as adults.

The reference to the Freud essay occurs in the brothel scene in which Ben sings "In Dreams," a song that contains the verse "The candy-colored clown they call the Sandman." The Sandman of the story Freud discusses is linked to the trauma of castration, of being beaten by the father and harmed because one has had sexual feelings for one's mother. How does the sequence that follows enact a similar scenario?

Frequently, the abuse of children shatters their sexual identity and makes it difficult for them to achieve a coherent adult identity. What about Jeffrey's story evokes both the possibility of such trauma and a response to it that might be considered fixed at an early adolescent stage of psycho-sexual development? Think of his comic book narration regarding Frank. Mental representation is one way of gaining a mature autonomous identity by turning one's object world into an object of cognition. How is mental representation thematized in the film? Jeffrey's style of mental representation seems especially infantile. How might this simple style of undifferentiated mental representation connect with Lynch's conservative attitude toward liberal sentimentality?

For heterosexual males, the shattering of sexual identity through abusive treatment by an adult can have the effect of inspiring panic regarding whether or not they fit the culturally mandated norm of heterosexuality. In this regard, it is important to note that Frank's assault on Jeffrey on the country road was originally scripted to include sexual assault and anal rape. Jeffrey wakes up on the ground with his pants down around his ankles. How might the inclusion of this scene have added to and expanded the psychological interpretation of the film?

What is the significance of Frank's fetishism? He loves the song "Blue Velvet" and fondles a piece of blue velvet as he listens to it, and achieves sexual satisfaction while gazing at Dorothy, a figure, we have noticed, of the mother. For Freud, children turn to fetishism when access to normal sexuality is blocked in some way. Is Frank someone who is fixated on an early stage of psycho-sexual development associated with the mother? If so, how would you explain his violence toward her?

Finally, what do you make of the erotic expression on the face of Dorothy at the end as she embraces her child? What is she thinking of? Is this a fantasy of a mother who dreams of being abused by her son? In other words, is Lynch's own filmic practice perverse, an attempt to circumvent the father's injunction against incestuous desire?

CHAPTER 6

Political Criticism: From Marxism to Cultural Materialism

Karl Marx did not invent the idea that economic equality – the notion that social wealth should be distributed equally throughout a population – is better than inequality. But he did more to link that ideal to the politics of literature and culture than anyone before him. Marx was not a literary scholar, but he did think about culture. And what he noticed was that different ideas were in dominance at different times in human history. Those ideas usually expressed the interests of the dominant social, economic, and political group of the era. They usually made economic inequality seem just and right, and they made the rule of those in dominance seem natural and legitimate. The purpose of the ideas, then, was to ensure that the dominant group or class remained in power.

Literature is one important way for ideas to circulate in a culture. Religion and educational institutions in the past, and film, television, radio, and other media in the present also play an influential role. Another way of studying literature, then, is to analyze its political function in sustaining the social power of dominant economic groups.

Marx contended that all societies are organized around the production of the means of sustaining life. In early agricultural societies, family-based tribal communities held property in common, but over time the division of property between those who own the means of production, such as corporations, farms, and factories, and those who work for them has become more and more unequal. Because material inequality is difficult to justify in itself, ideas and cultural values have become increasingly important for maintaining the unequal distribution of wealth.

For example, during the Middle Ages in western Europe, the social arrangement whereby the feudal aristocracy owned all the land while a class of landless peasants did all the labor was sustained by the circulation in the culture of ideals such as honor, fealty, and duty. The Catholic Church, which provided the only education that peasants received, gave them training in obedience and submission to authority from an early age. They learned to believe that their reward for a life of obedient labor would come in an afterlife. These ideas ensured that the peasants would not rise up against their masters, even though a simple sense of fairness would have led them to feel outrage at having to work so hard so that a small group of nobles could enjoy themselves so much.

A few hundred years later, a new group – the capitalist class – assumed economic power, and the social dominance of these shopkeepers, manufacturers, and merchants was accompanied by new ideas such as individual liberty and political equality. If you compare the literature of the Middle Ages with the literature of the capitalist era, you will notice remarkable differences. In the Arthurian legends or the Song of Roland, heroic knights fight for king and country or undertake quests that prove their virtue. In William Dean Howells' *A Hazard of New Fortunes*, business people are portrayed as being justified in their wealth, while those who argue for economic equality are depicted as disturbers of a social order that is deemed essentially right, despite inequality.

At their most determinist, Marxists hold that culture always is an expression of the prevailing social and economic situation. Shakespeare may have been a literary innovator, but in the end, he expresses the ideas and values of the ruling group of his era. Aristocrats saw their worldview reflected in his plays, while the poor would only find there a few bad sexual puns to keep them distracted. The interests of non-aristocratic social and economic groups might be evoked in the plays, but only to be dismissed. Edmund in *King Lear*, for example, gives voice to the newly emergent thinking of the merchant class in Shakespeare's time, the adversaries of the aristocrats whose interests and ideas Shakespeare usually endorses, but Shakespeare's play makes Edmund out to be an undeserving upstart. And he is killed while his more aristocratic brother triumphs and is made king.

Later refinements of the Marxist position argue that culture is more complicated than this reflection theory makes it out to be. Marx contended that all class-divided societies are internally contradictory. The merchant class ideal of individual liberty is contradicted by the reality of wage labor, which imposes a kind of servitude on the large mass of the population. A ruling ideology may make such societies appear unitary and coherent by contending that those who labor are in fact free, but the interests of subordinated groups can never be reconciled with those of their rulers. The extraction of value from underpaid labor in order to generate wealth requires a structural difference between those who own wealth, property, and power and those who must submit to working for them precisely because they do not have wealth. Fissures of this kind are inevitable, and they constitute a contradiction that the society cannot resolve.

Some Marxists argue that ideology is similarly fissured and contradictory. By studying it closely, one can find moments where the contradictions in a society express themselves as faultlines in ideology. French Marxist critic Pierre Macheray noticed, for example, that in Jules Verne's stories, the individualist ideology of the era dictates that a single individual is responsible for all the great technological accomplishments Verne describes. Verne gave expression to the capitalist assumptions of his era, which held that individuals, not social classes, make history. But in the stories, all the work on board the magical vessels is done by sailors who must remain silent and anonymous if the ideology of individualism is to succeed. Their presence is a silent absence that undermines the ideology. That ideology can never be complete, therefore, since to incorporate the sailors would be to suggest that in fact individuals are not the ones who make and create. Wealth is made by the underpaid labor of large masses of people.

Marxists in the dialectical tradition such as Theodor Adorno also argued that art can play an antithetical and critical role in capitalist culture: that culture turns everything into a commodity, and commodity culture creates a way of thinking or consciousness appropriate to it. Minds become routinized and uniform. We cease to be able to criticize intelligently the world we live in because we are pacified by consumption. Life comes to have a Disney-like upbeatness that no one can contradict without being accused of being a bloodsucking, Christian baby-eating communist or, worse, a liberal. We cease to be able to refuse to participate in commodity culture because all our needs and desires are routed through it. Being fulfilled as a human being consists of owning a car; being creative consists of choosing the right cellphone.

Art serves a negative function in relation to this culture of uniformity, routine, and pacification. In dialectical thinking, negation is a first step in developing a more complex way of seeing the world. According to the dialectical philosophy Marx borrowed from Hegel, our minds can accept sense data as truth, or they can negate that sensory perception and move back into the mental space where concepts are formed. Then, returning to the sense data armed with better concepts, the mind can perceive the data anew and look at them differently.

Our consciousness is naive when we take in messages from consumer culture without questioning them. Negation consists of refusing to credit them as reality. Instead of thinking "happiness = car," we negate that perception and replace it with a concept such as "consumer culture imposes routinized and uniform perceptions on us that make us more easily controlled and more readily manipulated into sustaining the unequal distribution of wealth under capitalism." Actually, it would take several negations to get to that point, but you see the thrust of the argument, I hope. By negating what we sense (see, feel, hear), we arrive at a very different conception of what the world is all about. Art is similarly dialectical. It is so different from our ordinary perceptions that by simply looking at it and experiencing it we are taken into a new realm of perception and thought. By forcing us to reflect on the world we live in, art suspends the routinized consciousness consumer culture under capitalism imposes on us. As an act of negation, it opens up for consciousness other possibilities of awareness and of being.

Materialist Marxism, best represented in the work of Antonio Negri, differs from dialectical Marxism in that it emphasizes the anchoring of culture in materiality. Materiality for Negri consists of a creative potential that expresses itself in human labor. That potential is harnessed and controlled by capitalism to generate wealth for a minority. But the force that drives the machine is human labor and the creative potential it embodies. Literary criticism derived from this approach emphasizes moments in literature that capture a democratic and communalist possibility in human life, such as the scenes of an egalitarian and democratic sailor community aboard the whaling vessel in Melville's *Moby-Dick*.

The theory of ideology has also been refined in recent years. Drawing on Jacques Lacan's psychoanalysis, Louis Althusser argued that one's sense of self-identity in a capitalist culture is delusory. We are in fact shaped and determined by the world we live in and by such institutions as families, schools, churches, and corporations. Yet capitalist culture nurtures in us the belief that each one of us is free and independent. In this way, our real relation to the means of production is misrepresented in our minds. We "misrecognize" our true place in the world.

Marxism survives as a tool of literary criticism in the insight that literature is produced in societies characterized by class differences and that such differences leave their mark on literature. It has also given rise to an increased attentiveness to the politics of culture amongst literary scholars. The English school of cultural materialism – from Raymond

Williams to Alan Sinfield – has been especially important in promoting such an understanding of culture. Sinfield contends that culture is a site of political argument with each side struggling to establish plausibility for its account of the world. In dominant ideologies, one can locate faultlines where the plausibility of the dominant ideology is in question. Such faultlines are inevitable in societies founded on inequality, since an ideology's account of the world it attempts to justify can never be fully universal, can never speak to or for everyone in the society. Capitalists may proclaim the utopia of freedom, but that exhilarating feeling presupposes the slavery of millions in factories all over the world.

Not all scholars who emphasize the social and political dimension of literature are Marxists strictly speaking. Mikhail Bakhtin, a twentieth-century Russian scholar, noticed that the novel is a literary form that incorporates multiple discourses from the social world around it. A discourse is a particular way of using language that characterizes a social group. Generations often speak different languages, and lawyers, of course, speak a notoriously different language from the rest of us. Teenage girls often create unique discourses that might vary from place to place and generation to generation. Any one society is cross-hatched by many different discourses, and novels usually incorporate them as the different modes of speech assigned different characters. In Scott Fitzgerald's *The Great Gatsby*, for example, a shady character named Meyer Wolfshiem says to the narrator, "I understand you're looking for a business gonnegtion." The odd pronunciation stakes out a line between morally inflected social sites. On one side of that line is the urban criminal underworld where Wolfshiem lives. On the other are such upper-class figures as Daisy Buchanan, whose remark "I think she's lovely" uses a phrasing that one would never encounter in Wolfshiem's world.

Novels, according to Bakhtin, are inherently "heteroglossic" in that they record a variety of different speech forms. They are also "dialogic" because they usually place these different discourses in contact with each other, as in a dialog. When a narrator adopts a character's point of view, he juxtaposes his own mode of speech with the character's. Narrators also engage in commentary on fictional events. When writers resort to parody or irony, they place their own discourse in antagonistic contact with another's discourse. Finally, writers sometimes engage in hidden polemics against other writers, as, for example, when James Joyce mocks W. B. Yeats in the Sandymount Strand episode of *Ulysses*. Stephen Dedalus writes a mock-Yeatsian poem, and then places a piece of snot on a rock before departing. Having compared the Irish literary aesthetics of his era to a used handkerchief, Joyce is suggesting a similarity between the two poetic "works" Stephen has just produced.

Bakhtin also introduced the concept of the "carnivalesque" into literary-critical discussion. In his study of the French writer Rabelais, he notices that Rabelais' exorbitant fictions depict the bodily life of giants in intense detail. Rabelais' work mimes the speech patterns of the medieval marketplace and of the medieval carnival, an annual ritual event in which normal social relations and hierarchies are temporarily suspended and overturned. He connects the carnivalesque to a distinction between what he calls the authoritative discourse of such institutions as the Catholic Church, which relied during the Middle Ages on fear and obedience to maintain a rigid social hierarchy, and the common speech of the market, which is full of bodily imagery and comic insults. Such taunts and insults deprive the serious discourse of the Church of its power to intimidate. Instead, such carnivalesque speech promotes a sense of the bodily nature of life, its incessant coming and going as death and new birth. Excrement and putrefaction give rise eventually to new life, and this sense of life's incessant renewal conforms to the more affirmative spirit of the carnival in which all are equal as natural beings. It denies the fear of an afterlife of punishment which the Church used to maintain control. Bakhtin contrasts the monologic style of discourse practiced by the Church, which is intolerant of dissent or opposition, to what he calls "internally persuasive discourse," which is more labile and fluid and which more readily accommodates itself to different discourses and different situations. It is flexible and more tolerant of being mixed with other discourses. It is dialogic rather than monologic.

Exercise 6.1　　William Shakespeare, *King Lear*

Does *King Lear* give expression to the ruling ideas of the ruling class? Or does it display fissures, contradictions, and faultlines in the dominant account of the world in 1606 that portend social change ahead? Is the aristocracy triumphant in the way in which the play suggests, or is it embattled and about to lose its collective head because it is not attending to the real material facts that contradict its ideological assumptions, facts that are discernible in the play?

A little historical information always helps when dealing with such questions. King James I assumed the throne in England in 1603 after the death of Queen Elizabeth I. He brought with him arcane feudal ideas about the divine right of kings to rule their lands autocratically. He compared his rule to that of God over his human family, and he expected as much reverence and obedience from his people. But this feudal idea was out of step with the emerging economic and social reality in England, a land in which a new merchant class was displacing the old nobility, whose life of unproductive consumption was increasingly at odds with the reality that wealth now lay with the merchants. The inflation of prices induced by trade and the influx of gold from the colonies in North America brought financial ruin to the aristocracy, whose income from tenant farmers remained constant, while that of the merchants increased. As a result, the nobility was obliged to sell land to non-aristocrats, and a new gentry of wealthy land-owners came into being. James even sold titles to raise money for his costly court. This resulted in an "inflation of honors" and a depreciation of the marks of nobility. The laws of inheritance, which left property to the firstborn, also meant that many nobles found themselves with title but no land. A new group of landless nobles came into being. Economic power had shifted, but political power remained in the hands of the nobles.

The merchants insisted on a role in governing the country through Parliament. They felt the king should not have absolute power. They argued with James over prerogative (who should make laws) and sustenance (who should pay to support the king's court). These conflicts reflected a deeper conflict. The new class felt the aristocracy should not rule by hereditary right, and they objected to the idea that society consisted of fixed ranks. They were committed to the egalitarian ideal of individual responsibility, which held that anyone might rise in society by being industrious and by gaining wealth through industry. While nobles felt that lineage earned one the right to a leisured lifestyle, the new class, many of whom were Puritans, felt that one proved one's worth through industry and frugality. The attitudes of the new class were also shaped by the scientific rationalism and empiricism of the era, which encouraged skepticism regarding previous accounts of the universe. For example, Ptolemy's idea of spheres held that the universe was a fixed, geometric order of ranks, and it sanctioned the aristocratic model of the universe, which held that some by nature were higher or better than others. While the aristocracy represented the residues of a society bound together by ideals of service, loyalty, duty, and obedience, the merchant class represented the beginnings of a social form characterized by relations of contract in economics and consent in politics. Those ideals would serve as the foundation for the new liberal constitutional order that would replace feudalism later in the seventeenth century. The economic fissure between old feudal nobility and new merchant bourgeoisie erupted into a political and military conflict that led, by the century's end, to a new political form in England, the constitutional monarchy.

How might this information aid a reading of the play? First, pay attention to how Lear is portrayed in the first scene of Act 1. He uses words like "recreant" and "vassal" that identify him as feudal. How else does he embody feudal ideas regarding obedience, loyalty, duty, and the like?

Does Lear play by the feudal rules? Or does he break them? Consider how Cordelia responds when he asks her to flatter him for land. She says: "I love your Majesty / According to my bond, no more nor less . . . I / Return those duties back as are right fit." Does she seem to represent feudal notions better than he does?

How might Lear be seen as corrupting the old, good feudal way of things by introducing new merchant class ideas? To Burgundy, he says "her price is fallen." That would seem to be the vocabulary of the new capitalists, not the language of honor and fealty.

Nobles felt that their value was inherent. Even if they had no money or land, they were still nobles. The new merchant capitalists felt differently. One had worth to the extent that one had wealth. Money mattered more than title or inner noble essence. The calculations of the economic market superseded traditional ideas of innate value. Think about this issue in regard to the way Cordelia is treated by Lear. How does he introduce market calculation into the discussion of her worth? Is she placed in an exchange economy at odds with the values nobles are supposed to adhere to, at least in their ideology?

What is France's role in all of this? What does it imply or mean for him to say of Cordelia, contradicting Lear, that she is "most rich, being poor" or that he calls her an "unprized precious maid"?

If the truly noble are supposed to be subtracted from the marketplace where merchants thrive, what does it imply for Cordelia to say to her sisters as she departs: "Well may you prosper"?

In the frame of the conflict between the feudal worldview and the emerging capitalist worldview, how should the actions of Goneril and Regan be interpreted? They are not exactly representative of capitalist ideals, although they do place material gain before family obligation.

Edmund is likened to the sisters by the word "prosper." He says: "I grow, I prosper." How is his way of thinking, especially in the first act, at odds with the old feudal way of conceptualizing the world? Consider what he says about Gloucester's way of thinking. How does he embody the new skeptical rationalism?

How does this new skeptical rationalism connect with the capitalist ideal of class mobility? If Edmund were properly feudal, how should he behave in regard to Gloucester and Edgar?

Edgar parallels Cordelia, and like her he embodies feudal ideals. He alludes to "Child Rowland," a reference to feudal initiation rites, since a young knight in training was called a "child." How else is he associated with feudal values?

How should the character of Kent be understood in the frame of this argument? How is his treatment of Lear after his fall significant?

And how do you read the Fool? He taunts the king, but he also advises him in ways that suggest his loyalty to feudal norms. How is he critical of the new capitalist ideology of calculation and private gain?

That all the characters associated with the breach of feudal norms and with the values of the new capitalist class are killed suggests that the play is fairly straightforward in its political allegiance. How might it be said to take sides with the aristocratic ideological position?

What seems to be the play's attitude toward the question of the right of kings to rule absolutely by divine authority? Notice how Albany summons divinity when he finally stands up to Regan.

How might the play, even as it resolves the conflicts it depicts, be said to display contradictions within the society of the time that are not that easily pacified?

The play struggles to establish the plausibility of its account of the world. Aristocrats, in its account, deserve to rule, and upstart capitalists do not. But does the play succeed? Or are there flaws, faultlines, in its account?

Does it show you, by denying it, a revolution about to happen? And does it show how that revolution might be justified? In 1644 the merchant class would finally rise up against the monarchy and the aristocracy, and a king would be beheaded. Can you see this on the horizon in the play?

Exercise 6.2   Elizabeth Bishop, "A Miracle for Breakfast"

This might be called Bishop's protest poem. Written in the 1930s during the Great Depression, it concerns a situation common during that time – breadlines of poor people waiting for a free meal from some charity.

The title suggests that Bishop will be evoking religion in the poem. But how can one have a miracle for breakfast? Or is the title ironic?

What does Bishop's attitude seem to be toward the difference between rich and poor? Notice that she calls the charity meal a "charitable crumb." Why?

And what does it signify that she compares those about to serve the meal to "kings of old"?

The first stanza concludes with an explicit, if humorous, reference to the Christ story – "One foot of the sun / steadied itself on a long ripple in the river." Why refer to Christ walking on water here? And why in this humorous manner? What might be unsteady about the son of God walking on water in the world the poem depicts?

The next stanza makes the Christ reference more explicit. Notice as well the reference to the sun that "was not going to warm us." Is Bishop referring to Christ again here? Or does she mean nature?

What is the attitude of the waiting people toward the rich man in the next two stanzas? What does Bishop seem to think of him?

What are the final two stanzas about? They seem to be a fantasy of some kind. What does the speaker fantasize about?

And how do you interpret the final two lines? What does Bishop mean when she says that the miracle was "working on the wrong balcony"?

Utopianism is a positive term in Marxist thinking. It means that people yearn beyond the limits that capitalism imposes on them and imagine a better world in which human desires and needs would be addressed rather than curtailed for the sake of endowing a minority of the population with excessive amounts of wealth. How might the poem be said to be utopian?

Exercise 6.3   Alice Munro, "Oh, What Avails"

How does this story register the effects of poverty?

It begins by noting that there is not much furniture in the house, and later we learn that only certain rooms are used to save money on heat. The narrator focuses on Morris, the boy with the one dark glass over one of his eyes. Why does he become her focus? How is the damage to his eye emblematic of their impoverished situation? Might there be a link between the thinking that prevents Morris from mending his eye and the fact that he earns money by selling a magazine called *New Liberty*? One of the primary justifications for capitalism amongst both the wealthy and the poor who play along with it is that it is based on a natural ideal of freedom or liberty. We all are free to pursue our economic goals; some win, and some lose. That accounts for poverty. But not all things are a matter of simple choice. How does Munro describe the mother in a way that might suggest that Morris is a bit of a victim, however much he may choose to think otherwise? Notice that the women at the outset are telling fortunes and that the word "misfortune" appears in the discussion of Morris' state at least twice. Which do you think Munro is emphasizing more here, chance or choice?

Wealth is often associated with fine manners, and poverty with their absence or lack, but one suspects that wealth allows one more easily to afford certain things. There is less reason to be resentful, angry, and impolite if one is comfortably settled in life with few material worries. The mother's behavior toward her neighbors is rude and mocking and a tad uncharitable. Is her behavior a symptom of poverty, do you think? What is wrong with "Mrs. Loony Buttler"?

The other emblematic character in the story is Matilda. Her beauty is of the "captive princess kind." How is her life story significant? How might we relate it to the fact that she is born into such poverty? Is her destiny in any way shaped by her economic, social, and even psychological context? Her mother's refusal of Morris' offer to take Matilda to the dance is a classic example of how people in poverty deal with the humiliation of their situation by elevating themselves over those slightly below them on the class ladder. How does Mrs. Buttler rationalize refusing Morris?

Is it possible to understand Joan's situation in part 2 of the story as somehow connected to her impoverished childhood? She seems to have gotten herself into a less than happy marriage. Why might she have done that? Is it an effect of poverty?

What in the mean time has Morris become? How does he deal with poverty differently from her?

In part 3, later in life, Joan, characterized now as a "lucky woman," expresses a fear of rubble. What is meant by that image?

There is another image of an underworld here as well. It is what Morris sees "underlying every human life," the "peculiar structure of earnings and pensions and mortgages and loans and investments and legacies." Money, in short, or at least income of some kind.

It or its absence can make or break relationships, and apparently it can make or break people. How might Matilda be said to be broken by it in the end? How is the magical, romantic relationship between her and Morris destroyed by the kind of financial trickery that might be expected to arise between people of very modest incomes who have to save, and not lose, as much as they possibly can in each financial transaction?

Why is it significant that Matilda more or less becomes her mother? What does it say about the way class situations reproduce themselves by instilling dispositions that make class location almost inevitable?

Finally, how do you read the relationship between the poem and the story? The poem seems to refer to Matilda, and it is about loss. The "form divine" and "every grace" are no longer the possessions of Rose Matilda in the poem. How might this apply to the real Matilda?

And what then would be the meaning of Morris' final remark that "I wasn't wrong"?

Exercise 6.4   *Working Girl*

The ideology that is most powerful in the United States is the ideology of "freedom." Freedom has a plausible political meaning – one has the right to be left alone to do what one wishes so long as one respects the law, and one has the right to determine one's own government. But freedom in economic matters is more problematic. Freedom in this sense applies most clearly to those with wealth. In a world in which being able to do something depends on the possession of money, those with a lot of money can do pretty much what they wish. They are free. But others have access to money only through working for others, usually the wealthy. And that work deprives them of freedom. They must remain in offices most of their lives, and they are not free to do what they wish while working. They must do what their employer tells them to do. Freedom ends at the factory or office door. The trade-off is that workers gain money to give them the freedom to do certain things like eat, own a house, and take vacations for a few weeks out of the year.

So can one really say that workers under capitalism are free? Conservative advocates of capitalism, who are themselves usually wealthy or at least quite comfortable financially, answer in the affirmative. Workers can always move up the class ladder if they have talent, initiative, and a good work ethic. But how many of them can move up? How far can they go? Can all of them move up? Is there room at the top for everyone? And if there is, who will do the work? Other countries, such as China, are ready to supply cheap labor to the world, but that available resource only replicates the initial problem on a global scale.

Someone still has to get by with less so that the system as it is currently constituted can function. Someone has to make less so that someone else can make more. And that means that some get to be free while a great many more are relatively less free – inevitably, it seems, under capitalism. The large portion of their lives will be spent in routine, uncreative, unfulfilling work for someone else whose resulting wealth provides him or her with the real basis for freedom.

In order to live and work and survive in a society, one must adopt its reigning ideas and adapt one's behavior and beliefs to them. Many members of the working class, those whose labor generates society's wealth but who are comparatively less rewarded than those who own the enterprises they work for, fully believe that their lives of routine daily labor constitute a form of freedom. They must do so because the illusion of freedom is one of the few rewards they are granted. It compensates for accepting the severe structural limits that are placed on their lives. But it also holds out the possibility and the hope that they too might rise to the top and be one of the lucky few. It is the cognitive equivalent of the lottery, the ticket that might make one instantly rich if the numbers by some trick of fate turn out in one's favor.

The best way to achieve acquiescence in a system of rigid economic inequality is to make it appear as if the system is open to all and that ultimate placement in that system is the product of a simple competition between varying talents or skills. Modern capitalist ideology is most effective when it manages to make the ideal of individual mobility cohere with a reality of stagnant segmentation and embedded class difference. Two things that would be entirely incompatible if considered logically are thus made compatible by virtue of a kind of thinking that eschews logic in favor of a more ego-reassuring and emotive-nostalgic kind of reasoning. Chains are made to seem a pleasing part of one's wardrobe.

Consider *Working Girl*, a film about a young woman, Tess McGill, who works as a secretary in New York and takes night classes in business and proper English in order to better her station. Through a convoluted plot, she succeeds in getting a much better job in a corporation, one far above the station she seemed to be assigned at the beginning of the film. In order to understand why this positive upbeat narrative might be an example of ideology, one must be aware that during this period – from the late 1970s through the 1990s in the US – income differentiation between the top fifth and bottom fifth increased dramatically: while the booming economy of the last part of this era benefited the top fifth enormously, the income of the bottom fifth declined. Most of the Tess

McGills of this world were going nowhere fast. Many at the time the film was made were being fired as a result of corporate downsizing for the sake of greater efficiency and profitability to benefit wealthy investors. Many were ending up in service sector jobs – cleaning houses, cutting hair, serving food, etc. Formerly middle-class Americans, in other words, were being pushed into menial, low-income lives with little chance of significant changes in income or status.

Why would so painful a reality be represented altogether differently in a major film of the era, one that takes suffering and anguish and transforms it into a chipper, feel-good evocation of hope, success, and self-transformation? It seems an unwritten rule of societies founded on radical inequalities of wealth and station that the culture not represent accurately those inequalities; otherwise the culture, instead of ensuring continuity and a commonality of feeling that holds the society together, might foster resentment, demands for change, and quite possibly revolution. Films are most ideological when, in the face of extremes of deprivation and potential anger, they foster false hope and futile aspiration, as well as a feeling that the society's institutions, regardless of what inequalities they consistently produce, are just and right. *Working Girl* is a very good example of this.

Here is the story of the film: Tess' boss Catherine is a wealthy, well-educated, and successful businesswoman. But when Tess brings to Catherine an idea of her own regarding the acquisition of radio stations by Trask Enterprises, one of Catherine's clients, Catherine steals it and pretends it's her own. When Catherine is laid up in Europe for two weeks after a skiing accident, Tess discovers her treachery and decides to pretend to be an investment banker instead of a secretary in order to pursue her idea herself. She takes on Catherine's identity, dresses up like her, learns to speak like her, and goes to meetings in her place. She accidentally manages to steal Catherine's boyfriend, Jack Trainor, from her, and he, a merger specialist, helps her to succeed with her idea. Catherine returns suddenly during the meeting at which Tess, Jack, and Trask are about to finalize the deal, discovers Tess' duplicity, and reveals to Trask and Jack that Tess is actually only a secretary pretending to be something and someone she isn't. She also claims the idea for the acquisition was her own, not Tess'. Tess seems defeated, but she finds a way of proving to Trask that the idea was actually her own and that Catherine is lying. Catherine is defeated, Tess gets a job at Trask Enterprises, and she and Jack, both dressed for business, are in the end shown living happily together and getting ready to go off to work.

It is important to note the class vocabulary of the film. How is Tess' class identity initially portrayed? What are the signs of her class location?

How does she contrast with Catherine in this regard?

What makes Tess different from her fellow secretaries? And why is she made to appear different?

Tess breaks out of the routine of her life by assuming Catherine's identity. But what do you make of her relationship with Jack? Does Tess lapse into a routine sexist stereotype with him?

Tess succeeds, but does her story actually reinforce the idea that class difference is justified?

What is the significance of Trask? Notice that he intervenes to save Tess and to use his authority to set right the wrong done her. He is like a patriarch and a judge in one. Does the film through his character endorse the hierarchies of capitalism against which Tess contends? Or does she really not contend against them? Is her story meant to reinforce them?

Moreover, who gains from Tess' idea? Is it the case that her self-annulment in favor of Trask's gain is her greatest achievement in the film? She gives him her idea, after all, and he will be richer as a result, more distant from her in the capitalist food chain.

The film takes the structural inequality between his station as owner and her station as worker devoted to increasing his wealth for granted. Does the story of her great success thus presuppose and reinforce an inequality of power which dictates that her upward mobility has a limit somewhere around his feet?

And what about her relation to her former friends in the secretary pool? Do they have to remain stable and fixed for her trajectory to be measured as success?

Tess can look down at her friends and be grateful she is no longer stuck with the mass of secretaries. But she will always also have to look up to where the Trasks of the world live, forever beyond her reach if she continues to define her identity, her virtue, and her trajectory in life in terms of the augmentation of their wealth and power. She merely pushes them further away up the ladder as she climbs up after. On this particular ladder of success, they rest comfortably on her head.

In watching the film and appreciating uncritically its story, we must endorse and celebrate inequality as much as individual success. We must give assent to a social system that designates certain people as less worthy than others. And we must accede to a regime of social power that allocates resources in such a way that a small minority (a single man in the case of the film) will benefit enormously from the accumulated labors of numerous others. A film is most successfully ideological when it gets us to lend assent in this way without realizing we are doing so. It gets us to see the world in one way but to interpret it in another. We see structural inequality but interpret it as individual success. We see a species of enslavement but think "freedom." To do so, we must know – but never think – that Tess will never be Trask. Her destiny is given in the final image of the film – rows of windows all alike, one of which is hers. It suggests that she is multiple, that her seemingly differentiated individuality is replicated in a mass of lives very much like her own, laboring away for the only real individual in the film, the only real individual success story, the man who owns, and who by owning rules. Tess rebels against her old life in order to be respectfully obedient in her new one. That apparently is all that the system allows.

CHAPTER 7
Gender Studies

Gender studies began as feminism and eventually became as well gay, lesbian, bisexual, and transgender studies. Feminism came into being as a school of literary and cultural study in the 1970s. Its initial impetus as a scholarly project was to ask why women have played a subordinate role to men in human history. It was concerned with how women's lives have changed over time, and it asked what about women's experience (including their writing) is different from men's. Some feminists claimed that women's experience is the result of an essential ontological or biological difference of identity, while others contended that it is the result of historical imprinting and social construction. Either women think and act differently from men for biological reasons or they are made different by the fact that human culture has always been male-dominated. Feminist literary criticism studies literature by women for how it expresses the particularity of women's lives. It studies the canon of male writers for how women have been represented in it.

According to feminist anthropologists such as Gayle Rubin, the subordination of women to men originated in early societies in which women were used as tokens of exchange between clans. The rule against incest forbade endogenous marriage, and exogenous marriages outside one's clan became a way of fostering peaceful relations between groups that might otherwise have been prone to conflict. The residues of such ancient patriarchy are still palpable in our own societies. While women occasionally become political or economic leaders, they are far outnumbered by the numerous men who run business, industry, and government. The assumed norm in many traditionalist societies in Africa, the Middle East, the American "heartland," and Asia is for women to be in charge of domestic labor while men do more public work. Moreover, the pressure of what Adrienne Rich calls "compulsory heterosexuality" ensures that women have no other options than to submit to more economically powerful men.

Whatever its origin – nature or society – this situation of gender inequality is sustained by culture. Most traditional religions such as Catholicism, fundamentalist Protestantism, Islam, and Orthodox Judaism assign women to secondary roles, and some forbid them from participating in public activities with men. In mythology and philosophy, women are often associated with danger, uncontrolled bodily urges, and madness, while men are linked to reason, courage, and independence. Even modern cultural forms such as film, because the industry is largely owned and controlled by men, foster assumptions that further the subordination of women. Images of strong, publicly competent women are still hard to come by in film culture, while images of women who are evil because they possess too much power are fairly easy to find.

The French feminist philosopher Luce Irigaray argues that images of frighteningly powerful, castrating women appear so frequently in male-dominated culture because man's first relationship in the world is with his mother. That mother is an overpowering being associated with the threat of engulfment. Men compensate for this initial state of powerlessness by engaging in an extreme rejection of the mother and of all that she represents in terms of care and empathy. For men to have an identity and to have power, the mother must be subordinated and anything associated with her must be depicted as evil. That symbolic early object in one's life gets transferred, of course, onto women in general. This would explain why in traditional societies women are often made to appear under the total control of their husbands. They are forced to live in confined interior spaces and forced to wear body-covering clothing that marks them out as their husband's property. That many women freely accede to such subordination is a sign of how successful cultural conditioning can be even when it works against one's interests.

American feminist scholars Sandra Gilbert and Susan Gubar add important detail to this argument in *The Madwoman in the Attic*. Women, they notice, are depicted either as monsters or angels in the male literary tradition. They are often objects of fear. Irigaray's account of how men compensate for the mother's early power over them helps account for the angel ideal. Men, she contends, learn to abstract from material life because it is associated with early experiences of union with the mother's body. Such speculative abstractions push matter away and keep it at a safe distance. Matter is replaced by spirit or ideality, a realm of pure mental abstraction that assures men of their ability to control the physical world. The angel ideal that Gilbert and Gubar study converts physical women into spiritual beings. In so doing, it essentially kills them, since they are rendered immobile and inanimate and deprived of autonomy.

Gender studies also includes gay and lesbian studies, as well as the study of sexuality in general. Increasingly, gay and lesbian studies programs are called gay, lesbian, bisexual, and transgender studies programs. Gender became unfixed from the traditional heterosexual binary in the 1970s and 1980s. Gay and lesbian studies theorists became interested in unearthing the hidden tradition of homosexual writing and began to study the gender dynamics of canonical literature. The unearthing of a counter-tradition of homosexual writing was made difficult by the history of the closet. While there have been many gay writers, from Sappho to Tennessee Williams, few of them wrote openly about their lives and experiences. Heterosexual culture was intolerant of gay perspectives both on the streets and in books, and while strong women might be put in the attic for being "mad," gay people were put in jail for being "perverse" or "against nature." Oscar Wilde is the most famous example, but writers like Elizabeth Bishop and Henry James, who remained "in the closet" for most of their lives, were more common.

Gay critics interrogate the very notion of gender identity and question the logic of gender categorization. They especially cast doubt on the idea that there is a necessary relation between gender, physiology, and sexuality. The relation of such categories as masculine and feminine to such supposedly stable bodily and psychological identities as male and female is, they contend, contingent and historical. Not only do traits like masculine and feminine circulate quite freely in combination with biological realities and sexual choices, but also the meaning of each of the terms is highly variable across cultures and over time. There is no guarantee that what one is biologically will line up in a predictable and necessary way with particular sexual practices or psychological dispositions. The normative alignment in mainstream gender culture of male and female with heterosexual masculinity or femininity must therefore be seen as a political rather than a biological fact.

The variability of sexuality and of gender identity is quelled by the dominant discourse regarding gender, which enforces what it describes. By assuming that there are stable identities such as masculine and feminine or man and woman or heterosexual and homosexual that give rise to the discourses that describe them, mainstream gender ideology enforces the normativity of such identities. The possibility of a masculine female or of a feminine male comes to appear unnatural. One contingent style of sexuality – reproductive heterosexuality – becomes naturalized through constant repetition and rote learning. It comes to appear "normal" while all other gender and sexual possibilities are rendered marginal or subordinate. In this way, a gender regime that limits legitimate sexuality to reproductive heterosexuality comes to be mistaken for an originating ground that defines and determines the difference between norm and margin, acceptable and unacceptable. What is or what is assumed to be the only possibly normal way of being becomes "what should be." In reality, however, the normative ground is simply one among many diverse sex/gender possibilities, all of which have equal claim to legitimacy. There is a plurality of sex-gender possibilities – masculine lesbian, masculine heterosexual female, feminine gay male, feminine heterosexual male, etc. This plurality is subsumed to the binary heterosexual norm in mainstream culture, but its reality is evident throughout society.

If normative reproductive sexuality and the identities that accompany it are one among many possible modes and vectors of sexuality, then supposedly marginal forms of sexuality, rather than being perverse deviations from a norm, may be manifestations of the basic multiplicity of sexuality. The norm, in other words, is less a center that defines deviations than one deviation among many. There is no central form of sexuality that can be declared to be the normative standard that allows other forms of sexuality to be declared deviant. All sexuality, in a certain sense, is deviant. There is no norm; there is only a variety of possibilities both for gender identity and for sexual practice.

These theories focus attention on the role of culture in establishing and maintaining gender norms. They assume that gender is enforced by, as much as it is expressed in, culture. Culture privileges certain sexual object choices and psychological gender dispositions while denigrating others. In the 1950s in the US, for example, melodramas such as *Written on the Wind* routinely portrayed women who were interested in sex and wore raving red cocktail dresses in the middle of the day as deviant, wild, and dangerous to patriarchy. In contrast, women and men who dressed in accordance with demure heterosexual standards, honored the norms of reproductive sexuality, ignored their homosexual urges, and played it straight were rewarded with happiness and success. Gender theorists such as Judith Butler have focused attention on the way gender is "performed" into being. We assume cultural accouterments are expressions of a gender nature or ontology, but these theorists contend that the repetitive imitation of normative gender standards in fact generates a sense in humans of having a coherent gender identity that does not include "deviant" possibilities.

Why are the ruling heterosexual gender groups so interested in making sure their norms are enforced? Gender theorists argue that the contingency of gender – that we could in reality be anything we wish to be in regard to sexuality or gender identity because nothing is naturally mandatory – inspires panic in people whose sense of identity is inseparable from the sanctity of the reigning heterosexual gender norm. At the heart of heterosexual culture's antipathy to gays is a panic fear that heterosexuality is not in fact normative. Indeed, if heterosexuality and homosexuality are on a fluid continuum of diverse possibilities, none more normative or central than the next, then homosexuality is less an "other" that is outside heterosexuality than an "alter" that is one alternative along with heterosexuality in a range of diverse and equally weighted possibilities. This argument is made more compelling by gender theorists' attention to the "homosocial" dimension of female friendship and male alliance. Both of these "normal" kinds of behavior contain elements of homosexuality. Indeed, such homosexually tinged homosociality is a primary condition of the male alliances that subtend particular kinds of behavior (in the military, for example, or in right-wing politics) that are supposedly connected in a necessary way to highly masculine forms of heterosexuality. If one looks at the numerous homemade trailers for the film *Brokeback Mountain*, especially the *Top Gun* parody, this point becomes quite clear.

The panic at the heart of heterosexual culture is most palpable in its fear objects. Loss of power often gets metaphorized in male-centered culture as anal penetration, for example, and perhaps the most feared monster in male fantasy is the masculine woman. Such women are often associated with confusion in the realm of mental representation, an inability to establish the identity of objects. If male heterosexual identity is predicated on having a passive, feminine female other as guarantor of male identity, then the masculine female upsets all of the cognitive processes and psycho-sexual assumptions that underwrite that identity. If the object that lends one credibility as a heterosexual male subject can so easily flip into its opposite, then the object world itself becomes unstable and unpredictable. The response is often violence against those objects. In films like *Disclosure* and *Basic Instinct*, for example, which are about such heterosexual male panic, one of the crucial motifs is the inability to see straight, to mentally represent the world in such a way

Gender Studies

that objects are clearly identifiable and categorizable. But if women can be men and men women, that becomes a vexed and flawed undertaking.

What these insights suggest is that homosexuality is not an identity apart from and completely outside another identity called heterosexuality. This sealed box theory might be replaced by another, called the ocean current theory. According to this approach, the fact that at different moments of history and in different cultures, so-called homosexual practices were routinely engaged in by people who were supposedly heterosexual suggests that we all have gay potentials with us, even if we are practicing heterosexuals. In ancient Greece, boys spent an initiation period in a homosexual alliance with an older male before being admitted into public life. If everyone is potentially gay, then it is only the laborious imprinting of heterosexual norms by the cultures in which we live that cuts away those potentials and manufactures good, norm-honoring heterosexual subjects. Yet latent and suppressed homosexuality is queered into being in the various forms of homophilia that pop up everywhere in heterosexual culture, from "good old boy" butt-slapping to the varieties of love-crazed fandom. Sexual transitivity is stilled for the sake of species reproduction, but in the realms of cultural play, the excess of desire and identification over norm and rule testify to more plural possibilities.

Exercise 7.1   William Shakespeare, *King Lear*

King Lear was written at a time when homosexuality – or "sodomy" – was outlawed, yet it was also a time when James I, the new king of England, was making it increasingly clear to his subjects that he was a practicing homosexual. He lived apart from his wife and child and lavished gifts – including Raleigh's last estate – on his young male lovers. Alan Bray's *Homosexuality in Renaissance England* tells us how one contemporary account, the *Memoirs* of Lucy Hutchinson, described James' court as full of "fools and bawds, mimics and catamites" who engaged in "debaucheries." That "mimics" is a word for actors and "catamites" a contemporary term for homosexuals suggests a possible connection between *Lear* and the court of King James, especially since the play was presented to the king's court on St. Stephen's Night, 1606, a festival that might be counted an occasion for "debaucheries."

Bray notes that the London theater was, like James's court, a locus of the homosexual subculture of early seventeenth-century England.

Parents were afraid to see their sons become involved with the institution for fear they might be "corrupted." Given that *Lear* was performed at court and may have been written for that occasion, it is possible that the play inscribes within itself the link between these two subcultural sites – the theater and the court. If this is the case, then those moments in the play that might be interpreted as making sly homosexual allusions – the Fool's remark that one should not trust "a boy's love," for example – or as lending a homoerotic slant to the play's social allegory – Kent's remark to Gloucester that "I cannot conceive you" – take on an additional significance. Indeed, once this perspective is adopted, the play can be seen as suggesting that not just homosociality but also homosexuality is good for the health of nations. Homosexuality is worked into the play both as innuendo and as a fairly explicit, if necessarily oblique, theme.

The play begins on a homosocial note that very quickly veers into an at least jokingly homosexual suggestiveness. "I thought the King had more affected the Duke of Albany than Cornwall," Kent remarks, drawing attention to the relation between male affection and affairs of state. The remark hints at the rashness and indecisiveness in Lear that will result in the destruction of the state; like a woman – as she is coded in Renaissance culture – he will act on the basis more of emotion than reason. The intimation that a man might behave like a woman seems to evoke a further expansion or crossing of gender boundaries and positions when Kent says to Gloucester "I cannot conceive you." He means he doesn't understand him, but Gloucester picks up on the sexual meaning: "Sir, this young fellow's mother could; whereupon she grew round-wombed." The possible reference to homosexuality is as quickly erased as it is evoked, and it is deflected into a heterosexual framework. That maneuver befits a culture dominated by the discourse and rituals of compulsory heterosexuality, which are enacted in the ensuing dowry scene, a culture that in its religion and its law was hostile to such homosexual acts as sodomy. As a result, homosexuality only appears in the play in glimpses whose fleetingness suggests repression as much as expression. One might even say that by evoking it in this opening dialogue, which is played out of view of the more public events that follow, Shakespeare is noting the closeted quality of life in the homosexual subculture to which he, as member of the theater, probably belonged.

But why make a coy homosexual reference at the opening of a tragedy about a father's betrayal by his daughters? The play depicts a crisis in gender identity, specifically a crisis of the institution of compulsory heterosexuality, an institution centered on an ideal of male masculinity which finds an enabling other but also a potentially subversive danger in female femininity. That social institution is depicted as pathological in its most extreme forms, and the play argues in favor of a new masculinity tempered by passage through the dangers of feminization. One cure for the failings of the old masculinity represented by Lear is retraction into homosociality from the troubled heterosexual sphere. In the mad scenes on the heath, a mock theater is created that offers therapy in the form of love between men, a love laced with homosexual allusions. Lear's mad fantasies are explicitly linked to theatrical exhibition, and one conclusion we might draw is that Shakespeare, by depicting a play within a play at a moment charged with homosexual references, is referring to the homosexual subculture of the London theater itself.

The play portrays compulsory heterosexuality as successfully healing itself and reattaining its dominant status and place after a fall into psychological fragmentation. But the play also depicts untempered heterosexuality as a weakness that has harmful effects. It is prone to incest and to the domination of women's lives for the sake of male vanity. "Better thou / Hadst not been born than not t'have pleased me better," Lear says to Cordelia in a line that is not meant to evoke sympathy from the audience. The incestuous character of his demands on his daughters is made evident when Cordelia points out that his desire for expressions of affection trespasses upon the rights of a husband. Later, he accuses his daughters of opposing "the bolt / Against my coming in." Edgar most explicitly articulates the play's critique of heterosexuality when as Tom he speaks of having "served the lust of my mistress' heart," which equates heterosexuality itself with demonic possession by the "foul fiend."

Heterosexuality is dangerous because it contains an instability: while it would seem to assure a man's identity as a masculine male, it leaves the man dependent on women for certification. Rather than be an identity, heterosexuality consists of a relation or an exchange, whereby male masculinity is confirmed by its other, the feminine – submissive and passive – woman. It is what it is not. Cordelia's "Nothing" in response to Lear's demands for tokens of affection exemplifies this dilemma. At the limit where the heterosexual male and the heterosexual female meet, there is always a margin of error where something needed can be lacking, where a required repetition that confirms by recognizing fails to occur. As the Fool reminds Lear several times, without heterosexual confirmation, Lear himself is nothing – "an O without a figure." Which is to say, given the slang meaning of nothing, he is a woman.

If women are the soft spot of the heterosexual regime, its point of proof as well as of vulnerability, it is because the exchange relationship that establishes that system is reversible. Lear's loss of sexual power is metaphorized as his feminization by his masculinized daughters. In a world shaped by compulsory heterosexuality and the cultural postulates of phallic normativity, the feminization of men results in a depletion of power and authority. If one cannot "command service" both as domestic and as sexual labor, one should not rule. In a world organized around aggressive relations between contending sites of power – a fact emphasized in the play through constant references to possible strife between such players as Albany and Cornwall – the need to survive dictates the subordination of weak characteristics and the privileging of strong ones. That these characteristics should be distributed along biological gender lines is not surprising for the historical moment. What is less clear is whether they are also distributed along the lines of gendered object choice. I say this because those left to rule at the end of the play – Kent and Edgar – are men who apparently love men not women.

The dangerous and destructive feminization of men occurs when women assume traditionally masculine powers, when they, as it were, become men. This places men like Lear, who are dependent on confirmation by feminine women of their masculine identity, in jeopardy. Their feminization produces a hysterical reaction that is figured in the play as madness. That Lear cannot ultimately survive the experience and must pass on power to Edgar suggests just how deadly feminization is conceived as being within the early seventeenth-century cultural gender codes.

Within the Renaissance bodily code, Lear's loss of temper and rash actions based on momentary emotions are coded as female. In relinquishing his power to his daughters and thereby masculinizing them, he says that he will follow a "monthly course," a reference to menstruation. By entering the realm of uncontrolled bodily and emotional processes, he abandons the realm of principle, reason, and law – the realm assigned men in the play and in patriarchal culture generally. He breaks his quasi-legal agreement with Burgundy to provide land as dowry for Cordelia, and he subverts the principles of fairness and justice by depriving her of everything for nothing. The price he pays for behaving like a woman is to become a woman.

When his Fool speaks of him as "nothing," he adds a sexual spin to Lear's loss of power: "Thou hast pared thy wit o' both sides and left nothing i' the middle. Here comes one o' the parings." The use of "Nothing" suggests that Lear will be obliged to adopt a "feminine" sexual posture of passivity to penetration, and indeed, Goneril, who assumes masculine phallic proportions as a result of the territory and power Lear attributes to her, makes him bend to her will in a manner that Albany characterizes in symbolically sexual terms: "How far your eyes may pierce I cannot tell." The Fool's preparation of the encounter between father and daughter is more explicitly sexual: "thou mad'st thy daughters thy mothers . . . thou gav'st them the rod and putt'st down thine own breeches." The image of punishment suggests the submissive sexual position and the feminization of the man deprived of power. He can now be had from behind by his phallic daughter.

Earlier, the Fool had compared the division of Lear's kingdom to the breaking of an egg into two ends or crowns: "Why, after I have cut the egg i' th' middle and eat up the meat, the two crowns of the egg. When thou clovest thy crown i' th' middle and gav'st away both parts, thou bor'st thine ass on thy back o'er the dirt." "Ass" refers to servant ("Thy asses are gone about [getting your horses]," the Fool tells Lear at one point), and because servants were known to be used sexually by their masters in Renaissance England, the image, in addition to social inversion, also suggests the adoption of a submissive sexual posture in regard to someone more powerful, someone who would be quite literally on Lear's back. Something similar is implied by Lear's statement "Persuade me rather to be slave and sumpter / To this detested groom." A sumpter is a pack animal, but it also carries the connotation of putting something (or someone) on one's back. That someone, of course, is Goneril, who now possesses the quality of firmness ("marble-hearted fiend") Lear lacks. When he wishes sterility upon her, he more or less completes her sex-change operation, and when she taunts her husband with "milky gentleness," she assumes masculine power in her own household. It is at this point in the play that the Fool's sexual taunts most concern castration and the loss of sexual power on Lear's part: "She . . . / Shall not be a maid long, unless things be cut shorter." "I am ashamed," Lear says, "That thou hast power to shake my manhood thus." And he is described as suffering an "eyeless rage."

In contrast, one important feature of the new masculine figure who takes Lear's place as ruler is his detachment from women. Edgar's martial power, his capacity for violence, leaves him immune to feminization. He is not dependent on women for heterosexual confirmation because his aggression enacts a successful separation from the feminine that is best instantiated in the fact that he has no conversations with women throughout the play. His capacity for violence or aggression also distinguishes him from the old king, who in one crucial moment is incapable of saying what violence he will wreak on his daughters: "I will have such revenges on you both / That all the world shall – I will do such things – / What they are yet I know not."

Edgar and Kent, the two characters most capable of restorative violence, are also those most associated with homosocial relationships. Kent says he is "not so young . . . to love a woman for singing, nor so old to dote on her for anything." Edgar's repeated warnings against heterosexual attachments during his mad speeches align him with a similar male separation. One consequence of the instability of compulsory heterosexuality is a parallel structuring of relationships between men and women on one side and men and men on the other. The dangerously feminizing dependence inscribed in heterosexuality provokes a violent response against women, the agents of potential feminization, which enables a safe separation of the male from the female and from femininity. The emotional needs and dependencies that leave a man vulnerable to feelings of feminization within a culture that proscribes "woman's tears" on a man's face and that mandate a more aggressive, emotionally sanitized posture toward the world are transferred into the realm of homosocial, isomale relations.

This ideal of isomale relations is not only homosocial, but also homosexual. Lear, by virtue of a passage through a healing homosexuality, moves from pathological heterosexuality ("I have sworn. I am firm") to an acceptance of his own "infirmity." If emotional dependence is disallowed between men and women under the regime of compulsory heterosexuality because it represents a dangerous feminization, it is permitted in relations between men.

Undercover homosexuality is a parallel social structure to compulsory heterosexuality in early seventeenth-century England, and in the play, a parallel world of explicitly homosocial and implicitly homosexual relations offers a counter to a dangerous heterosexual realm. The danger of being refused "service" by women is compensated by affectionate and trusting isomale relations. If the phallic woman feminizes Lear, deprives him of power, and transforms him into a sexual servant, Lear discovers in Kent someone who subordinates himself to Lear's will. "What wouldst thou?" Lear asks him. "Service," Kent replies. "Service" has throughout the play the dual meaning of obedient labor ("The dear father . . . commands . . . service") and sexual labor ("one that wouldst be a bawd in way of good service," "To thee a woman's services are due"). In isomale relations, the feminized heterosexual male can be repositioned in a dominant masculine posture if he receives "service" from another male.

With Kent, the Fool is a figure of homosocial healing who is also suggestive of homosexuality. Called a "pretty knave" upon entering, he is a male correlate of Cordelia, who is referred to later as Lear's "fool": "And my poor fool is hanged." Both are romanticized figures of affection untainted by expediency. The Fool remains loyal to Lear when it is foolish to do so, even in his own cynical terms. And Cordelia accepts loss for the king's gain, even after he has imposed great losses on her. Both are linked to emblems of retraction from the storms of the world – the Fool with the hovel and Cordelia with the cage. If the Fool provides the same "nursery" to Lear that Cordelia in her absence cannot, he disappears in the play in large part because Cordelia returns to take up once again her role of providing service. She is called fool because in some respects she is the Fool.

What these cross-gender confusions (or continuities) suggest is that the sites of retraction – hovel and cage – are curative because they are outside the exchange system of compulsory heterosexuality. The Fool can be replaced by a woman, and Cordelia (a part acted by a boy) can take the place of the healing men because the play moves us temporarily outside the world of compulsory heterosexuality and into another gender and sexual realm altogether – one that we would characterize as the homosexual underworld of London which has to appear under the sign of madness because it was so outside normalizing acceptability. If Lear is to be cured of the pathological heterosexuality of which he was initially guilty, he must turn to homosexuality and the possibility it affords of adopting a feminine posture of emotional dependence without stigma. We witness that turn in the mad scenes on the heath.

Edgar is the character who is most capable of enacting the new masculinity the play demands after compulsory heterosexuality has been shown to be both deficient and dangerous. Like Kent and the Fool, he is markedly nonheterosexual; he doesn't even talk about women, at least while sane, and while insane, all he talks about is why one should avoid them. Misogyny protects him against possible feminization, and from him, Lear learns not to trust women in the way that he has up till now. He is also placed in a subordinate homosexual position without suffering feminization.

When Lear sheds his clothes and joins Edgar in nakedness (save for Edgar's blanket), the visual display evokes homosexuality, and so as well does Edgar's vocabulary of possession, which at the time was associated with sodomy. Sodomites or homosexuals were often linked to witches, were-people, and evil spells, and Edgar's mad speeches are full of such images: "Flibbertigibbet ... squinnies the eye and makes the hare-lip ... aroint thee, witch." Lear immediately develops an affectionate attachment to the "learned Theban" and will not let him go. His characterization of Edgar as an "Athenian" slyly situates their encounter within the homoerotic Greek tradition of master and pupil, and indeed, Lear adopts a student's posture toward the younger man, a posture in keeping with the prevailing image of homosexuality at the time as a relationship between an older man and a younger one or "Ganymede."

Edgar undergoes with Lear the experience of liquefaction that is effeminization. He and Lear are naked in the storm together, and Edgar's "friend" is associated with water: "Frateretto ... tells me Nero is an angler in the lake of darkness. Pray, innocent, and beware the foul fiend." In the source for this passage in Chaucer, Nero is called a fiend and is associated with incest. "Angling" is a term for sexual penetration, and "darkness" is linked to the vagina later in the play: "Beneath [the waist] is all the fiend's; there's hell, there's darkness." What Edgar would thus seem to warn against is the incestuous desire of which Lear has been guilty. The reference to Nero also evokes Nero's other crime – having his mother dissected so that he could see her womb. Edgar does not encourage Lear to violence, but Lear picks up on the reference when he exclaims: "Then let them anatomize Regan." The way out of the water into which women dissolve men when they destroy their masculinity is, it would seem, a violent aggression that desexualizes women and reaffirms masculinity re-firming men.

If Edgar is teacher, he also refers to himself as a "childe" or young knight about to be initiated, since his encounter with Lear prepares him for his assumption of the king's place. That transformation is foreshadowed by the acting he engages in at this moment in the play. That he can adopt a role suggests his malleability and the possibility of a change in social place. Theatricality thus supplies the model for repairing the state, for installing a new person in the role or part of the king. But it also provides the model for an all-male, homosexual group of the sort that ultimately reclaims state power. The small acting troupe on the heath that enacts the trial and imaginary dissection of the offensive daughters plays not only with the emblems and rituals of justice and statecraft but also with those of gender. The scene of "Greek" tutelage between the learned Theban and Lear prepares the substitution of

younger ruler for older king, and constitutes an endorsement of homosexuality as a reparative alternative to heterosexuality.

Nevertheless, in the end, Lear must be repositioned in relation to a
woman, Cordelia. That the woman is someone with whom he cannot
legitimately have sex and that her character forms a continuum with a
healing homosocial male companion – the Fool – suggests some of the
complexity of homosexual experience at the time, its closeted character,
while also embodying the difficult representational strategies
Shakespeare was, as a result, obliged to adopt. A play about how good
homosexuality is for heterosexuality must necessarily attempt to have
it both ways, while having it neither way in the pure form (of sexual
identity) mandated by compulsory heterosexuality. For this reason,
Cordelia, who finally fulfills Lear's desires (that they die in each other's
arms should at least evoke the possibility of the Renaissance coding of
death as sex, something which has to occur under the cloak of metaphor), is the Fool in drag, but she is also the heterosexual Cordelia
because the reigning cultural imperatives mandate that semen shall
make its way to the gilded cage rather than the dirty hovel.

The play's ending is noteworthy for its emotionality. In contrast to
their earlier fear of taint by women's tears, the men seem to cry in
abundance. Their hearts burst asunder, and their love for each other is
manifest. Lear's "I am firm" no longer seems to have a place. The
pathological masculinity he initially represents is now replaced by
another that seems to incorporate what the play depicts as femininity.
If women have been like men in the play, men now become like women.
Culturally certified traits seem to shift if not circulate. The play is at its
most gender-radical when it seems to suggest that those traits are contingent rather than ontological or natural.

It concludes on a note of aristocratic gay romanticism ("Speak what
we feel, not what we ought to say") that privileges subjectivity over
social convention, the pride of the closet over the mandates of compulsory heterosexuality. It does so, I would argue, because Shakespeare
himself no doubt experienced the play's equivocal subject position,
which is inwardly gay and outwardly straight. As we know Shakespeare
to have probably been gay yet married, we know Edgar to love men, yet
he must, like James I, stand up in a public forum at the end and pretend
to submit to the rules of compulsory heterosexuality. That no sign of
that mandate is evident (Edgar is still not linked to a woman) suggests
just how tentatively or grudgingly it is accepted. But it is there nonetheless, inscribed in the anti-sodomy laws and in the religious culture that
could not tolerate gay coupling. Only in such enclaves as the theater and

the court was a gay subculture possible because only under assumed roles could men act out their love for each other. That James' gay court was known for staging plays like *Lear* says something about the necessary theatricality of gayness at the time, as much as it says something about the gayness of the theater. The tragedy of *Lear* is in part that of pathological heterosexuality, which must in the course of the play learn to reform itself. But it is also that of the homosexual man who must live out the form of compulsory heterosexuality while yet experiencing feelings that must remain silent.

Now consider the play from a feminist perspective. Notice how women are portrayed in the dowry scene. How does the depiction of women reproduce traditional stereotypes regarding women?

Men traditionally usurp values such as reason and logic for themselves, while assigning irrationality to women. In a more positive stereotype, women are thought to be submissive and virtuous. How do these stereotypes appear in the opening scene?

After the opening scene, Goneril and Regan change dramatically. How might that also be the expression of a stereotype in male culture regarding women? How might changeability be linked to a troubling danger that women might represent for men?

Goneril and Regan become viler and viler as the play proceeds. But they also become increasingly powerful, and the moral assessment of them seems to grow more negative the more power they acquire. Is the play about female power and the danger it poses for men?

A feminist might be tempted to read against the grain of the play and to see in the negative depiction of the two sisters a positive possibility. What might that be?

What do you think a feminist critic would say about the play's conclusion? What are we to make of the fact that all the women die, even the loyal, virtuous Cordelia? Is there a symbolic connection of some kind between that fact and the fate of patriarchy in the play?

Exercise 7.2   Elizabeth Bishop, "Roosters," "In the Waiting Room," and "Exchanging Hats"

That one of the three expressly lesbian poems that Elizabeth Bishop wrote – "Exchanging Hats" – had to go unpublished (while one of the others – "The Shampoo" – was refused publication by Bishop's usual outlet, *The New Yorker*, because of its sexual allusions) says something about the problems faced by gay writers in the recent past.

"Roosters" might also be read as a lesbian poem, but I place it here more because it offers such a spectacular critique of male culture from a woman's perspective.

It will become clear fairly quickly – by line 3 at least – that by "roosters" Bishop means men. Notice how she uses a simple descriptive vocabulary to characterize male culture. What colors are used and why?

What is her attitude toward the roosters? How is it registered in description and choice of setting?

Why does she call their cries "traditional"?

What is the role of "wives" in all of this male display? And why are they characterized as "despised"?

Bishop eventually begins to lend thematic significance to the roosters. What do they mean in her eyes? What feelings do they evoke? And why does she associate them with "unwanted love, conceit, and war"?

She mocks their combativeness and seems to relish their deflation and death. But then she turns oddly away from her theme and begins what appears to be a reflection on the role of the rooster in Christian symbolism. She refers to the story of Christ's betrayal by Peter. Peter was told by Christ that he would betray him by the time the cock had crowed three times.

Why does Bishop turn to this story? What do you make of the lines that begin "There is inescapable hope, the pivot"? "Pivot" might refer to the way the cock on a weathervane turns on a pivot. But here the turn seems to have to do with Peter's sorrow over his sin of "spirit." How might the meaning of the cock change or be changed by Peter's story?

The final five stanzas seem to offer a different version of a morning that contrasts with the first one described in the opening stanzas of the poem. How is this morning different?

"In the Waiting Room" is a remarkable and debatable poem. Some read it as a story of a girl coming of age and realizing her identity. Others – myself included – read it as a story about a girl coming to realize that she is a lesbian.

When the poem was written, lesbians could not live openly. They were considered deviant, and it would have been a very troubling realization for a young girl to come to if she began to see herself as being more drawn to women than to men. Heterosexuality was compulsory at the time, and she would have been expected – unless she wished to be branded a "spinster" and considered odd – to grow up to marry a man. Her youth, one might say, would consist of being "in the waiting room" of heterosexuality. Now consider how heterosexual sex might appear to such a young woman. It might seem both violent and a violation, a source of pain rather than of pleasure, like going to the dentist. Quite literally, a man would have the right to poke around in one of your essential cavities, and you would have to grin and bear it.

The girl in the poem reads *National Geographic* while her Aunt Consuelo is inside with the dentist. Back then, this magazine often contained photographs of African women with exposed breasts, and it was one of the few places in the culture where one could see images of nakedness. It had a reputation as a form of mild pornography. Notice how the girl qualifies what she is doing – "(I could read)" – in parentheses that suggest a kind of inside that is parallel to the "inside" where the aunt is. This inside, one might say, is her inside self, and one senses that the poem will explore her psychology. What she describes, in other words, may be her own reactions to things as much as the things themselves.

Why would she "carefully" study the photographs? What does that word suggest about the quality of her attention? Imagine you are a young person seeing an image of a naked person for the first time. It would grab your attention probably, and it might light a fire of sexual interest in you. Notice what happens next to the girl – an exploding volcano, rivulets of fire. What do you make of that image?

The image that follows is of two explorers, one female, the other male, but you don't realize that immediately from the names. Why might the girl focus on how they are dressed? Can you tell which is male and which female?

The next image is troubling – a dead man slung on a pole. How might it fit in? "Long pig" is a very derogatory term. How might it be explained by a young lesbian girl's awakening hostility to compulsory heterosexuality?

A similar hostility might be said to inform the next images – women who seem bound to childbirth and child-rearing. Why the repetition here?

What do you make of the word "horrifying" applied to the girl's sense of their naked breasts? Given that her own reactions are so bound up with the things described, what about her reactions might provoke a feeling of horror in the girl? Are the breasts frightening, or are the feelings the breasts inspire frightening? And if so, why?

What do you make of the insistently reassuring quality of the following two lines – "I read it straight through. / I was too shy to stop"? There seems to be a small element of guilt here, as if she wanted to assure herself and readers that she didn't dawdle over the potentially erotically arousing photographs, taking pleasure from them. Notice that she implies that she wanted to stop to look longer, but she was "too shy" to do so.

She seems to seek even more reassurance in the lines that follow. By looking at the cover, she pushes the photographs (and her troubling reactions to them) inside. You might say, she represses the feelings they inspire by "covering" them. Notice the image of boundaries here – "margins" – as well as the punctuality of "date." In space and time, she wants to fix a boundary between herself and the feelings now safely "inside" the magazine.

All of this makes the next line striking and interesting – "Suddenly, from inside." Here "inside" refers or seems to refer to the dentist's inner room where Aunt Consuelo has gone and where the girl imagines her experiencing an "*oh!* of pain." That "oh" sounds like "O," and as in *King Lear*, it suggests the vaginal opening. If the dentist is a figure for a feared painful heterosexual experience the girl does not want to have, then that allusion would make sense. Compulsory heterosexual sex is pain for a lesbian.

What follows suggests that things are not clear-cut for the girl. She confuses herself with her aunt, but of course, that would be what a young girl trying to form her own identity from identifications with older relatives would be expected to do. Why would she begin this section by saying that she knew her aunt was "a foolish, timid woman"? If we generalize, what might that suggest about women who submit to a regime of compulsory heterosexuality that would turn them into beings like those in the magazine photographs, whose whole lives seem to be reduced to sex and child-rearing?

In the sentence "she was a foolish, timid woman," where do you think the stress falls? If it falls on "she," then the girl is marking out or trying to mark out a difference from her aunt. The girl knows SHE, meaning the aunt, may be timid and foolish, but she herself is not. Does that seem like a plausible reading?

If so, what do you make of her confusion of herself with the aunt? Why would she imagine that she is her foolish aunt? Is she imagining growing up to be like her aunt and wondering what that would mean? Or is her confusion more an expression of what we have noticed about her feelings in the previous stanza – an expression of preference for women over men?

That would seem to make a certain sense. After all, to be "like" someone in the sense of identifying with them in order to form one's own identity can easily be confused with to "like" them, as in having affection for them – just as in love we often mold our own identity on that of our love object. It all depends on how you read the line "Without thinking at all / I was my foolish aunt." Does she mean that she WAS her foolish aunt, but she didn't realize it? Or does she mean that she did not think she was her foolish aunt?

But why would the girl feel that they are "falling, falling" together, and why would their eyes be "glued" to the cover of the magazine? Does "fall" mean something like "caught in the act" and therefore "in sin"? Or is it more that the girl is falling back into the feelings awakened by the photographs in the magazine, disturbing lesbian sexual feelings, that make her yearn for the security and safety associated with a "cover," a boundary that seals off the dangerous affect somewhere inside?

Read the rest of the poem on your own. Take note of the interplay of identity and identification and notice how she uses "like" and "unlikely" in this regard. The black wave has to do, I would suggest, with the powerful affect released by the girl's awakening sense of herself as "unlike" others. If that is so, then the final stanza seems to re-evoke the possibility of some punctual, well-marked boundary where the danger both of the affect and for the girl of that realization can be controlled or concealed. Notice as well the odd configuration of inside and outside in that stanza, and think about how that might bear on this reading.

I will not say much about "Exchanging Hats," an unpublished poem about the fluidity of gender identity, other than to draw your attention to it and to say it is very interesting! You might take the trouble to look up "anandrous" and "avernal" and ask why she uses these words.

Exercise 7.3 Henry James, *The Aspern Papers*

The narrator of *The Aspern Papers* clearly adores Jeffrey Aspern, but does he love him? Is this a love story between men, one of whom is dead and remains accessible only through letters he wrote to a woman and one of whom is desperate to see the letters for purely "literary" reasons that seem to just barely conceal a much stronger passion?

Consider how Aspern's relations with women are characterized in the first chapter. How does the narrator describe those relations? You might look up the story of Orpheus to find out what that allusion means. To compare Aspern's female companions to Maenads is not flattering, since these followers of Dionysus were known for tearing people limb from limb. Notice how the narrator disparages women and asserts that Aspern was "not a woman's poet." Why does he seem so bent on diminishing the significance of Aspern's relations with women?

Do you get any sense of the narrator's sexuality in this chapter? He uses a sexual allusion to distance himself from the erotic attachment to women Aspern seems to have cultivated. The narrator says, "it struck me that he had been kinder and more considerate than in his place – if I could imagine myself in any such box – I should have found the trick of." It's a strangely convoluted way of saying something, and a psychoanalytic critic would latch on to that fact and suggest it is significant of a psychic conflict between desire and repression. Is the narrator imagining himself as Aspern or as one of Aspern's women? There are two sexual terms in the quoted passage – "box," a slang term for vagina, and "trick," a slang term for the sexual act. For the narrator to say that he can't imagine himself in any such box is a bit like saying he cannot imagine heterosexual sex. The name of his partner – "Cumnor" – also contains a sexual pun. To not "come" means to not ejaculate, and that might also be a symbolic signal of sexual detachment.

Are there other ways in which sexuality seems implied in the setting, action, and characterizations in the story?

Consider the discussion of the garden in chapter 2, for example. And there is another curious sexual pun at the end of that chapter. The narrator says of Juliana Bordereau that he "could pounce on her possessions and ransack her drawers." "Drawers" is an old slang term for women's underwear.

So what do you think the tale is about then – a man with sexual yearnings toward a maternal figure, or a man with negative feelings for women who clearly prefers other men?

Why do you think Juliana is described so negatively at the end of chapter 2? What significance does it lend her? What does it mean that the narrator seems to fear her so much?

Psychoanalytic theorists describe masochism as a process that converts pain into pleasure. In masochist fantasies, there always seems to be a strong, quasi-maternal figure who inflicts pain. Are there any indications that one aspect of the narrator's sexual make-up might be masochism? Notice how, at the beginning of chapter 4, he is described as "whimpering" in his friend's salon.

One of the more homoerotic moments in the text occurs in this chapter. The narrator imagines Aspern talking to him about being in

Venice together in a "mystic companionship." Even the world seems to dissolve in an image of erotic bonding – "the marble of the palaces all shimmer and melt together."

Juliana's name contains a similar image of liquidity – "border" and "eau," which means "water" in French. If she is maternal and Aspern paternal in the fictional fantasy of which the narrator is the subject, then it is significant that she is associated with a dissolution of boundaries and with charged sexual imagery some of which focuses erotic energy on her. If a mother does not respect clear boundaries between herself and her male child, if she eroticizes his body through either inappropriate attentiveness or punitiveness, what results is very much like what one sees in the narrator. He idealizes and idolizes the paternal figure as an alternative, and he has strongly charged negative feelings toward the mother, some of which are erotic in character.

He imagines himself pelting her door with flowers, and the door "would have to yield." He has fantasies of her as someone characterized by "impenitent passion." And later, of course, the goal of his quest, the papers, will be hidden in her mattress, as symbolic a hiding-place as one could imagine.

What does Aspern represent? If Juliana is a death's mask who inspires fear and makes the narrator whimper, one should expect Aspern to offer a strong contrast. Notice the way he is characterized at the end of chapter 4. How is that significant in this context?

The relationship with Tina is tinged by expediency. It is also a kind of trial heterosexual relationship. The expediency works to remove any sincerity from the relation, and that would seem to confirm the gay theme by relieving the narrator of any responsibility, any sense that he really means this mock-heterosexual courtship. He is just playing for the sake of his more important goal – union in "mystic companionship" with Jeffrey Aspern. How does the narrator think through his motives regarding Tina? Do you detect signs of bad faith, of reasoning that excuses what should not be excused?

As the narrator nears the goal of his quest, the erotic imagery intensifies. He speaks of nearing the "climax of my crisis," and the papers are in a box in a mattress. He is close to being an object of Aspern's love, since the letters he seeks are written to a love object. Does the narrator want to be in Juliana's place in order to enjoy Aspern alone?

And what do you make of his intense feeling of shame upon being discovered? If his actions have the homoerotic meaning I have been attributing to them, the intensity of his shame would seem to be accounted for. What would a feminist critic say about how Juliana is characterized in this scene?

The final encounters with Tina are remarkable for the way they bring into direct relation the two gender-sexual strands at issue in the tale. The first would be compulsory heterosexuality, since that in part is what Tina represents. Juliana mocks the narrator for not being manly enough, and tries to push him into a heterosexual relationship with someone who moans with "ecstasy" when he takes her out on a date. The second would be the subcultural homosexuality whose name cannot be spoken in the culture of the late nineteenth century but which manifests itself latently and marginally in the narrator's quest for some connection, through the love letters, with a man he idealizes and loves. When Tina proposes marriage, notice how she characterizes the proposed gift of the papers. How does she eroticize them and suggest their sexual symbolism? She almost proposes playing doctor when she says "You could see the things – you could use them." How is the narrator's reaction significant? How does his homosexuality manifest itself at this moment? How does his connection with Aspern "save" him?

Finally, we've discussed the possibility of masochism. How might the ending be read as evidence of masochism?

Exercise 7.4   *The Silence of the Lambs* and *Paris Is Burning*

Most mainstream films deal with heterosexuals and their lives, but in recent decades more and more films have begun to be made about gay, lesbian, and other gender identities and sexual preferences. Many of these films, such as those by Greg Araki, represent gay life from a gay point of view and treat it as being as "normal" as any other gender or sexual preference. Many other films, however, still express the prejudice and hostility that mainstream heterosexuals have for many centuries directed against gay and lesbian people. This prejudice, hostility, and even violence rest on the assumption that homosexuality is abnormal and deviant in relation to a heterosexual norm that is valid and absolute. Yet if this were the case, homosexuality would not so easily and so repeatedly emerge within heterosexual culture as one of its possible permutations. Heterosexual Pashtun tribesmen still take young boys as lovers because their culture limits interactions with women to marriage. And homosexual sexuality is also widely practiced in all-male prisons.

This suggests that heterosexuality and homosexuality may not be absolutely distinct, hermetically sealed identities; rather, they may exist on a continuum and may overlap considerably.

Heterosexuality is made to seem normal and normative only through the repression of behaviors that might betray its apparent absoluteness. This possibility is confirmed by studies of sexual behavior, such as the famous Kinsey Report (1949), which found that many more people experience homosexual feelings than is assumed to be the case. Those feelings are not acted on because heterosexuality is assumed to be the most normal kind of sexual identity in all societies and cultures. Homosexual inclinations are repressed for fear of appearing "abnormal." As a result, heterosexuality is further reinforced as a norm because it reflects "reality." But the trouble is that reality may be manufactured by the norm. The judgment that homosexuals are "abnormal" has the effect of making people curb homosexual feelings, and that in turn makes heterosexuality seem even more the norm. An assumption thus reproduces itself. A circle is created that ensures the transformation of one among many sexual options – heterosexuality – into an absolute and a norm. The gender choice of one segment of the population is thereby made into a universal in regard to which alternative gender forms appear deviant or deficient. And the apparently wide range of human sexual identities and preferences is forced into one large and one small box labeled "normal" and "deviant." The majority's rather unstable commitment to heterosexuality is only made to seem normative by bundling all the other options, some of which heterosexuals themselves are capable of embracing, into the category of "deviancy." In this way, a plurality of sex and gender options is inaccurately divided into an opposition with moral overtones, the purpose of which is to expel and stigmatize sex/gender alternatives that are very little different from those declared to be normative.

This hierarchical ordering of the sex/gender universe is sustained by other traditional ways of structuring the social world through conceptual oppositions. One such opposition is reason and emotion, or rationality and irrationality. A social or cultural norm must seem reasonable; that is, it must seem to exist for rational reasons and not as an expression of one group's power. Yet the standard of reasonableness has a way of playing into the hands of power. Those who control society – male heterosexuals for the most part – can make their own norms appear reasonable because to be in control is to have the safety and peace that allow one to promote one's interests without much effort or emotion. There is no need to be angry or upset at mistreatment or subordination. To rule is to appear reasonable, and this has the effect of making one's rule appear rational. Those without power or those who are subordinated by another group are more likely to be angry and emotional. They will appear irrational, and as a result, because reasonableness seems to justify the right to rule, they will appear to deserve exclusion.

Another version of the reason/unreason or reason/emotion dyad is the mind/body opposition. Those who rule appear to rely more on their minds than on emotion, which is associated with the body. If reason connotes a sense of control and expresses the control of the ruling group in society, the body connotes things out of control and the dangers of emotion that threaten reasonable control and controlled reason. Reason is associated with logic and rules that create order and harmony in society; the body and emotion are associated with an absence of logic and a breaking of rules that upset order. Subordinated peoples, from women and blacks to homosexuals, are often associated with uncontrollable bodily urges for this reason. They challenge the rationale of rule, the reasons that justify rule and the air of rationality that attaches to it by virtue of being in the ruling position. The heterosexual norm advertises itself as being reasonable, and it is associated with the mind and with a sense of being in control. Homosexuality, in contrast, in order to be banished as deviant, a danger to the reasonable norm, is associated with emotion and irrationality, as well as the uncontrollable urges of the body.

Silence of the Lambs replays some of the most common stereotypes of gays but also puts on display the mechanism for constructing a "reasonable" heterosexual identity that seals itself off from the "irrationality" of homosexuality. Clarice Starling's progress consists of the putting aside of emotion, weakness, and being out of control in order to achieve a professional identity associated with reason, strength of mind, and control. Her progress is overseen by two "fathers" or mentoring guides – Carpenter, her FBI manager, and Lecter, a doctor who is a cannibal – and both of them are characterized as possessing a powerful mind or as figures of control. Her adversary in her quest for a certificate of approval by male-dominated, heterosexual society (the graduation ceremony at the end of the film) is an out-of-control, irrational homosexual who is associated with emotion and the body. If the two fathers work logically to establish the identity of Jamie Gumm, the serial killer who longs for a sex-change operation to make him a woman, he in turn represents the subversion of proper identities, the mixture of distinct elements that confuses reason and eludes control. If reason operates by assuming a norm that then makes the control of deviations from the norm necessary, Jamie has no sense of that distinction and operates in a realm of mixture that confounds the difference between norm and deviation. If the heterosexual norm arises out of a sense of identity that supposedly expresses nature, Jamie cuts and stitches to make a nature of his own, thus reversing the proper order of identity. His identity does not derive from nature; rather, he manufactures an identity by rearranging nature. He is an emblem of pure deviation and change, and his symbol in the film, fittingly, is the pupa that molts into a butterfly or moth.

Jamie has not learned to repress his urges, to submit to the law of the father, to be in control and to act reasonably. Lecter, in contrast, urges Clarice to adhere to first principles and to see what things are in themselves. "What is its nature?" he tells her to ask of Jamie. Things in themselves have boundaries, distinct natures, identities of their own. Jamie is linked not only to bodily threats to mental order but also to women and mothers, people whose association with emotion has always been figured as a threat to a patriarchal dominance that portrays itself as rational. Jamie lives in the house of Mrs. Lippman, and when Clarice searches the house, she finds Mrs. Lippman's body, now a brown liquefied mess, in a bathtub. Liquid is traditionally associated in patriarchal imagery with what threatens the boundaries of identity, the control lines of male heterosexual rule. A male child who remains too close to his mother and does not learn to separate and to acquire an identity based on his father is associated in this film with the failure to achieve a proper heterosexual identity.

Male heterosexual rule is linked from the outset with control over the body. As Clarice at the outset runs through the FBI training course, she passes a sign that speaks of hurt, agony, and pain, and concludes "love it." The FBI's exercise of scientific reason against the irrational threat to both legal and rational order is thus coded as the power to make the body submit. Later, she and her friend Ardelia are portrayed memorizing FBI rules (and bear in mind the double meaning of the word "rule" as both imperative and mode of control). Yet Clarice's first visit to Lecter in his prison associates her with emotional weakness and bodily processes. Meigs flings cum at her and says he can smell her cunt. Outside, she collapses and cries. Narrative fictional films typically move characters like Clarice from initial positions of weakness or negativity to positions of strength or positive accomplishment. By the end, she will have achieved a professional identity molded on the male heterosexual model of Carpenter, but the film initiates that process in the edit that follows this scene of collapse. The immediate cut takes the viewer to an image of Clarice aiming and firing a gun, an image of toughness that also connotes the rejection of the "feminine" side of her personality linked to bodily life and emotions. Later, when Catherine is kidnapped violently by Jamie, who clubs her with a fake cast over his arm, the film cuts from this scene to an image of Clarice in training fending off blows from another male FBI student. Her ability to maintain her bodily boundaries suggests an antidote to Jamie, who connotes a breakdown of boundaries.

A hint of Lecter's role in helping her to transcend the body and learn to be more rational and in control is given when he sniffs in the initial prison hospital encounter and says he cannot smell her sex. He exists on the boundary between body and mind, reason and unreason, and he helps her sort out the mucky bodily messes that Jamie leaves in his wake on his quest to castrate heterosexuality and identify with femininity. Both Jamie and Lecter are positioned in underground spaces, a topographical metaphor for the body "below." Jamie is incapable of transcending this positioning and indeed revels in it (the place where he keeps his liquefied mother-figure and plays with women's bodies and with his own). Lecter's powerful mind allows him to escape his dungeon, to kill Meigs, and to conquer that other subverter of rational rules by inappropriate emotional and bodily urges – Doctor Chilton. While Lecter is, like Carpenter, linked to the rules of courtesy and reason that maintain boundaries and that aid Clarice's transcendence of the body in favor of the mind, Chilton makes a pass at her and reduces her to bodily life. He thus more resembles Meigs in the film's structuring of characters than does Lecter or Carpenter.

The more important parallel for Lecter, from Clarice's perspective, is with Carpenter, her teacher and mentor in the FBI. How does this evolve? How does it parallel her relation to her other mentor, Lecter?

How does Clarice finally manage to catch Jamie? What skills does she rely on? How in the end does she achieve both professional and gender identity success? How does she evolve? How is success associated with both the achievement of reason on her part and the expulsion of the irrational Jamie?

In a different culture, reason would have a different function and meaning, of course, and it is possible to imagine a story in which reason attaches to the acceptance of a diversity of gender positions and a more complex vision of gender identity. From such a perspective, the homophobia of *Silence of the Lambs* might seem quite irrational and reactionary, a fear projection that seeks to assure heterosexist culture that its prejudices are reasonable. The curious thing about the film, of course, is that it really is about a successful sex-change operation. Clarice does, in essence, become a professional man, or at least, the image of a professional man. In a society dominated by heterosexual male imperatives, people of either gender seem to have little choice, if this film is to be believed, beyond identifying in one way or another with the father.

Paris Is Burning displays high levels of tolerance for a playful approach to gender identity. Gay and transgender black and hispanic youth dress up in costumes and "vogue," participate in fashion contests in which they imitate certain roles such as corporate executive or college student.

How does this film allow one to reinterpret the violence done to Jamie in *Silence of the Lambs*? Again, it is important to think of Jamie as a metaphor for gay men and for homosexuality rather than as a literal serial killer. How does *Paris* provide a very different sense of gender violence?

In a culture characterized by intolerance toward homosexuality, homosexuals are obliged to live in the "closet," a metaphor for keeping their gender identity hidden from the dominant heterosexual population. They must "pass" as heterosexuals in order to avoid verbal and physical violence. This is especially true of those gays and lesbians whose gender identity includes cross-dressing or dressing in a manner more suited in the dominant culture to the biological gender that is the opposite of their own (i.e., gay men dressing as heterosexual women). How does the film depict "passing"? What does it mean to appear to be "real"? Why is appearing to be "real" so important as a costume choice at the balls?

Consider some of the roles that the gay men assume at the balls. What is the irony of some of their choices from a class perspective?

Silence of the Lambs subtly suggests that there is something threatening about the working class and that there is something redemptive about corporate-suited professionals like Carpenter. *Paris* looks at class from the bottom up. How does this change the way class is portrayed and perceived? The film cuts away from the balls at certain points to portray "normal" men and women on the street. What is the effect of these images? How does the film allow one to rethink the relationship even in mainstream or majoritarian heterosexual culture between dress and gender identity?

How does this film challenge the implicit assumption of a film like *Silence of the Lambs* that heterosexuality is natural and normative and homosexuality deviant and unnatural? How might *Paris* be said to side more with Jamie's vision of gender as something fabricated? Think of what it means for a gay man to teach heterosexual women how to walk like heterosexual women. What does this do to the traditional assumption that nature generates gender behavior?

CHAPTER 8

History

Arguments about the meaning of a literary text are often easily settled by turning to history. History is such a powerful analytic tool because it usually provides a fairly firm ground on which to stake a claim regarding meaning. Once one knows, for example, that *King Lear* first played at King James' court and that many things in the play refer to conflicts between Parliament and the court, one can more readily grasp what the play is in fact about. It is less a tragedy with universal values than a quite partisan polemic whose meaning is provided by the historical world in which it was produced.

The historical study of literature has waxed and waned over time. Before World War II it enjoyed enormous popularity in the United States especially. Scholars of Shakespeare pored over his works for allusions to historical events. Mention of a ship called the *Tyger* in *Othello* was seen as a reference to factional disputes in Queen Elizabeth's court, since the *Tyger* was an actual ship associated with the leader of one faction. This kind of study passed out of favor after World War II, and was superseded by the close reading of texts for internal meanings. History disappeared and was replaced by "literary history." Literary history limits its range to literary matters, and studies such movements as modernism or sentimentalism. Occasionally, it touches on extra-literary historical concerns such as how the marketplace affects the thinking of writers.

In Britain, the historical study of literature and culture thrived after World War II. Historian E. P. Thompson renewed interest in the study of culture in his *The Making of the English Working Class* (1957). Raymond Williams became the most important scholar of the relations between literature and history during this period. In *The Country and the City* (1956), he studied the evolution of English

literature in terms of the way literature depicts the tension between rural
and urban life.

In the wake of the social movements of the 1960s, scholars in the
United States once again turned to history as a source of meaning for
understanding literature. With the claims of women, ethnic and sex-
gender minorities, and people of color from around the world newly
placed on the table, it became difficult to continue to study literature
for "universal" themes that invariably looked white, male, and heterosexual when they dressed for dinner.

These "New Historicist" scholars did not return to the older form
of historical study, however. They drew on French post-structuralist
theory especially, as well as anthropological theories of culture. Such
scholars as Stephen Greenblatt argued that literature should be understood in relation to the collective beliefs, social practices, and cultural
discourses that prevailed when it was written. Greenblatt sees the same
rhetorical operations in literary works that he finds in adjacent texts
from the work's historical context. For example, he notices that English
settlers deceived natives by pretending to possess "invisible bullets" that
in fact were European illnesses. By pretending such bullets were evidence of God's intervention on the Europeans' behalf, the Europeans
seemed to subvert their own religious beliefs. If religion is merely a
device to dupe credulous masses so they will be more submissive, how
can it claim to be true? In fact, the Europeans furthered the ultimate
ends of those beliefs by converting the natives. In a similar way,
Shakespeare in his *Henry* plays incorporates elements such as Falstaff's
revolutionary speeches that seem to undermine the legitimacy of the
monarchy, but these subversive moments ultimately are folded back into
the overall rhetorical goal of the texts, which is to legitimate a strong
monarchy. The apparent subversiveness is contained and its negativity
converted into a positive condition of power.

The historical interpretation of literature poses problems for first-
time students of literature. It usually requires reading well beyond the
literary text into the historical archive. I have found that the best historical analysis arises when one immerses oneself in primary works of historical study written by professional historians. What passes as "literary
history" or as "literary historical" study is often quite limited when
compared with what actual historians do. For example, in studying
Nathaniel Hawthorne's *The Scarlet Letter*, I found that Hawthorne
scholars avoid going too deeply into the historical roots of the work in
the nineteenth-century debates between Whigs and Democrats. They
focus instead on the fact that the story is about seventeenth-century

Puritan society and argue that Hawthorne, who was an avid Democrat, was too ironic and ambiguous in tone to have written a political novel invested with his democratic values. But if you read the historians, a very different picture emerges. In nineteenth-century polemics, Whigs were referred to by Democrats as "Puritans," and the characteristics that made their values repugnant to Democrats like Hawthorne are exactly those that Hawthorne assigns to his seventeenth-century Puritans in *The Scarlet Letter*. Like the seventeenth-century Puritans, the Whigs worked for a union of church and state, religion and law. And they had a bad habit of peering into the hearts of others to monitor their moral well-being – exactly the gravest sin committed by the most negative character in the novel. So, a novel that literary historians claim is about seventeenth-century America is in fact about nineteenth-century America, but one would not know that if one did not read actual historians of the period.

Historical evidence of this kind can help blunt the claims of those who assert, almost in a religious manner, that literature is so ambiguous that its meaning must be akin to spiritual truth. It is more a matter of faith than of evidence. Words like "irony" and "ambiguity" have a bad habit of licensing a host of hermeneutic sins. In Hawthorne's case, they allow his frequent gestures of commitment to democratic politics to be declared to be ironic and his one fictional reference to himself as a "modern Tory" to be declared to be indubitable evidence – entirely unironic – of his conservatism. So history has its uses. It makes us as readers of literature more responsible to the truth. It gives us one possible standard of historical truth to measure our work against. And it provides us with a handy rule of thumb in our interpretive work: if you cannot justify a claim with evidence, do not make it.

Exercise 8.1   William Shakespeare, *King Lear*

In working on *King Lear* for this section, I began with several well-known works of social history such as Lawrence Stone's *The Crisis of the Aristocracy, Social Change and Revolution in England, 1540–1640*, and *The Family, Sex, and Marriage in England, 1500–1800*. Those works led me to other, less well known, historical sources such as Paul Slack's *Poverty and Policy in Tudor and Stuart England* and Catherine Drinker Bowen's *The Lion and the Throne*, which concerns Edward Coke's conflict with James I. Those historical works led me in turn to primary sources such as J. H. Jessie's *Memoirs of the Court of England*

and the works of King James – *Basilikon Doron, Demonologie,* and *The True Lawe of Free Monarchies.*

I chose as my starting point the relations between the way Lear is depicted and James I, the king who ruled England in 1606 when the play was presented at court. A traditional historicist essay on the play might be entitled "Lear and James I," since the character of the fictional king and that of the real one so resemble one another. A fitting title for a New Historicist essay might be "Shakespeare and the Judges," for reasons I shall explain shortly.

The Scottish James I, the heir to the English throne upon the death of Queen Elizabeth, was not greatly loved by his new English subjects. His attempt to unify England and his native Scotland soon after his ascension to the throne in 1603 was turned back by a recalcitrant Parliament. He was a rash and imperious ruler who was given to delivering intemperate, oath-filled lectures to Parliament when they did not meet his wishes or provide monies to support a court lifestyle that cost twice what it had under Elizabeth. The king also had difficulties with the people he ruled. His right to demand housing and food for himself and his numerous notoriously ill-mannered retainers while making his rounds of the country in pursuit of the hunt, something he preferred to sitting at court in London, provoked complaints. One day, one of his favorite hunting hounds disappeared and returned with a note around his neck begging the king to depart, since he and his followers were eating up the countryside: "it will please his Majestie to go back to London . . . all our provision is spent already and we are not able to entertain him longer." The complaints began to verge on outright rebellion in November 1605, when Guy Fawkes and some followers were caught attempting to blow up the king and Parliament.

The parallels with *Lear* scarcely need underscoring. It is a play about rebellion against a king that hinges on a denial of hospitality. Lear assumes that those who owe him "service" will provide food and shelter to his retinue of ill-mannered knights and courtiers, who are given to "pranks," debauchery, and drink. The negative characters in the play refer to them as a "disordered rabble" that make "servants of their betters." James was well known to dislike the duties of office, and Lear's first act in the play is to divest himself of the "cares of state" in order to go hunting, James' favorite diversion. James valued "plain" speech, and the play privileges such speech in the character of Kent as well as, ultimately, in Lear himself ("I am a very foolish, fond old man / . . . And, to deal plainly"). James himself resembled Kent, who like James swears a great deal and shuns pomp, and like Kent, who cares little what people think of his bad manners, James was blunt rather than politic. His disgruntled behavior during his extravagant welcoming procession in 1603 was so obvious it offended his new subjects.

The shift in the play from an initial language of flattery, circumlocution, and courtly elegance to one of simple plainness by the end can be seen as a figural rendering of the changes James brought about in Elizabethan court culture. He disliked the extravagant dress of the likes of Raleigh and kept his clothes until they were completely worn out, a practice which seems to be echoed in Lear's own disregard for dress when he is on the heath. Of all the meanings of Lear's gesture of undressing, one is the rejection of the court style, with its emphasis on external appearances as opposed to the inner virtues James favored. James' intemperateness as well as his penchant for oaths also seem to be echoed in Lear's behavior and in his oath-filled speeches with their references to classical mythology, a characteristic of James' own literary works. James loved "fooleries," and his court was full of jokes and pranks, much like the court of Lear, in which a Fool plays a prominent role. Fond of masques and burlesques, James staged scenes with comic or moral effects of the kind Lear arranges for his daughters' mock trial. The daughters' behavior seems all the more reprehensible given Lear's generosity toward them, and indeed, James himself was caught in a similar dilemma: known for his extreme, indeed reckless, generosity, he also had trouble getting those responsible for his upkeep to cover his needs. Finally, James and his Scottish followers were looked upon by many in much the same way as Lear's followers are by Goneril: they sought to govern their "betters."

The link between Lear and James becomes more evident if one compares the play with *Basilikon Doron*, James' advice book to his son, an English-language version of which appeared shortly after he assumed power in 1603, and with his *Demonologie* (also 1603). In many respects, *Basilikon* provides both a thematic and linguistic dictionary for the play. Given the importance of the word "plain" and the value of plainness in the play, it is important that James' book begins with a sonnet that argues that kings should "Reward the just, be stedfast, true, and plaine." James returns to the virtue of plainness on numerous occasions ("be plaine and truthful") and contrasts it with "the filthy vice of Flattery, the pest of all Princes." It is as if he has Lear himself in mind when he counsels his son to "love them best, that are plainest with you, and disguise not the trueth for all their kinne." Plainness is a necessary virtue of a good monarch, as is control over one's own sexual appetites, something Kent and Edgar demonstrate positively, and Goneril and

Regan negatively: "he cannot be thought worthie to rule and command others, that cannot rule . . . his owne proper affections and unreasonable appetites." James, in terms that echo the sexual advice Edgar delivers to Lear, tells his son to "abstain from fornication" and to avoid "the filthy vice of adultery," and warns of women who use "their painted preened fashion, [to] serve for baites to filthie lecherie." As if he were counseling Goneril, who places private interest over national security ("I had rather lose the battle than that sister / Should loosen him and me"), James says the king should subject "his owne private affections and appetites to the weale and standing of his subiectes, ever thinking the common interesse his cheefest particulare." He uses the same terms Shakespeare uses to characterize Cordelia (who "was a queen over her passion") when he promotes Temperance which "shall as a Queene, command all the affections and passion."

Shakespeare also seems to have James in mind when he has Lear take note of poverty and advocate charity on the part of wealthy nobles: "O, I have ta'en / Too little care of this! Take physic, pomp; / Expose thyself to feel what wretches feel, / That thou mayst shake the superflux to them / And show the heavens more just." James advises his son to "embrace the quarrel of the poore and distressed . . . care for the pleasure of none, neither spare ye any paines in your own person, to see their wrongs redressed." Similarly, Shakespeare has Gloucester argue that "distribution should undo excess, / And each man have enough."

Finally, James condemns disobedience of parents in terms ("a thing monstrous," "unnatural") that echo the play: "I had rather not be a Father, and childlesse, then be a Father of wicked children." Lear gives vent to a similar feeling when he says he "would divorce me from thy mother's tomb, / Sepulch'ring an adult'ress." Like Shakespeare, James refers to parental authority and filial loyalty as the "order of nature" and characterizes writing against parents as an "unpardonable crime."

James, in his *Demonologie*, describes the power of devils to "transport from one place to another a solid body" and speaks in the same passage of the possibility of falling "from an high and stay rock." One is reminded, of course, of Edgar and Gloucester at Dover, where Edgar speaks of a "fiend" standing next to Gloucester before his mock fall. The "foul fiend" is an imaginary symptom of Edgar's feigned madness, but the fiend also represents disobedience and the danger of broken contracts: "Take heed o' the foul fiend. Obey thy parents; keep thy word's justice." The first mention of the fiend coincides with Lear's banishment by his daughters. Later in the play, the associations are more ominously demonic. "See thyself, devil," Albany says to Goneril. "Proper deformity shows not in the fiend / So horrid as in woman." In the *Demonologie*, James is particularly critical of women who are prone to become witches and succumb to the "greedy desire" for power or for "worldly riches . . . their whole practices are either to hurt men and their goods." Shakespeare, in this play at least, would seem to agree.

One might conclude that Shakespeare with Lear ingratiates himself with the new ruler of the land in which he did business. James himself had brought a gift of cloth for the playwright upon his ascension to the throne, and Shakespeare seems to return the favor in this play by painting a portrait of a tragic king whose flattering resemblance to James himself would easily, it seems, have been recognizable to those in the audience at court on St. Stephen's Night 1606. But Shakespeare might also be said to take the king's side in a number of quarrels in which he was engaged and thereby to help further royal power at a time when it was vigorously debated in England. Perhaps the most significant of those disputes concerned the character of monarchical rule itself, whether it should be absolute or limited by law and by Parliament. And it is in regard to this issue that a New Historicist concern for discursive negotiations and representational exchanges becomes essential.

In *The True Lawe of Free Monarchies* (1598), James, king of Scotland at the time, makes a statement that would not sit well in England, the land over which he would become king five years later. Arguing that kings rule at God's behest and therefore are deserving of absolute obedience, he writes: "the King is above the Law . . . And therefore general lawes, made publikly in Parlamente, may uppon knowne respects to the King by his authoritie be mittigated, and suspended upon causes onely knowne to him." To the English, who had fought hard to secure their liberties against monarchical power and who believed in the sanctity of the common law tradition, that well of legal precedents that was binding on all, including the king, such statements were troubling, if not alarming. The future Chief Justice of Common Pleas, Edward Coke, was especially disturbed. In 1607 he would advise Parliament: "There is a maxim. The common law hath admeasured the King's prerogative." James, in Coke's eyes and in those of many other Englishmen, was wrong.

In an encounter famous in legal history for establishing the superiority of law to political power, Coke entered into a direct argument with James concerning Fuller's Case, which concerned the rights of dissident Puritans. James's loyalists, who felt that judges were "delegates" of the king and therefore that the king was the ultimate judge in all matters, wanted to force the Puritans to testify under an inquisitorial oath that deprived them of their common law rights. As Chief Justice of the Common Pleas Court that fought for jurisdiction with the loyalists' Ecclesiastical High Commission regarding the judgment of lay matters, Coke disagreed, and the issue came before James. When the loyalists claimed that the ultimate decision lay with the king, Coke replied: "The King cannot take any cause out of any of his courts and give judgment upon it himself." James accused Coke of speaking foolishly and said he reserved the power to decide jurisdictional issues, adding that he "would ever protect the common law." Coke responded: "The common law protecteth the King." At this point, James accused him of treason. "The King protecteth the law, and not the law the King," he declared. To which Coke replied "The King should not be under man, but under God and the Laws." He nevertheless flung himself at the king's feet and seemed to submit. But the next week he commenced once again to issue rulings at odds with the Commission.

I recount this anecdote to give a sense of what the discursive ambience was at the time *Lear* was written. The topics of monarchical power and judicial authority were publicly discussed and debated. The limits of monarchical power were at stake, and the conflict between king and Parliament would eventually lead to civil war and the overthrow of the monarchy in mid-century. In 1605, the year *Lear* was probably written, things had not yet come to that point, but Guy Fawkes and his followers took the debate over prerogative to another level in the Gunpowder Plot in November of that year. Rebellion was not only in the air; it was also underground.

James' *True Lawe* is an argument against such rebellion. Its principal rhetorical strategy consists of *warning*. James begins by warning his audience of just how abusive monarchical rule can be. The monarch will, James warns, quoting the book of Samuel, take your sons and make them servants, take your daughters and make them "Cookes and Bakers," take your fields and give them to his servants, "take the tenth of your seede . . . and give it to his Eunuches," and "all that ye possess shall serve his private use and inordinate appetite." He concludes "and ye shall be his servants." If one weren't aware that one was reading a work by a reigning monarch, one might at this point think that the author was Guy Fawkes himself trying to raise a following. The warning is subversive of the very power it ostensibly legitimates. It suggests that kings do abuse their power, and it quite accurately and vividly describes those abuses.

Yet the warning also serves to further power. By quoting scripture, James places the question of monarchical rule within the frame of the paradoxical parables of the Bible, parables whose very incomprehensibility serves to reinforce God's ultimate authority, his transcendence of mere worldly logic. "Yet it shall not be lawful to you to cast it off," James argues of monarchy, because absolute rule is "the ordinance of GOD" and "your selves have chosen him unto you, thereby renouncing for ever all privileges, by your willing consent," especially that one which would allow people to "call backe unto your selves againe that power" given to the king. In other words, despite all the great abuses of monarchical power that have just been so vividly depicted, you will have to put up with it. As in biblical parables in general, which argue that one has to learn to accept rough treatment at the hands of God since it is for one's own good, one must, according to James, also put up with abusive kings, because the king is a step down from God. Hence, he has the loyal people say to Samuel: "Al your speeches and hard conditions shal not skarre us, but we wil take the good and evill of it upon us, and we will be content to bear whatsoever burthen it shall please our King to lay upon us." If the king is bad, God will judge him – but no one else shall. He has the "power to judge [his people] but to be judged only by God."

The king, for James, is like a father in a family. If the people must fear the king "as their judge," they must love him "as their father." To displace the king through rebellion is to invert "the order of all law and reason," so that "the commanded may be made to command their commander, the judged to judge their Judge, and they that are governed to governe their time about their lord & governer." Obedience is the "duty his children owe to" a father, and hence also to a king. It would be "monstrous and unnatural to his sons to rise up against" either father or king. Fittingly, rebels who claim a higher allegiance to the commonwealth, "as to a Mother," are condemned. James concludes the text by denouncing what he twice, using language echoed in *Lear*, refers to as "monstrous and unnatural rebellions" against an absolute monarch. It is wrong for one party to break a contract "except that first a lawful trial and cognition be had by the ordinary judge of the breakers thereof."

What *Lear* depicts is in many ways what James describes and denounces – a "monstrous" and "unnatural" rebellion against both paternal and monarchical power. The play literalizes James' metaphors. Lear is both father and king; the rebels are his daughters. They invert the right order of government when they "command the commander" and refuse him "the duty his children owe to him." They enter into a contract – land in exchange for love and hospitality – and break it unilaterally. Regan's language of rebellion recalls the legal language of arguments in favor of parliamentary prerogative: "In my right, / By me invested, he compeers the best."

It is as if Shakespeare had James' concluding argument in mind when he has Lear summon his daughters forth for an imaginary trial, which enacts the lawful reinstatement of the appropriate judge so that "cognition" can be taken of "the breakers." If Shakespeare would seem to take James' part in his argument with parliamentary dissenters, he also seems, especially in the trial scene, to take his side in his debate with the common law judges, especially Coke. "You are o' the commission; / Sit you too," Lear tells Kent. This is not the first reference in the text to the Ecclesiastical Commission that supported James' claim to absolute authority over the common law judges. Already in Act 3, scene 2, Lear speaks favorably of "These dreadful summoners," a reference to the police or summoners who served warrants for the Ecclesiastical Commission or court. Given James' antipathy to the common law judges, it is probably of some significance that the trial scene concludes with Lear's cry "Corruption in the place! / False justicer!"

But what are we to make of Lear's vision of a judge and a thief as interchangeable and his provocative suggestion that judges favor the wealthy over the poor? It is one of the most subversive statements in the play. Yet like the mock trial scene, it is framed by an implicit pledge of allegiance to James's absolutist position regarding the superiority of monarchical power to the common law. Coke was one judge who had become quite wealthy while in office, and justices of the peace, upholders of the common law, were great obstructors of the poor relief James advocated. The 1590s were a time of harvest failures and of famine. As a result of the enclosure of common land for the sake of more profitable pasturing, more and more farm laborers turned to vagrancy, giving rise to laws regarding poor relief and charity. James was a promoter of charity, and the Statute of 1604 was meant to provide such relief on a more uniform basis. Its implementation was overseen by his Privy Council, but it met with a resistant negligence on the part of justices of the peace, who were in charge of tax collecting and the enforcement of statutes on the local level, even when prodded "by extraordinary directions derived from the prerogative power of his Majesty by proclamations, letters, and commission." Perhaps this is why one of the most sympathetic characters in the play, Edgar as Tom, mentions charity twice: "Do poor Tom some charity . . . The country gives me proof and precedent / Of Bedlam beggars who with roaring voices / . . . Enforce their charity."

Other seemingly subversive statements by Lear can be interpreted in a similar manner. When he speaks of "the great image of authority; / A dog's obeyed in office," he refers not to the king, whose position as a divinely ordained ruler was above "office," but rather to the holders of political office – the parliamentarians – who circumvented the king's wishes. The lustful beadle who hypocritically punishes the whore in the next lines describes a similar enemy of the Catholic king whose court was renowned for loose sexual morals – the Puritan clergy. And the "Robes and furred gowns" that "hide all" vices in the following lines refer to the Elizabethan courtiers, like Raleigh, whom James loathed.

If Shakespeare is critical of judges and of justices in a way that echoes James' absolutist positions, the one positive reference to justices in the play also serves the interests of absolute monarchical power. Of the quick death of Cornwall after Gloucester's blinding, Albany says: "This shows you are above, / You justicers, that these our nether crimes / So speedily can venge!" Heavenly not earthly judges are the guardians of justice in the play. The rebels are also subject to "the judgement of the heavens, that makes us tremble." "The gods are just," Edgar remarks, after having vanquished Edmund and set right the kingdom. He is presented as an instrument of divine justice, while also evincing a natural royalty. The force of someone endowed with royal power ("thy very gait did prophesy / A royal nobleness") is needed because legal measures are subject to the contingencies of broken agreements and the failure of judges. "[T]he laws are mine, not thine," Goneril claims defiantly, "Who can arraign me for 't?" A divine judge, James might respond, and in his place, a king or would-be king like Edgar.

The seemingly subversive critique of justice and of judges in the play is a maneuver within a discourse that seeks to legitimate absolute monarchical rule by warning of its abuses in order better to plead for its divinely ordained necessity. "[W]e will resign to him, / . . . our absolute power," Albany says of Lear at the end. Rather than directly advocate such power, however, the play enacts a subversive vision of inversion and disorder whose ultimate purpose is to reinforce that which is overturned and to further power. Initially, monarchical rule is presented negatively. The play begins with a warning regarding the abuses to which kings are prone. Lear rules in an abusive manner. In a single scene, he banishes his favorite courtier and deprives his favorite daughter of her dowry. He is intolerant of dissent and commands absolute obedience. His behavior seems "rash," but it is also typical of how kings should be allowed to behave, according to James, and still command obedience. Kent's and Cordelia's remarkable fidelity in the face of the king's abusive exercise of monarchical power are the positive examples that complete what one might call the warning plot of the play. Kings may be rash, it argues, but we must, like Kent and Cordelia, obey them absolutely nonetheless. Even the infirmity and fury of a king, like that of a father, must, according to James, be "borne." Even as a madman, Lear is told "You are a royal one, and we obey you."

Exercise 8.2   Henry James, *The Aspern Papers*

The narrator of the tale is an aesthete, and aestheticism was an important cultural movement in England at the time the tale was written (in the 1880s). But the narrator, oddly enough perhaps, is also a tourist, a relatively new cultural invention. One point of departure for a historicist reading might therefore be James' use of these two cultural makers in the tale.

The desire to see picturesque places, especially landscapes, animated the Romantic movement in art and literature from the late eighteenth through the early nineteenth centuries in western Europe. Jeffrey Aspern has elements of Romanticism about him, and the prototype for Juliana Bordereau – Claire (Jane) Clairmont – was the lover of one of the great English Romantic poets, George, Lord Byron. As Byron's aristocratic title suggests, travel is search of the picturesque began as the private pastime of the English upper classes in the eighteenth century, who traveled to distant places such as Scotland in search of the right vista. In 1848, however, Thomas Cook, who had up till then devoted himself to the cause of temperance amongst the urban laboring classes, took note of a new invention – the railroad – and decided to adopt a different approach to the task of moral reform. Rather than uplift the laboring masses, he would instead send them on vacation – or on excursion, as he called it. Cook established the world's first travel agency and began organizing weekend trips to such places as Bath, which were quickly overrun by crowds seeking accommodations that did not exist. Modern tourism was born.

By the early 1860s, Cook, taking full advantage of the prosperity as well as the power of the British empire, then at its peak, was busy wardening groups of middle-class professionals and their families through Europe, Africa, and the Middle East in search of picturesque landscapes and cities. What had been a matter of private appreciation by the wealthy few became a very public matter indeed, one characterized by crowds embarking and disembarking on boats and trains in search of their own version of the picturesque, one often now capturable in newly invented photographs. Those who had been used to having the picturesque to themselves were understandably upset. "The fortunate generation is passing away," Leslie Stephen wrote at the time. "The charm is perishing. Huge caravanseries replace the hospitable inn; railways creep to the foot of Monte Rosa . . . The tourist dispatches Switzerland as rapidly and thoughtlessly as he does Olympia; and the very name of the Alps, so musical in the ears of those who enjoyed their mysterious charm, suggests little more than the hurry and jostling of an average sight-seeing trip."

A tourist publishing industry came into being, ready to supply the new travelers with guidebooks filled with advice and descriptions of their favorite destinations. Many writers, including Henry James, made an income supplying magazines back home with accounts of their travels to such places as Italy. These books served in part as training manuals in how to find and see the picturesque. In his *Transatlantic Sketches* (1875), for example, James writes of his arrival in Siena: "As I suddenly stepped into this Piazza from under a dark archway, it seemed a vivid enough revelation of the picturesque." And what the picturesque consisted of in part was a sense of the artistry of the world viewed: "There is to an American something richly artificial and scenic . . . in the way these colossal dwellings are packed together." The Jamesian tourist is guided by a sense that the world is art, something to be appreciated in the same manner as a picture in a museum.

But such tourism had its limits. If earlier tourists felt that their private contemplation of places like the Alps was disturbed by the hordes of middle-class barbarians, another kind of privacy limited the scope of the art of travel, and that was the privacy of the inhabitants of the picturesque. James writes again of Siena: "My friend's account of domiciliary medievalism made me wish that your really appreciative tourist was not reduced to simply staring at black stones and peeping up stately staircases." He goes on to wish he might mount the stairs, "Murray in hand," and get favored by the local aristocrats with "a little sketch of their social philosophy or a few first rate family anecdotes." The trouble with so public a venture as tourism was that it precluded intimate engagement with the goal of one's quest. Between the role of tourist and that of inhabitant there was a small but significant difference.

How might these historical developments aid a historicist reading of *The Aspern Papers*? Consider how the tale alludes to the new tourist industry and what role it plays in the portrayal of the narrator. It would seem a significant choice on James' part that the narrator goes touring after he has essentially killed Juliana. How else is tourism portrayed in the tale?

The aesthetic movement came into being in the mid-nineteenth century at the same time as mass tourism. It emphasized either the otherworldly and moral or the subjective and private qualities of art and of artistic experience. The two great works of the aesthetic movement were John Ruskin's *The Stones of Venice* (1849) and Walter Pater's *The Renaissance* (1873). The first argued for a moral vision of architecture, while the second celebrated the sensuous experience of art. James was aware of both books. "It is Mr. Ruskin," he writes in his *Portraits of Places*, "who, beyond any one, helps us to enjoy [Venice]." The trouble was that he also helped crowds of others to enjoy it as well. In celebrating Venice, Ruskin advertised it to the masses and helped make it a favorite stopping-place for tourists.

Paterian aestheticism exalted a less crowded ideal. Favoring the pleasurable experience of art over its moral value, it emphasized private contemplation and singularity of experience. James gives voice to this ideal when he notes "There is no simpler pleasure than looking at a fine Titian." However, he adds "or than floating in a gondola . . . or taking one's coffee at Florian's." Aesthetic experience could be of anything; art had entered life to that degree. When, in his famous "Conclusion" to *The Renaissance*, Pater celebrated a consciousness that sought out experience as an end in itself and burned always like a "hard, gem-like flame," he was not that far from James' gondola-rider. But the inclusion within aesthetic experience of Venetian coffee-sipping repeats Ruskin's dilemma. Aesthetic pleasure might be available to anyone who could afford a gondola or a coffee on St. Mark's Place, but, as a result, it ceased to be singular and original.

Meditation in a jostling crowd is difficult at best, as James himself notes on numerous occasions: "The sentimental tourist's only quarrel with Venice is that he has too many competitors there. He likes to be alone; to be original; to have (to himself, at least) the air of making discoveries . . . [T]he little wicket that admits you is perpetually turning and creaking, and you march through . . . with a herd of fellow-gazers. There is nothing left to discover or describe, and originality of attitude is completely impossible."

By entering circulation as a form of cultural capital, the ideal of aesthetic appreciation lost not only its uniqueness and originality but also its subversive power. As a celebration of sensuous experience, especially as it was most riotously embodied in the life of Wilde, it threatened Victorian respectability and morality. Just barely subliminal in its homoeroticism, its obvious delight in bodily pleasures was a scandal to the regime of Victorian sexual repression. But as a celebration of such potentially mass activities as gondola-riding, church-gazing, and coffee-sipping, it could be turned to uses more suited to the maintenance of the reigning stabilities. It diverted potentially troublesome energies into more pleasurable pastimes. Laboring classes on excursion were less likely to engage in "agitation."

How is aestheticism represented in *The Aspern Papers*? Look again at the passage in chapter 4 where the narrator thinks about the "moral fraternity" of devotees to art. Consider as well how the tale depicts the conflict between the singularity of aesthetic experience and a more public kind of appreciation. The contrast between Juliana and the narrator would again seem important. Note how her room is described and how her early life is characterized. Think again about how he and she represent contending attitudes toward the aesthetic.

Exercise 8.3   Elizabeth Bishop, "Twelve O'Clock News"

Bishop, after living in Brazil for nearly two decades, returned to the United States in the mid-1960s, in time to witness the public uprising against the Vietnam War. The Vietnamese had liberated their country by defeating the French in 1954 at Dien Bien Phu. The peace treaty that settled that struggle divided Vietnam between the North, controlled by the liberation forces, and the South, still essentially under colonial control. The government in the South was little more than a foreign-funded puppet regime, and the liberation forces continued to press the war, hoping to liberate the South as well. Throughout the 1950s and early 1960s the US was drawn further into the war, first by sending advisors to aid the South Vietnamese army, then by sending US army troops to conduct the war themselves. Since the liberation forces were aided by communist countries, the war became part of America's struggle against world communism as that was embodied in the Soviet Union (made up of Russia and a number of other contiguous "republics"). But the war was widely perceived to be an illegitimate foreign intervention in a domestic civil war as well as an attempt to impose imperial will on a "backward" country.

Bishop's poem, she herself noted in an interview, is about the war, although she had written a first unsatisfactory draft while still in college in the 1930s. That draft never matured into a poem, and it seems to have required the combined experience of her time in Brazil, where she acquired firsthand knowledge of what it is to live in an underdeveloped country like Vietnam, and of the opposition to the Vietnam War on the part of friends like Mary McCarthy (with whom Bishop had lunch shortly before McCarthy left for one of her trips to Vietnam) to allow her to turn that early draft into a poem. A New Historicist interest in the transverse connections between discourses might lead one to compare the poem to McCarthy's own writing on Vietnam. Here is an excerpt from her book on the war:

> The Saigonese themselves [Saigon was the capital of South Vietnam] are unaware of the magnitude of what is happening to their country, since they are unable to use military transport to get an aerial view of it; they only note the refugees sleeping in the streets and hear the B-52s pounding a few miles away. Seeing the war from the air, amid the crisscrossing Skyraiders, Supersabres, Phantoms, observation planes, Psywar planes (dropping leaflets), you ask yourself how much longer the Viet Cong can hold out; the country is so small that at the present rate of destruction there will be no place left for them to hide, not even under water, breathing through a straw. The plane and helicopter crews are alert for the slightest sign of movement in the fields and woods and estuaries below; they lean forward intently, scanning the ground. At night, the Dragon-ships come out, dropping flares and firing mini-guns.
>
> The Air Force seems inescapable, like the eye of God, and soon, you imagine (let us hope with hyperbole), all with be razed, charred, defoliated by that terrible searching gaze. Punishment can be magistral. A correspondent, who was tickled by the incident, described flying with a pilot of the little FAC plane that directs a big bombing mission; below, a lone Vietnamese on a bicycle stopped, looked up, dismounted, took up a rifle and fired; the pilot let him have it with the whole bombload of napalm – enough for a platoon. In such circumstances, anyone with a normal sense of fair play cannot help pulling for the bicyclist, but the sense of fair play, supposed to be Anglo-Saxon, has atrophied in the Americans here from lack of exercise. We draw a long face over Viet Cong "terror," but no one stops to remember that the Viet Cong does not possess that superior instrument of terror, an air force, which in our case, over South Vietnam at least, is acting almost with impunity. The worst thing that could happen to our country would be to win this war.

Consider what connections can be made between this excerpt and Bishop's poem. Note how each one uses irony, and think about how Bishop might also be said, albeit implicitly, to rely on a notion of fair play.

The title "Twelve O'Clock News" refers to the fact that the reality of the war was mediated by television news. The poem therefore draws attention to the issue of representation – how do we know something foreign if we must know it through our own representation, our own concepts and mental images as well as our own media? The poem playfully describes objects on the writer's desk as if they were objects in the world. Consider how this strategy bears on the question of representation and knowledge. Think as well about how it is a comment on the war, on how and why it was conducted as it was.

Exercise 8.4 *The Official Story* and *Las Madres de la Plaza de Mayo*

In recent history, the troubled economies of Latin America spawned many egalitarian movements that occasionally attained political power in places like Cuba and El Salvador. The American response was to support military coups that restored conservative economic elites to power. Liberals were critical of these actions and of the enormous loss of life and of civil liberties that they entailed. But knowledge of the events was frequently curtailed by policies of official secrecy. Many of the most violent acts, such as the forced "disappearance" (kidnapping, torture, and murder) of leftists in places like Argentina after its coup in 1976, were kept from public knowledge. Only after the military junta was overturned and a Truth Commission agreed to trade amnesty for information did the facts emerge. In Argentina alone, during the "dirty war" against egalitarians from 1976 to 1983, over 30,000 people "disappeared."

The Official Story and *Las Madres de la Plaza de Mayo* are liberal films dealing with these issues. That is, rather than endorse the conservative position that the violent repression executed by the military junta in Argentina was necessary to prevent pro-egalitarian "subversives" from coming to power and overthrowing governments that pursued economic policies favorable to the wealthy, the films explore the human consequences of that repression.

Both films hint at US involvement in the military repression of the egalitarian left. Up through 1976, US foreign policy was directed by conservatives such as Henry Kissinger, who did not shirk from arranging the overthrow of governments unfavorable to US economic interests as he perceived them or from supporting military dictators so long as they supported US economic and political aims.

We might begin by comparing how the two films deal differently with US support for the military junta. How are the American characters in *The Official Story* portrayed?

Each film follows a progression from lack of knowledge to increased knowledge, and with each progression come other changes. How is the expansion of the movement of *Las Madres* similar to the progressive change in Alicia's life in *The Official Story*?

Las Madres is a documentary that seeks to provide more of a historical understanding of the context of the events in Argentina. *The Official Story* seems to take much more for granted. How would you explain that difference? How might the absence of that context in *The Official Story* be appropriate to the story it recounts?

What information does *Las Madres* provide that helps you to understand the fictional film better?

What other similarities are there between the two films? You might consider the representation of the role of the Catholic Church or of the role of the business class in the events they portray. Note as well that the fictional film uses visual metaphors, such as the German shepherd Roberto plays with, that are explained by a viewing of the documentary. What is the significance of the dog and why link it to Roberto? In a similar vein, why is Enrique, Roberto's brother, dressed as he is? Who in the documentary dresses this way?

Are the Madres represented differently in the fictional film than in the documentary? Why might that be the case? How does this aid the film's argument or its rhetorical approach?

The title *The Official Story* refers to the idea that those with political power also have the cultural power to tell "official stories" about events that conceal the real character of those events. The film compares the experience of dealing with the official story regarding the disappearances in contemporary Argentina with Alicia's experience in teaching Argentine history. How does the film compare the two kinds of storytelling? Bear in mind that the Spanish word for "story" is "historia."

The film also seeks to make connections between the present and the past. What are those connections? Think of the way the students recite passages from Moreno. Who was Moreno and what is the connection between him and events in Argentina in the 1970s? Similarly, what does Roberto's father represent? Roberto calls him an anarchist, refers to the

Spanish Civil War, and taunts him as a "loser." What is Roberto referring to? Who won and who lost in the Spanish Civil War? What bearing does that have on the events in Argentina?

The film uses several different yardsticks to measure Alicia's progressive enlightenment – Benitez, Costa, Roberto, and Anna. How are her relations with others transformed by her growing awareness of the true origin of her child?

The movie makes a theme of the question of knowing and not knowing: how does it use terms and expressions concerning ignorance and knowledge? If you know Spanish, pay attention to what Roberto says to Alicia. His locutions often have to do with this issue, and they are not always translated in the subtitles.

Knowledge is often visually associated with glass, windows, and mirrors. How does the film use such imagery? Knowledge and ignorance often also are suggested using light and darkness. What images in the film come to mind?

The director, Luis Puenzo, often modulates our attention, directs our allegiances, and orchestrates our own discovery process in the film by pointing the camera at certain people or putting it in certain places. For example, why does he place the camera as he does during Alicia's interactions with Sara Reballo, the woman from the Madres? Can you find other examples of such camerawork?

Note as well the way compositions and composed arrangements between characters are used to convey emotional and psychological information or to describe changes in relationships. This is true especially of Roberto and Alicia's interactions. How does the scene in the bedroom when she confronts him and he finally confesses work in this regard?

The use of close-ups between these two characters is especially significant, although in each instance the meanings are quite different. Find a close-up for each character and consider how they are used differently.

Finally, successful political arguments cannot afford to grant too much credence to the opposition's point of view. How do the two films make it difficult to identify with the conservative position? How especially is emotion summoned in *The Official Story* to ally the audience with the liberal position? Note the way music especially is used.

The documentary does not mention the fact that leftist urban guerrilla movements were active in Argentina in the period before the coup. Would inclusion of this information have made the documentary less forceful?

CHAPTER 9

Ethnic Studies

While science casts doubt on the idea that the human species breaks down into sub-species called races, ethnicity remains a powerful category for organizing human experience. Most of us probably identify ourselves with one ethnic group or another. Despite our often strong feelings about such ethnic affiliations, the members of ethnic groups usually have little in common other than a particular "look" – fair hair, dark skin, almond eyes, etc. Ethnicities are breeding patterns that over time generate a similarity of external traits. But those traits are accidents that emerge at a particular moment in historical time, are sustained by social practices of marriage and reproduction usually within geography-specific communities, and can easily disappear if practices, communities, or migration patterns change. We tend to assume that external traits such as skin color express internal racial essences that are pre-social, but in truth black skin is about as relevant as blonde hair as an indicator of an internal biological reality. Rather than being the biological ground that gets expressed in social practices, it is an effect of social practice. It may distinguish people who have been bred along certain lines from others of different breeding lines, but that is about the extent of the significance. If you were to change the pattern of breeding, the "race" would disappear. As a result of cross-breeding, it is hard to tell a Eurasian from an Asian, a mixed-race African and Euro-American from a Euro-American (itself a fairly mongrel breed in most instances). Racists mistake accidents for essences, traits for truths, and meaningless markers of chromatic distinction for meaningful expressions of natural difference.

For all of its contingency and irrelevance, ethnicity nevertheless remains one of the most powerful reasons for either bonding together or falling apart. While external traits such as skin color cannot be construed as expressing internal racial essences, such traits are the visual language of human identity and human community. History speaks a different language from science, and race and ethnicity, for all their imaginary qualities, are not easily erased or ignored. Indeed, they are some of the most compelling determinants of cultural difference and of literary specificity. Even if black skin is ultimately meaningless as a biological marker, it is nevertheless a sign of a scarred historical reality with resonances in the present. To read Toni Morrison's *Beloved*, one of the most celebrated examples of ethnic writing in the late twentieth century, is to realize why blackness cannot be dismissed as a theme of literary discussion. Indeed, the painful reality of its history in America still weighs heavily on the present. Ethnic difference persists most palpably as economic difference, since race was often connected in the past to the economic exploitation of one group by another. Slavery is probably the most obvious example, and the legacy of such practices is palpable in the continued difference in wealth and economic power between ethnic groups. What the historical reality of ethnic difference means is that there are grounds for arguing that there are specific ethnic experiences of the world. Ethnic literature records quite distinct cultural, social, and psychological realities.

Ethnic literary study has also questioned the hitherto unexamined ethnic norms of a supposedly race-neutral literary study. For all of its efforts to secure a sense of literary universality, the New Criticism may in fact have been White Male Southern Literary Studies disguised as a more capacious ideal. The emergence of ethnic literary study displaced the notion that universality spoke a white dialect, and it focused attention on the bleaching out of other-than-dominant ethnic experiences by the privilege, always implicit and sometimes explicit, given whiteness in Eurocentric, North American literary study. In recent years, the challenge to the assumed white norm of the literary canon has taken the form of arguing that ethnic literary voices should no longer be confined to "programs" and should instead be integrated into the canon as equals with the usual white voices. The Heath *Anthology of American Literature* has led the way in displacing whiteness from its traditional centrality and replacing it with a more multiethnic vision of American literary history.

Ethnic studies has also provoked an interest in the imbrication of the dominant white culture in America with that of its ethnic others. In *Playing in the Dark*, Toni Morrison argues that white American literature often uses African Americans and African American experience as instruments for such projects as achieving an identity or realizing a quest. White freedom often defines itself in contrast to black servitude, and blacks often appear in white culture as happy supplements to white-only projects of achieved self-identity. The long association of blacks with slavery means in part that whites continue to think of them as lesser beings whose role in life is to assist whites in various ways. From Jim to Bagger Vance, blacks get to pole the raft or carry the clubs that allow whites to gain freedom or win the game.

A good example of blindness to racism in American literary studies is the case of William Faulkner. Because Faulkner was a white south-erner who spoke the same universalist language as they, the southern New Critics enshrined him as an example of great literature that gave expression to timeless, placeless truths. As a result of this canonization, Faulkner has been an unquestioned member of the "great tradition" in American letters from the 1930s down to the present. But one could just as easily compare him to the viciously anti-semitic writers of Europe who helped foster the culture that gave rise to Nazism. Faulkner's "aw shucks," it-couldn't-help-but-be-so version of the "ordinary southerner" is, from an African American perspective, as pernicious and as reprehensible as European anti-semitism appears from a Jewish perspective.

In *Light in August*, for example, one of his more offensively racist efforts, Faulkner tells the story of a man who appears to be white but who in fact is part African American. This "blood" stain ensures that Joe Christmas falls on the negative side of the dichotomies such as mind/body, universal/particular, light/dark, and civil/savage that Faulkner uses to organize his racial universe. Joe murders a white woman with whom he is having an affair. She is a representative of the northern reformers who sought to "reconstruct" the South and to end racism against blacks. That someone who represents the fruit of that labor – a free black who behaves arrogantly toward whites – kills her is, in the novel's argumentative scheme, an example of an appropriate lesson to those who would seek to tamper with natural folkways. Those folkways should be allowed to work their own way toward redemption.

Faulkner casually characterizes blacks as idiots who are akin to children. Their role in the novel is either to be the occasion for humor (tweaking the nose of villainous representatives of institutional religion) or to be representatives of a mindless, violent depravity. Whites, on the other hand, pertain to the realm of the universal, of timeless truths and events such as the white southern cavalry charge that Gail

Hightower hangs on to as a token of the South's enduring sense of tragic honor. He represents a good non-institutional spirituality and affirms the ideal of restraint against natural, especially sexual, passions. Joe, on the other hand, indulges those passions, with an aging, fat white woman whose physical characteristics are highlighted as a way of placing her below the more spiritual characters, especially Hightower. The whites experience life as tragedy, as something fated that cannot be changed, and blacks are part of the tragic legacy whites must live with.

This sense of the "immemorial" quality of human life assists Faulkner in engaging in acts of historical inaccuracy that further his racist argument. The first is that blacks lamented the loss of their white masters in the Civil War. Just the opposite was likely to be true, and blacks fled willingly from plantations once given the chance to do so. The second is that white southern communities were peace-loving and non-violent; they pursued justice in cases of inter-racial violence slowly and judiciously. Yet the actual story that lies at the origin of the novel is more accurate – a mob lynched a black man who murdered a white woman. The only thing slow and judicious about how white southern communities responded to black infractions against Jim Crow culture, which required deference by blacks toward whites and especially toward white women, was the preparations for the lynching. In the South in the years prior to the publication of the novel in 1932, as many as a hundred blacks were lynched each year.

Yet in the novel Faulkner portrays a white southern community determined to see justice done properly. It is a representative of the North, a man who represents federal government interference in the natural folkways of the South, who kills Joe. That dichotomy – bad northern government/good southern folkways – would continue to underwrite southern, "states rights" resistance to federal governmental attempts to end southern institutional racism down through the late twentieth century. The novel, therefore, is less a good example of universal ideas than it is a good example of a quite particular, southern conservative racist culture. It succeeds in portraying African Americans as either idiots in need of white paternalism or depraved victims of natural passion who are incapable of moral restraint. The only thing universal about the novel is the banality of the racial prejudice that informs it and the cowardly posture it assumes toward a violent culture of racism that should have provoked courageous opposition on the part of white writers.

A complacent sense of "literary" value probably accounts for the fact that Faulkner is still taught as an example of "great literature" and not as an example of a racist culture. One important effect of the emergence of ethnic studies is that it brings to the table of literary discussion things that are not "literary," in the sense that they do not pertain to writing form or do not express putatively universal ideas. Ethnic studies forces on literary studies a need to attend to the specifics of history and to the complex social dynamics of particular times and places, the loci of people's actual lives. Literary study inevitably shifts, as a result, toward the study of culture. And when that happens, someone like Faulkner becomes less easy to excuse. He may be a good example of the kind of literary style that the ethnic group with access to educational goods as a result of occupying a superior economic position promoted as the mandatory mark of "literary" greatness. But if one puts the literary aside for a moment and takes the real historical context of that literary situation into account, the sense of what Faulkner "is" also changes. There are few southern black competitors for the title of great southern writer in the 1930s because of the very racist culture that Faulkner describes and endorses so well. In his picture of the world, blacks are incapable of the cultural achievements he himself attains. But that is so precisely because the culture he endorses requires such a high degree of subordination and enforces such a violent diminishment of blacks that any exception to the picture would be more than surprising. Pictures of reality have a way of bringing the reality they depict into being. By insisting that blacks are inherently less than whites in all the ways that his novel says count – mind/body, spirit/matter, tragic gravity/comic irresponsibility, etc. – Faulkner helped ensure that his culture would continue to enforce the exclusion of African Americans from the education that would have allowed them to contradict the white picture of them. In Faulkner's view, they are "tragically" uneducable because of their "blood," and by making that argument as well as he did (in as "great" a "literary" language, one might say), he helped ensure that they would indeed be denied education. Significantly, of course, it was his home state of Mississippi that was the focus of African American efforts in the 1960s to gain access to higher education on an equal footing with whites.

By questioning the ideology of "the literary" in this way, ethnic studies has helped push literary study toward cultural studies. It has made it more difficult to isolate texts from their social context or to abstract universal themes from specific acts of ethnically inflected characterization in the literary work.

Exercise 9.1   Elizabeth Bishop, "Faustina, or Rock Roses"

"Faustina" is both the name of a species of rose and the name of a black servant who tends a white woman in this poem. Study the use of rose imagery in the poem. What are the different ways roses are used as images? Why might Bishop choose to give the servant the same name as a kind of rose?

Bishop often uses simple descriptive terms, but often as well they are weighty with implication. Notice how she describes the room and the bed in which the old woman lies. How does the setting become a way of characterizing the woman and her life?

Bishop is also a skillful shaper of sounds that give emphasis to her descriptions. Notice in stanza 3 the way she develops a string of "wo" and "ow" words – "two glow-worms / burning a drowned green." Those sounds create a dense feeling; they are made deep in the mouth; and they accompany the image of drowning. Why might they be associated with "drowned green"?

Often, she uses such sounds in striking contrast with other sounds. Notice the line that follows. Read it aloud after reading the preceding two lines. There is a sharp difference between the "ow" and "wo" sounds and the "e" and "i" sounds that follow. Why does she do this, do you think? How might light "betray us all"?

Why do you think Bishop emphasizes the woman's poverty so much? Notice the details in the next stanza. What is the significance of wall-paper held up with tacks? Or of a hole in the wall in which glistening silica is visible?

What about the woman is betrayed by the light?

Notice how Bishop repeats the word "white" and uses other words to suggest whiteness such as "bleached" and "pallid." Why does she do this?

She refers to herself as "the visitor" and remarks that she is embarrassed less by age and pain or nakedness than "by its reverse." How might the woman's mode of dress be embarrassing?

The arrival of Faustina, the black servant, is the most interesting and the most puzzling part of the poem. How do you read her character? How does Bishop present her? What does she emphasize?

Faustina's relationship to her employer is the heart of the puzzle. How would you characterize it? Why might a black servant of a white woman place the white woman in a situation whose meaning is not altogether clear?

Faustina seems to bring quite contradictory qualities together –
"sinister" yet "kind," for example. What might be sinister about her
kindness to the old white woman?

Bishop even suggests the possibility of cruelty. What do you think
she means by that? And what is a "coincident conundrum"? How is the
situation a conundrum?

What do you think the white woman gains by having a black servant?
And what does she risk? How might economic difference play a role
here?

What might Bishop mean by the "unimaginable nightmare"? It seems
to have occurred before. How might that be the case? What about the
relationship between the two women might hint at something like a
nightmare rather than a dream of freedom?

And what, finally, do you make of the snake-tongue image in the next
stanza?

The poem ends by suggesting that there is "no way of telling" what the
answer to the question posed in stanzas 9 and 10 is. Whose eyes do you
think she is referring to in the next line – "The eyes say only either"?

How might this balance of possibilities help explain the title of
the poem?

Exercise 9.2   Toni Morrison, *The Bluest Eye*

The novel begins with an emblematic scene of race and class difference.
The difference is not enormous. It hinges on bread and butter and a car,
but it is enough to provoke the strong emotions that are summoned by
class distinctions organized around race. On the one side is arrogance
and smugness, and on the other resentment and anger. As so often is
the case in multiracial societies, this class situation also gets configured
along the lines of racial difference. Rosemary is white, while Claudia
and Frieda are black. The paragraph depicts how self-regard operates
in contexts that might deprive one of self-esteem for reasons that are
outside one's own control. No one controls the economic situation into
which they are born. Children in poor situations especially must find
ways to balance an awareness of the negative judgment leveled at the
poor (for being irresponsible) with their need in a non-nurturing social
context to compensate with a strong sense of self. Notice that Claudia
says that "our own pride must be asserted by refusing to accept" when
Rosemary, after being beaten by the sisters, offers to pull down her
pants, a gesture of submission. Why does she say this?

Are there other places in the novel where people develop an exaggerated sense of themselves to compensate for being born into a subordinate situation?

Claudia clearly grows up in a very poor environment. What are some of the signs of poverty? What effect does poverty have on family relations, and especially on the relations between parents and children?

How is Claudia's mother characterized? Why do you think she behaves as she does? What effect does her behavior have on her daughter's emotions? Her sense of self?

Claudia at least has a home. The boarder, Mr. Henry, does not, nor do the foster children like Pecola Breedlove, who comes to live with Claudia's family. Their condition makes Claudia think about the difference between being "out" and being put "outdoors." How does the threat of homelessness affect people's aspirations? How do they shape their identity around it?

Another identity-creating object is the white doll. Claudia rejects it, but this inspires recrimination from her older relatives. Why are they willing to overlook the fact that the doll is white?

From Claudia's mother we get a sense of the role of culture in fabricating a means of enduring poverty. How does she use song to deal with her situation? How do blues songs function in black culture?

Poverty is humiliating. We sense that in Claudia's feelings of shame. How is it central to the Breedloves' experience of the world? Why does Morrison choose to use the image of ugliness as a figure for their humiliating condition in life? How does this sense of personal ugliness affect their lives?

Race-based poverty often breeds violence, domestic abuse, and broken homes. The Breedloves are a case in point. How does the bad domestic situation of the parents affect the children? Why does Morrison devote so much attention, do you think, to taking stock of those effects?

Morrison concludes the first part of the book by focusing on the prostitutes. What role do they play in the novel?

Racial difference is registered in several other anecdotes throughout the novel – the conflict with Maureen Peal, Pecola's encounter with Geraldine, the light-colored black woman from Meridian, and Polly's job in the wealthy white home.

How does Maureen Peal's story further our sense of the harm ethnic thinking does? How, for example, is she different from Claudia in her effect on other people? And why does that matter so much? How does it affect Claudia's sense of her own identity?

What do we learn about how color shadings and class shadings operate from Geraldine's story? What effect does the ideal of upper-class existence have on her and on her relations with others? What does Pecola notice about the life of someone with relatively more wealth than her? Why does Geraldine reject her so violently? Would you call Geraldine a racist?

What is the significance of the girls' visit to the house where Polly works? Why is it significant that Mrs. Breedlove becomes "Polly"? How is the anecdote a lesson in misdirected affection and in the skewing of human relations that class difference fosters?

Polly and Cholly are significant characters in that they are the two whose life stories are told almost in full. Why does Morrison choose to do this with these particular characters? What is significant about Polly? How is her psychology worth examining for gaining an understanding of how people who are made to feel subordinate because of race or class come to terms with their situation and try to compensate for it?

What about Cholly's life background accounts for his later behavior? How does poverty breed pathology? In a remarkable passage, Morrison says of Cholly that he "was free. Dangerously free." What does she mean? And why does she say that "the pieces of Cholly's life could become coherent only in the head of a musician"?

Soaphead Church is a study in ideology. He stands in contrast to Claudia, who rejects white culture. How does Church behave toward white culture?

Exercise 9.3   NWA, "The Nigga Ya Love To Hate"

This rap song presents an argument about how African Americans should behave in a racist society. Let's begin by asking what Ice Cube takes for granted as the counter-position or counter-discourse against which he is arguing. Who is the "you" in early lines such as "You gotta deal with a nine-double-m" (a reference to a 9 mm pistol)?

He is criticizing African American life in America. How does he portray the position of African Americans? And what does he mean in the first stanza by "I never / Tell you to get down, it's all about comin' up"?

What is the argument against which Ice Cube is contending? And what is his response? The crucial lines are "The mothafucka that say they too black, / Put 'em overseas, they be beggin' to come back." Who does he have in mind here and how does he think being sent overseas will change their attitudes?

What does his position seem to be about the involvement of African American youth with "gangs and drugs"?

The first chorus, which begins with "Fuck you, Ice Cube!", also addresses another discursive position in the debate about African American life. In the 1980s, Bill Cosby's very positive television show about an upper-middle-class African American family was associated with the argument that young African Americans should work within the white-dominated system in order to become responsible members of society. How does the chorus evoke this argument? What does NWA seem to think of the argument?

The second stanza (which begins "All in the muthafuckin' cycle") evokes the possibility of white violence against blacks ("You getcha ass ready for the lynching"). What is gained for his argument by this move? The possibility also obliges Ice Cube to announce a different argument that comes most clearly in lines 45 and 46: "Thinkin' not about how right and wrong ya live, but how / Long ya live." Link this to his evocation of prison and to the line "I like to clown." Who is he referring to in the line "We got 'em afraid of the funky shit / I like to clown"? Why does he advise blacks to "pump up the sound in your / Jeep"?

What do you make of the gender debate raised in the second chorus? The chorus responds to Ice Cube's sexist use of the word "bitch" for a woman, but does it change anything?

The final stanza explicitly takes on other cultural agents in African American life such as Soul Train (a dance show modeled on American Bandstand), Arsenio Hall (who imitated white talk-show hosts) and Hammer (a hip-hop artist whose dancing was featured on MTV in the 1980s). The latter two might have been considered "role models" for African American youth. What does Ice Cube think of them? What might explain his position? What might be implied by the idea of a role model that he might find suspect and why?

And how does his final advice to black youth emerge out of his argument?

Exercise 9.4   *Falling Down* and *Hate*

Conservatives and liberals tend traditionally to take very different approaches to the issues of race and ethnicity. In the US, liberals promote a broadening of rights for minority ethnic groups, and they favor government assistance and legal remediation for past racism by conservatives against ethnic minorities. Liberals do not identify the country with one particular kind of ethnicity and are generally more open to ideals of ethnic diversity or multiculturalism.

Conservatives are less likely to accept ethnicity as a reason for special or remedial treatment. Individual initiative, industry, and enterprise guarantee success in life, and conservatives as a result take less seriously the idea that racism acts as an impediment to social and economic advancement. Opposed in principle to government intervention in economic and social life, conservatives feel that no remedial action, such as civil rights laws or "affirmative action" hiring designed to remedy the effects of past acts of discrimination by conservatives, should be taken to assist economically disadvantaged ethnic minority groups. The difference between conservatives and liberals has been most evident in recent decades regarding the issue of immigration to the US of non-European ethnic groups. Hispanics especially have been targeted by conservatives who believe immigration should be restricted.

Conservatism in the US has traditionally been the political philosophy of large property owners, the heads of the business class who see government as an instrument of economic and social egalitarianism and so seek to limit its powers. But lower-class males who accept the conservative argument regarding the individual character of social advancement tend as well to embrace conservative positions. Their economic lives are made precarious and unstable as a result of the search for profits in other parts of the world on the part of the investment class. But they do not understand or see the invisible structural cause of their misery, and instead of blaming the real wrongdoers they blame ethnic minorities, who seem to be responsible for taking their jobs. That has been especially true in the contemporary era in the US, a period characterized by enormous swings in the economic fortunes of such men and by a successful conservative cultural backlash against liberal ideals of ethnic equality and diversity. Other factors, such as the increasing social and economic presence and power of immigrant groups, have also contributed to the feelings of resentment and anger such men experience, feelings that make conservative hostility to ethnic mixture and multicultural pluralism more attractive.

Falling Down dramatizes these issues from the point of view of such a conservative white American male who has lost his job and his family and who feels resentment against new immigrant groups. He castigates an Asian American grocer, for example, for not being sufficiently

American, and he gets into a fight with Latino gang members when he challenges their cultural assumptions. The film seems to endorse the man's harshly Americanist feelings about ethnicity. He is initially linked visually to two emblems of conservative white Christian culture, the ideal of individual freedom and the Christ story of personal suffering and sacrifice. As he waits in a frustrating traffic jam at the beginning of the film, he looks at bumper stickers that mention "freedom" and "he died for your sins." In this film, the white American male has lost his freedom, and he does die standing up for his rights against a multi-ethnic society whose corruption and inhumanity is lent a particularly conservative codification: Asian American grocers who charge too much, Latino gang members who show no respect for a hard-working white man, restaurants that are overly regimented, poor people who are in fact exploiters of hard-working people, public workers who do make-work jobs to keep the public tax money flowing, wealthy people who enjoy leisure while hard-working lower-class men struggle to survive, etc.

In the film, white American males are portrayed as under attack from a harsh economic climate, hostile non-white ethnic forces around them, and women who emasculate them. Bill, the unemployed defense worker who gives up in frustration at waiting in line and goes on a quest to reach the home of his divorced wife on his daughter's birthday, and Prendergast, the policeman who tracks him, are both disempowered by women. Bill's wife refuses to let him come home to see his daughter, and Prendergast's wife bullies him on the telephone, an emblem for both men of excessive ties to powerful women. Prendergast's wife is portrayed as a physical and emotional mess, a trope typical of misogynist films that portray heroic men subdued by more powerful women. In the dual narrative, Prendergast succeeds in reclaiming his masculinity, defined in the film as the ability to act successfully in the public world and to exercise violence against others. Prendergast tells his wife finally to "shut up" and severs the symbolically umbilical phone connection to her that has kept him from his work all day. Bill fails because he continues to define his existence through his wife and fails to find a source of happiness and success apart from her. Sent back to live with his mother by his wife, he fails to "reach home," literally the house he lived in with her but also, more symbolically, the masculine ideal of a successfully achieved familial and sexual life.

Bill complains that he is no longer "economically viable," but no cause is given for his loss of economic status. That lack of information or explanation befits, however, a consciousness that fails to pierce the empirical economic reality around it and is incapable of deciphering the structural causes of its own suffering. Instead, it turns its anger and resentment against more empirically visible, surface annoyances, such as an Asian American grocer who charges too much for a soft drink, that are misread as structural causes.

In contrast, Prendergast's sidekick is a sympathetically portrayed young Hispanic woman who admires him. While Bill gets enraged at ethnic minority grocers and street gang members, Prendergast more rationally accepts his ethnic minority partner. The strategy of placing two quite different characters in similar situations or relations allows the film to indulge in an exploration of racist attitudes while nevertheless appearing to endorse a much more anti-racist position embodied in the police detective. The strategy is at work especially in the sequence in the used military supply store. The owner is a neo-Nazi racist and homophobe, and before Bill kills him, he characterizes him as a "sick motherfucker" in contrast to himself: "I'm an American." This differentiation has the effect of distancing the more extreme forms of ethnic hatred associated with the radical right. It nevertheless lends endorsement to Bill's more mainstream conservative "American" brand of ethnic animosity, which he turns against the "extremes" of the street gang and the rude, unhelpful, and apparently exploitative grocer.

The visual portrayal of the characters in the two scenes of ethnic conflict endows Bill with a sense of virtue and respectability, while the non-white characters are made to appear "greasy," dark, threatening, vicious, uncivil, and irrational. Bill wears a white shirt and tie, has a neat haircut, and is lit usually in such a way as to make his actions and statements appear rational and virtuous. Mr. Lee, the grocer, is in contrast dressed in a motley dark shirt that appears too tight, is unshaven and rough-looking, and is lit in such a way as to connote deceptiveness and incivility. His dark store seems more the cave of a brute animal than a well-lit and transparent place of fair dealing. His windows, drawing on an old racialist code for Asians, are yellow. The young Hispanic men circle Bill like prowling animals on the hunt while he sits and minds his own business. Their faces in close-up are dark and sweaty, another emblem of animality, and their hair is thick with oil. That these supposedly angelino gangsters speak with New York Hispanic accents, dress in New York style, and do not use the usual weapons of Los Angeles gangs (the Tech 9 automatic pistol) adds to the sense of a badly constructed depiction of ethnic conflict. It is told at such a great distance from actual Latino culture that it cannot even get the codes of dress, speech, and behavior right. Bill's hostility toward the two ethnic groups focuses on themes common in conservative complaints regarding modern multiethnic mixing in the US. He points out to the Latinos that he would not want them living in his backyard, and to both them and Mr. Lee he remarks that they do not know English. When they point out that he has failed to read their sign marking their territory, he says: "Maybe if you wrote it in fucking English, I could understand it." Conservatives during this time argued that immigrants should be forced to learn English and that English should be declared the national language of the country.

Mean humor is used in the sequences to make acts of destruction and cruelty on Bill's part appear comic. Laughter is provoked by his use of a baseball bat to smash Mr. Lee's goods and "reduce" his prices after asking how much they cost. When the Latino boys crash their car and are lying on the ground, their weapons around them, Bill picks up a gun and gives one of them a lesson in shooting straight by shooting him in the leg. Such mean humor is, of course, itself an expression of violent feelings toward others. It gives expression to the tough attitude conservatives believe is needed to survive in the economic marketplace, and it also expresses the dis-empathy that accompanies that toughness. Conservatives usually mock the liberal tendency to feel empathy for socially and economically disadvantaged people, and such empathy springs from a psychological disposition that sees others less as antagonists and more as fellow members of a community, people with whom one has some commonality. For conservatives, no such commonality exists, except perhaps with members of one's own ethnic, social, or national group. Others are competitors, and the social world is atomized into individual parts (one meaning of the conservative ideal of "freedom"). As a result, society consists of a war against all in which the government's role is simply to maintain order and prevent property from being stolen from the more advantaged by the less advantaged.

That the death of the free white male comes at the hands of a police officer doing his job well can thus be read as a vindication of the conservative position. The role so many films play of symbolically purging its dysfunctional members in favor of more functional ones is fulfilled. The world is portrayed as a conservative jungle of contending, atomized powers – ethnic, economic, etc. – and if white males are depicted as failing or falling down, they also succeed in purging that failure and moving on, wounded but stronger. Prendergast kills off the weaker member of the white gang so that the white gang can ultimately be better equipped to survive. That Prendergast is the last standing member of the gang in the film suggests that it ultimately endorses a more accommodational position, one that makes its peace with ethnic mixture. But the new ethnic groups must absorb themselves into the white social system (metaphorized by the multiethnic police department) and not ask for special or separate consideration.

Hate is a polemical story of three young French boys – one Arab, one Jew, one African – set in the working-class suburbs of Paris. What is gained by so carefully arranging the choice of characters so that they all come from different ethnic groups?

The film's narrative is structured both as a journey and as a circle. The boys go away to Paris, then return home. The time period covered by the journey is roughly twenty-four hours. Is there some reason for arranging the narrative in this manner? Think about the joke that is told in voiceover at the beginning and the end – about the man who is falling from a building and who says to himself as he passes each floor, "So far so good." What is the point of the story? How might it relate to the circularity of the narrative?

Are there other moments in the film that emphasize redundancy, stasis, and the feeling of going nowhere fast? Consider those cuts or edits where one expects to move away from a setting to another; yet the film is on the same shot after the edit. How might this editing strategy be linked to the circularity of the narrative? How else does the film suggest the walled-in character of the boys' lives? Note the brief mention of school. What is Hubert's particular significance in this regard?

The boys seem at ease in a multiethnic culture, yet they encounter ethnic-based hatred on their journey. Why is it so significant that Hubert loses his temper and asks Vinz to use the gun when they encounter the racist skinheads? This scene precedes the penultimate scene, in which Vinz relinquishes the gun to Hubert, who all along has been pleading with him to give it up. How has the encounter with the skinheads changed the two boys? Vinz decides not to use the gun because in a scene preceding the skinhead encounter he, while separated from his friends, has seen a gun used against someone. Why is that scene so crucial to his evolution? How is it filmed to dramatize its psychological significance?

The boys' culture is dominated by verbal play, storytelling, taunts, curses, and posturing. Masculine pride is a crucial feature of this culture. How is masculine pride depicted? Consider the scene on the roof and the encounter with the police. In what other ways is pride an important element of the action? How does it ultimately infect even the police and make them betray their role as upholders of the law and protectors of citizens?

The depiction of the police is complex and multi-sided. What does their acquaintance, the "Lieutenant," represent? What is the point of the torture sequence? Consider how the third policeman behaves.

A certain amount of irony is to be found in the film's rendition of the contrast between the actual limits on the boys' lives and the various "feel good" slogans that surround them on billboards and signs. How are those slogans ironic? The visual style of the film also draws attention to this contrast. Compare how the film uses close-ups and a rotating camera in the police station with the use of a zoom out of the Paris street once they reach the city. How does the style in the police station characterize the boys' relationship to that important institution in their lives? And how, conversely, does the zoom out work to characterize their relationship to the world of the city?

The ending, of course, is also ironic. Why?

Said doesn't understand why the man in the bathroom tells them the story of Grunwalski. Why do you think he does? What have the boys just been arguing about and what point might the man be trying to make? The anecdote is about several things – individual survival in a harsh setting, sticking together or going off alone, pride versus accepting help – that are also issues in the film. How does the anecdote relate to the themes of tolerance and violence in the film?

CHAPTER 10

Post-Colonial and Global English Studies

Post-colonial studies takes two forms – the study of writing by "post-colonial" writers, usually natives of countries colonized by England – and the study of the discourse and literature of imperialism. Post-colonial studies is by now a largely historical undertaking, but it has a contemporary existence as global English studies. The words "imperialism" and "globalization" might be said to be the central organizing terms for each intellectual enterprise.

The colonization of the non-European globe began when European countries with navies began to discover that many foreign countries that had eluded contact with Europe until then were inferior militarily. It was a fairly simple matter, the Europeans found, to conquer and colonize them. This was the case from India to Africa to America. This extraordinary venture in conquest had some positive consequences that are difficult to separate from the numerous painful and deleterious consequences that attended them. Entire indigenous populations disappeared; civilizations and cultures were destroyed; people who had enjoyed freedom became slaves; their pillaged natural resources such as gold would make Europe a storehouse of wealth down to the present. Europe brought modern political forms and institutions to the conquered countries, along with educational systems and common languages that bound the world together for the first time. English became a prominent language in south Asia, parts of Africa, and the Americas as French and Spanish, for similar reasons, became common in other parts of the non-European globe.

But the natives, as is often the case with subordinated peoples, were restless. From Plessy in 1775 to Dien Bien Phu in 1954, they manifested an ingratitude surprising only to the most placidly self-deluded of imperialists. Native people resented their political and military subordination to the Europeans, the deliberate destruction of their cultures and languages for the ends of cultural homogenization, and the wholesale plunder of their natural wealth. Empire could not have sustained itself in any event, since the very commercial spirit that motivated it came accompanied by an independence of spirit at odds with passive subordination. Once injected into the local cultures, it combined with nationalist yearnings for independence that proved potently combustible. The British and French especially found they could not practice democracy at home and autocracy abroad. Empire quite literally blew up in their faces in places like Ireland, Iraq, Algeria, and India. And such blowing up continues down to the present in the Middle East, where the Euro-American colonization of Palestine remains an enduring lesson in how not to behave toward others if one expects to live peacefully with one's neighbors.

Imperialism grew out of ignorance, arrogance, and greed – common human motivations and dispositions but not the best grounds on which to build a global community in which all can thrive and survive equally. Nevertheless, it supplied the grounds for achieving such a community by linking the different parts of the globe culturally and economically. Such linkages are quite common in the contemporary world in the form of economic globalization and in such trans-geographic cultural phenomena as the "Black Atlantic." Old centers and dominant assumptions are displaced by such linking and mixing. Writers of mixed post-colonial ethnic and cultural roots – Caribbean, African, English – now in some respects are more English than the English. They generate the kind of compelling fictional prose that in the past made writing by Anglo-Saxon English writers universally admired.

Post-colonial literary scholars study both sides of the imperial equation. Some concern themselves with the discourses that justified or obliquely registered the existence of empire in the metropole or imperial center. Most of us grew up reading *Jane Eyre* as a tale of Victorian womanhood, but post-colonial critics taught us to see it as a story of empire. The second Mrs. Rochester (Jane Eyre) could only come into her own if the first Mrs. Rochester (a madwoman of Caribbean descent) was immolated and symbolically removed from the narrative. Numerous examples of such colonial shadowing of imperial literature could be adduced, from Spenser's Ireland to Austen's Antigua, from Huck's Jim to Natty Bumppo's Chingachgook.

Other post-colonial scholars examine the cultural fronts where imperial and subaltern cultures meet in such places as India. Natives often mimicked the cultural patterns of their conquerors but with a sense of sly difference that asserted their own yearnings for independence. If foreigners tried to impose their own cultural beliefs through education, natives often rejected imperial culture and language in favor of indigenous national cultural forms and languages that underscored differences that could be the basis for political mobilization for independence. Still other post-colonial scholars attend to the indigenous movements such as writers' leagues that attempted to use culture as a political tool to bring about national liberation.

There are several important names and concepts associated with post-colonial studies. Edward Said's *Orientalism* is an important diagnosis of how imperialism worked in the realm of intellectual and cultural discourse. Empire had to be justified, and it gave rise to fields of knowledge such as Orientalism that turned colonized cultures into objects for scholarly analysis. Often, the Orient became a cluster of stereotypes that rationalized imperial management. Frantz Fanon's *The Wretched of the Earth* examined the psychological wounds inflicted on natives by the imperial relationship, and it examined the role of a sense of one's own national culture in the resistance to empire.

Important concepts in post-colonial study are diaspora, hybridity, ambiguity, mimicry, mestizaje, and creolization. Most former imperial countries are now diasporic in the sense that people from former colonies have moved to imperial metropoles such as England and become English. Ideas regarding national or even ethnic cultural identity become more difficult to apply in situations where traditional and metropolitan cultural norms and identities meet and mix. The characters in Zadie Smith's *White Teeth* are difficult to pin down in regard to ethnic culture for this reason. Their identities are hybrid in that they consist of two or more different strands that intertwine. Colonialism had always been ambiguous, but such mixing and matching of identities makes its legacy even more so. Colonialists sought to impose their own culture on a quite different culture so that it would mime or imitate that of the imperial center. The desire for a homogeneous identity of ruler and ruled was confounded by the unequal relation of power which meant that such imposition was disturbed implicitly by tendencies toward noncompliance and willed dissonance. What resulted often was mimicry with irony rather than imitation. Some natives sought refuge in indigenous, often oral cultures or in ideals of a national culture based in their own experience and language. The assumption was that language bears worldviews within it, so that to adopt the imperial language was in effect to adopt the point of view of imperialism, with all of the arrogant assumptions that ran counter to one's own interests as a subject of colonialism. But other writers and intellectuals embraced the opportunity for creative mixing that the colonial and post-colonial situation afforded. From this way of thinking resulted such terms as "mestizaje" and "creolization," the idea that identities and languages from both sides of the imperial equation can combine to generate new subjective and linguistic possibilities. A mestizo is a mixed-race person, and a creole is a mixed language that combines elements of a language like English or French with local indigenous dialects.

Many of the new cultural possibilities in global English arise from the situation of economic inequality that still characterizes relations between metropole and periphery, imperial center and former colony. The characters in *White Teeth* are for the most part economic migrants who came to England seeking a higher standard of living than was available in their much poorer, less economically developed homeland. The migrant experience is often central in contemporary global English literature. But so are many other experiences from diverse geographical locations that are now made available by the common international currency of the English language. That such cultural internationalism is inseparable from the ongoing soft imperialism that is economic globalization – the quest for higher profits from cheaper labor that permits a small metropolitan minority to live hyper-wealthy lives at the expense of roughly 90 percent of the world population – is, of course, problematic. Tallying the relation between the costs and benefits of such globalization for local peoples is difficult, and, as with imperialism proper, one can probably only imagine benefits by ignoring the structuring unequal power relationship between the two players. One question to entertain would be to what degree the new popularity of writers like Jumpha Lahiri or Kieran Desai is merely a reflex of such globalization, a cultural version of the search for better value in the exotic and other. But such writing can also be a delivery system for consciousness-transforming experiences that educate the reading public living in the central sites of economic world rule even as it entertains them. And from such consciousness-raising an end to the viciousness of economic globalization might eventually ensue.

Exercise 10.1   Joseph Conrad, *Heart of Darkness*

The reputation of this novel is a lesson in point of view. If you are white and an inhabitant of a formerly imperial country or a member of a colonizing group, you may be inclined to support those who for years thought this work a critique of imperialism. But some time ago, with the African writer Wole Soyinka leading the way, people from former colonies in Africa began to point out that the novel is in fact quite racist.

What do you think? Is it possible the novel is both things at once?

It all depends on how you assess the portrait of black Africans that Conrad draws. To my mind, he comes dangerously close to identifying them with the "darkness" in the human heart, a darkness he seems to equate with our animal side, our ability to behave in "savage" ways. Early on in the novel, one encounters this theme. Speaking of people he seems to consider good imperialists, the Romans, who built civilizations where they went conquering, Conrad says: "They were men enough to face the darkness." He speaks of a "decent young citizen in a toga" who feels "the savagery, the utter savagery" around him when he lands "in a swamp," "the mysterious life of the wilderness that stirs in the forest, in the jungles, in the hearts of men."

Savagery suggests an ability to commit violence against others without any sense of moral restraint. Racist thinking would say that some peoples or races are savage in this way. And it has been a commonplace of racist thinking regarding blacks especially that they are incapable of civilization, of the restraint that curbs such savagery.

Notice in the passage above that savagery is associated both with a geographical location – the jungle – and with a psychological one – the "hearts of men." The "heart of darkness," then, will be something to do both with the African jungle and with a natural quality or propensity in humans toward "savagery."

My own hunch is that Soyinka and others are right in claiming that the assignment of such savagery to Africans is racist. It associates them with the primitive, animal side of human nature, the one that fuels our ability to violate one another. Civilized restraint, on the other hand, is white and European.

Yet not all Europeans are portrayed positively in the novel. Some are brutally greedy; others are ineffective and incompetent; the religious crusaders who would bring light to the darkness are fools. The Belgian project of extracting natural resources from the Congo is portrayed as misguided and inefficient. Kurtz goes to Africa with high-minded liberal humanist ideals and returns a reactionary committed to the conservative position of the time that there are race differences and that some races are "higher" on the human scale than other, "dark," ones. He gives voice to the reactionary idea that Africans should be exterminated. Only a few decades later, in Europe, similar conservative reactionaries – the

Nazis – would try to carry out such a program against people they too considered sub-human.

How do we put all of these different pieces together?

It helps to bear in mind that Conrad is criticizing a particular kind of imperialism, that practiced by the Belgian government. It was known to consist of the brutal treatment of the native population in order to extract raw materials. There was no effort to promote education or the development of social institutions. As Conrad puts it quite early on: "They were no colonists; their administration was merely a squeeze. . . . they grabbed what they could for the sake of what could be got."

A few lines further down, he adds: "What redeems it is the idea only." He distinguishes this idea from a "sentimental pretence," something that at the time would have been associated with women and with sentimental literature, as well as with liberal humanism, the belief that all people are equally "human." The liberals would have been the ones inclined to think Africans can be "raised up" to European standards and norms of civilization.

Think about female characters who might be associated with such a pretence about Africa. You have already gotten a sense of a masculinist bias in Conrad's assessment of the varieties of imperialism. Some people are "man enough," as he puts it, to face up to savagery; others are not.

What do you think he means by "the idea only"? How might an idea make colonialism acceptable? If he thinks blacks are a lesser race, then the idea might have to do with bringing European civilization to them. But how is this effort portrayed in the novel? Is Conrad's conception much "darker" or more pessimistic? Does he even think blacks are redeemable at all? Are they merely savages in his eyes?

You get a sense of what the idea might be when on page 4 of the novel he describes what he clearly considers to be good colonialists, people like Francis Drake and John Franklin, "knights all, titled and untitled – the great knights-errant of the sea." This is silly schoolboy stuff, something you might expect of Rudyard Kipling, who at the same time was writing horrifically racist anthems to imperialism. But then Kipling and Conrad admired one another. So perhaps they shared a puerile way of thinking about the world – all worship for "knights-errant," all blindness to the racism of it all? The silliness goes on. They were, according to Conrad, "messengers of the might within the land, bearers of a spark from the sacred fire." They carried with them the "dreams of men, the seed of commonwealth, the germs of empire." Is this the kind of "idea" that Conrad feels justifies a good colonialism? If so, how does it make colonialism good?

In fairness to Conrad, we should bear in mind that his racism was not "his." It was quite common amongst even educated people to hold racist ideas at the time. One senses such thinking early on in the novel: "The old river in its broad reach rested unruffled at the decline of day, after ages of good service done to the race that peopled its banks." You would have a difficult time finding such a sentence today; people no longer think in such explicitly and dubiously racial terms. But back then, at the beginning of the twentieth century, it was common.

When English audiences first read the novel, they felt it portrayed Kurtz and the liberal humanism he represents as misguided, that it depicted blacks as a lesser species, and that it justified colonialism. Since then, the consensus, amongst whites at least, is that Conrad is a great ironist who would never do something so unironic as endorse colonialism or racism, despite what his contemporaries thought, probably more accurately given that they read it in its original context. Think about the nonsense about knights-errant and examine carefully how he depicts blacks in Africa. Think about the words he uses. Then, decide for yourself.

Here are some prompts for reading the rest of the novel.

Conrad was a conservative. In his youth, he aided the rightwing, proto-fascist side of the Carlist conflict in Spain. In that conflict, interestingly for how women are portrayed in the novel, a male pretender to a throne tried to make sure the daughter of his brother did not become queen. Conrad did not believe in liberal ideals of human progress. Early twentieth-century conservatives held a quite pessimistic view of human nature. It cannot be improved; it is given over irredeemably to natural appetites that are evil. Restraint must be imposed on the lower classes especially if social order is to be maintained, just as firm restraint must be imposed on the body and its natural urges. In this way of thinking, nature is frequently portrayed as something dangerous. And the lower classes are often associated with the body and with natural passions that warrant control (very often that worst of human passions – the desire for economic equality). Some people – the wealthy conservative elite – are better than others. They are tough, have won at the battle of life, exercise self-restraint, and are best qualified to run society. The noisy, uneducated, democratic rabble need to be governed by their betters. Such conservatives tend frequently to be racists. At least, they often feel other races are lower on the scale of things because they are poorer or have not attained the same marks of "civilization" that some wealthy white Europeans, at least, have attained. That wealth arose largely through their pillage-and-burn approach to other peoples around the globe, but that violence was civilized while resistance to it was a sign of "savagery" and "barbarism."

Consider how Marlow's aunt is portrayed. Why does Conrad call her a "dear enthusiastic soul"? What is the significance of "enthusiastic" as a modifier? Think of a phrase conservatives often use for liberals – "bleeding heart." Any relationship?

How is the ideal of progress treated in this part of the novel? Why is the city characterized as a "whited sepulchre"?

Conrad describes two women knitting "black wool feverishly." How might it be a reflection on what Conrad feels the promoters of progress are trying to do to blacks? Why "feverishly"?

In Africa, Marlow encounters Belgian colonialism for the first time. How is it portrayed? What does he seem to think of it?

What does Marlow think of the characters he meets along the way upriver? How is the manager different from the accountant? Why? Does it make a difference that he is a "young aristocrat"? How might that fit with Conrad's conservatism? Conservatives usually feel that an elite, usually also wealthy, should rule society.

How are the pilgrims portrayed? What does Marlow seem to think of them? How are they associated with lying? Think back to what he has said earlier about women being afraid of truth. How might the pilgrims be afraid of truth? And what truth do you think Marlow has in mind? One suspects it has to do with the themes enunciated earlier regarding the darkness and savagery of human nature. How might the pilgrims be afraid to face up to that? Notice how the metaphor of "pretense" carries over from the aunt to the pilgrims.

What do you make of the Eldorado expedition at the end of chapter 1? How is it a fitting way to conclude this stage of Marlow's journey, just before he sets off upstream to meet Kurtz and the heart of darkness?

The racism of the novel begins to become more evident as you enter chapter 2. What signs of racism do you notice as you read? What, for example, is the significance for notions of racial difference between Europeans and Africans to say that going upriver is "like travelling back to the earliest beginnings of the world"? Does that suggest that blacks are lower on the scale of evolution? Evolutionary thinking was quite powerful in Europe at this time, and it was often used to justify a racist belief that some ethnic groups are superior to others.

An interesting exchange occurs just after this remark. Marlow says that the "inner truth" of the jungle "luckily" remains hidden. And he begins to mock his interlocutors for their cowardice until one retorts: "Try to be civil, Marlow." It is an interesting symbolic moment. How might "being civil" be juxtaposed symbolically to what Marlow is describing?

Civility seems in the novel to be equated with ignoring the conservative truth that savagery lurks in the human heart as our animal existence and as our early evolutionary history. Africans, lower on the evolutionary scale than whites, are closer to that animal existence.

Notice the discussion of human and "inhuman" as Marlow thinks about the meaning of his approach to the heart of Africa. Is there something racist about Marlow's thought that he might feel a "remote kinship" with the wild Africans? And what do you make of the fireman who is compared to a "dog in a parody of breeches"?

How might Marlow's reflections on the cannibals be construed as racist? It is racist enough to reduce all of Africa to a group of cannibals, but notice how he thinks about their significance for the "principles" that characterize civilization. What does it mean that those principles do not apply to these people?

And notice another animal metaphor: "I would just as soon have expected restraint from a hyena prowling amongst the corpses of a battlefield."

Kurtz seems to bring together two quite distinct qualities. He is associated with the savagery in humankind but also with "the pulsating stream of light." What do you make of this confluence of qualities? How might it prepare us to accept his judgment on the natives: "Exterminate all the brutes!" Does this seem to be a judgment Conrad endorses? Has the racist depiction of Africans prepared us to embrace it?

Why is it so important that Kurtz had such high motives and yet seems, on encounter with the savage darkness of human (and especially African) nature, to have capitulated to what a conservative would call a more realist position regarding the truth of nature? How might this further Conrad's conservative argument? Notice that in the end even the pilgrims are reduced to firing rifles into the jungle to save themselves. What does this say about their altruistic idealism? How does that confirm Conrad's conservative argument in the novel?

Upon returning to Europe, Marlow says he remains loyal to Kurtz in the face of the "irritating pretence" of life amongst "commonplace individuals." Why does he do so? What aspect of Kurtz does he seem to have in mind?

Civility, the forms and rituals of civilized life, is a kind of pretense, and Conrad associates it with women. It is contrasted with being "man enough" to face up to what a conservative pessimist would term the truth of the darkness in all.

Given everything so far, why am I tempted to think that the "extremist party" Marlow says Kurtz might have led would be a rightwing, pre-fascist party? The fascists, especially in Germany, were extreme conservatives who based their politics on racist assumptions not that distant from those in this novel.

Notice how in the end women are once again associated with the cowardly need to live with delusions rather than face the brute reality of human nature (or, on a more racist note, the brute savagery of the dark-skinned races).

I have always found it fascinating that Marlow, in a highly symbolic act, tells Kurtz's betrothed that his final words were her name. In fact, they were "The horror! The horror!"

Given how much the novel privileges masculinity and associates it with conservative tough-mindedness about the brutality of the world and about being manly enough to face up to that truth, how in fact might women equal horror? How might they represent something horrifying for men who accept the ideas this novel advertises? Go back and consider the example of Kurtz's black consort in Africa. How might she represent what men like Conrad fear in women? And why might a conservative man who feels that masculine toughness is a virtue be afraid of a powerful woman? One might note that the masculine ideal seems to be intrinsically connected to a denigration of women. Real men are true; women are false. Real men are tough; women represent weakness. Real men see the world as a place of primitive savagery that must be faced up to unsentimentally. African brutes must be colonized, if not exterminated. Women are more inclined to be progressive-minded liberals who seek to bring light and sympathy to people who, despite poverty and racial difference, are human and capable of progress. But why then is the most powerful metaphor for the heart of darkness a black woman with power?

Exercise 10.2   Elizabeth Bishop, "Brazil, January 1, 1502" and "The Burglar of Babylon"

For many years Bishop lived in Rio de Janeiro, and she wrote poems about both the Brazilian colonial experience and relations between ethnic groups in twentieth-century Brazil.

"Brazil, January 1, 1502" concerns the arrival of the Portuguese colonialists in Brazil and their conquest of the indigenous peoples. Read the poem and try to determine what Bishop's attitude toward the colonialists is.

The first part of the poem is a little confusing. She begins by saying that she is seeing the Brazilian world as they, the Portuguese, must have seen it. But notice that she seems to be describing the natural setting as if it were a painting or a tapestry – "every square inch filling in with foliage." Why does she make this deliberate confusion?

Note that the epigraph for the poem suggests just this confusion – "embroidered nature . . . tapestried landscape." How in the first stanza especially does she make nature seem like a work of art? How would you characterize the nature she describes? And how does the last remark about it being freshly taken off the painter's frame add to the characterization? Why might she wish to compare nature to art?

The next stanza seems to continue the description of nature, but you soon catch on that a major change has occurred in the poem. She is now describing an actual painting or tapestry. We are used to seeing paintings on walls, but back in the sixteenth century – the historical moment of the poem – people would have been more likely to hang tapestries, enormous pieces of embroidered cloth with pictures on them, on walls. Often these were allegorical stories in natural settings, and they often told stories having to do with Christian morality or Greek and Roman mythology. The moral stories often had to do with the Christian virtues.

How does this tapestry relate to or follow logically upon the nature described in the first stanza?

What are some of its important traits or features?

Notice the contrast between positive terms that suggest artistic delicacy and the terms assigned to the overly obvious moral allegory – "big symbolic birds." What does Bishop's attitude toward the Christian allegory seem to be?

What is the significance of her choice of adjectives in the description of the allegorical picture? Notice "massy" and "sooty" especially.

How are the big, undelicate allegorical figures at odds with the natural setting? How does Bishop emphasize this?

Notice the way the rocks are described as being "worked with lichens, gray moonbursts." Why are the rocks "threatened from underneath by moss" and "attacked above by scaling ladder vines"? Nature seems to be fighting the allegorical story the painter injected into the painting or tapestry, but why?

There is a very odd characterization here – "in lovely hell-green flames." "Hell" is a word from the Christian allegory, but here it is "green" and it is "lovely." Why might nature be associated with hell?

In the Christian story of the world, natural sexual passions are immoral and should be controlled. What do you think Bishop thinks of this position? She has remarked that the tapestry is about "Sin," but then she describes a beautiful nature that seems at odds with the allegory of sin. She even links that beautiful nature which resembles art to "hell," that place of punishment in the Christian story for, among others, those who indulge sexual passions. Does she feel that the imposition of an allegorical story about sin on this beautiful natural world is unnatural? But what is unnatural about a story about sin?

What do you make of the next line of this stanza? It seems to describe words put into the tapestry in Portuguese. But why "yes" and "no"? What might this have to do with the allegory of sin? It suggests a simple choice, but does the painting seem to allow such simplicity?

The final four lines might explain this. What is going on here? Notice the use of the word "wicked." What are some of its meanings – both positive and negative? Why might Bishop use it, and is it ironic?

The lizards are clearly filled with lust for the female, and the painting is instructing the viewer to think that such lust is "Sin." Bishop seems to think otherwise. Her nature is vividly beautiful, and it is hard to imagine her thinking anything natural would be sinful, especially lust. She's trying, I think, to make us feel that there is something wrong with imposing those kinds of moral meanings on nature. Nature is beautiful in itself; it is like art, and we should appreciate it as such.

Bishop begins the final stanza by comparing the Christian colonialists to the lizards. This is not a very complimentary thing to do, of course. And it gets worse. They are "hard as nails, / tiny as nails." Why? What does being like "nails" suggest about them and their purpose in coming to Brazil?

In this stanza, she brings together the two ways of thinking about art and nature she has summoned in the first two stanzas. In stanza 1, nature resembles art. In stanza 2, art resembles nature. Here, the colonialists encounter a nature that is "not unfamiliar" because it is somehow linked to "lovers' walks" and "bowers" and "lute music." These are all things you might expect to see in tapestries in Europe at this point in history. Many of the tapestries having to do with mythological stories portrayed nymphs and lovers and had to do with courtship. That may explain the racy line "no cherries to be picked," which refers to a slang term for breaking a hymen. Why does Bishop characterize European art in this way? What does she seem to think of it? How does her negativity toward the colonialists carry over into her assessment of their art?

The nature the colonialists encounter is not like the tapestries, but it corresponds "nevertheless / to an old dream of wealth and luxury." What might this mean? You might try to find a picture of the kind of tapestry she has in mind, one in which nymphs and young aristocrats gambol and play in natural settings, usually ornate gardens that suggest wealth and luxury.

Why does she emphasize that this picture of the world is already out of style in 1502?

We all carry images in our minds that oftentimes correspond to reality and sometimes do not. The most obvious kinds of images might be those having to do with other countries or ethnic groups. And the most obviously inaccurate ones would be prejudicial. They reflect our desires and fears rather than reality. But they nevertheless affect our behavior toward the world or the people about whom we have those mental images. That said, what kinds of images do the Europeans have in their minds? And what are the implications for their actions of holding those images? How are the images inaccurate?

The "old dream" imported from Europe includes a "brand-new pleasure." You soon learn what that is. The Portuguese colonists seek out the Indian women, each wanting one "for himself." What they want, of course, is sexual pleasure, and that should remind you of the second stanza and of its meditation on the Christian notion of "Sin." How does Bishop alert you to the contrast between the Christian account and the actions of the men? How does she alert you to the violent nature of their desire? And why does she refer to the natural landscape as a "hanging fabric" here?

Finally, how are the Indian women portrayed? Does Bishop indicate resistance on their part to what is being done to them? And why does she underscore the sexual character of this act of colonialism? How does it allow her to critique the Europeans?

The next poem, "The Burglar of Babylon," concerns life in the slums around Rio de Janeiro. The city is surrounded by *favelas* that have grown up the mountains surrounding the city.

Read the poem through and ask yourself why it has such a sing-song rhythm. What might Bishop's point be in writing it in this, for her, very anomalous form? It seems reminiscent of a ballad, and ballads often were about popular heroes.

But can Micucu be called a popular hero?

Much time has passed since the Portuguese invasion, but have things changed in Brazil? Notice that Micucu has an Indian name. The rich, who are seen through the binoculars used to observe the soldiers' hunt for the renegade, are probably, given the way economics and ethnicity divide in South America, descended from the Portuguese colonizers. Many of the poor on the hills are probably economic migrants from inland and are probably of Indian descent. What is the significance of Bishop's characterization of them as a "fearful stain"?

Why does she take such care about translating the names they have given the hills on which they live? And why translate them literally? What effect does it have? What is the significance of the different names? What does Babylon refer to?

How does Bishop try to humanize Micucu? Notice his relationship with his aunt, and his interactions with those he meets. Bishop calls him an "enemy of society," but can she be said to side with him?

Notice how she treats the soldiers, especially the one who shoots the officer in command. What is significant about her characterization of him? And why does she note of the officer that he was "the youngest of eleven"?

Micucu's attempt to live as long as possible is juxtaposed to elements of ordinary life, such as people going to the beach. Why does Bishop do this? How do such juxtapositions add an element of sympathy to the portrait of Micucu?

What do you make of the slightly comic conversation that takes place amongst patrons of his aunt's shop after he dies? Bishop was a liberal, and the liberal position regarding crime is that it is the effect of economic environment. Does Bishop do anything to advance that idea here?

Exercise 10.3   Toni Morrison, *The Bluest Eye*

Frantz Fanon in *Black Face, White Masks* describes the painful encounter between former colonial subjects and their masters when blacks visit the metropolitan center as being vexed by almost tragic psychological dynamics. The blacks, many of whom have internalized the racist assumptions of the masters and who, as a result, believe blacks are inferior because they lack the marks of civilization the whites possess such as a better language, try to emulate their masters. They adopt metropolitan modes of speech especially, but they often make gaffes regarding social etiquette that betray their colonial origins. Fanon is describing a period in the distant past, roughly the 1940s and 1950s, and much has changed since then. The colonies are gone and so are the relations he describes.

Morrison in *The Bluest Eye* describes such a colonial subject – Soaphead Church. Go back and read her account of him. How is he harmed by his colonial experience? How does he behave in relation to the culture of the colonial masters?

Exercise 10.4   Kieran Desai, *The Inheritance of Loss*

This is a funny/sad novel in which Desai paints a complex portrait of contemporary India in a language and style that draw on both traditional literary forms and elements of Indian oral culture, the spoken language especially of different classes or groups of people.

You might begin by locating places where the two different styles – traditional English and popular oral – are used. What might be the point of this stylistic mixture? How does it fit with the world the novel depicts and the attitude Desai demonstrates toward it? Are there moments when the two styles are in direct contact?

The story is framed by the Gorkhaland uprising in the mid-1980s. You might consult the following website for information about the conflict: <http://countrystudies.us/india/78.htm>. How are the Gorkha nationalists depicted? Do you get a sense that their cause is just? How does Desai balance a record of their grievances with a depiction of the wrongs they do?

The novel is structured as an alternation between Biju's experiences in New York and Sai and the others' experiences at home in West Bengal. How do Biju's experiences act as a counterpoint to what is going on at home? How is life for Indians in the US portrayed? What are the major concerns and aspirations of migrants? How are these different from life at home?

The natural landscape plays a strong role in the novel. How is it used? Try to find moments where the landscape and the environment have a significant place in the characters' lives. How is the landscape itself a commentary on the events of the novel?

India is divided into regions that are often specific to one ethnic group. But, clearly as well, there is quite a bit of migration and ethnic mixture. How is ethnicity a feature of the story? Where do you see it become a source of conflict?

In a country that is so poor, class difference can also be an important feature of people's lives. Where do you see class difference at work in the novel?

Another dimension of class and ethnic difference in Indian history has to do with British colonialism. The British controlled India from the late eighteenth century down to 1947. They were different ethnically, and they were more powerful economically. Those differences warped relations between the Indians and the British, and they distorted the kinds of life aspirations Indians could have. How do you see these issues played out in the life of the judge especially? How is his life warped by British dominance in India? What does he lose by virtue of his aspiration to become a British civil servant?

In part, the novel is about the clash between tradition and modernity. How is traditional Indian life portrayed? What are its significant elements? Modernity would be everything having to do with life in England or America. How does that enter into the story? Where do you see clashes between the two erupting? Think of the Christmas tree dispute between Sai and Gyan.

Sai and Gyan are central characters. How do they bring into focus many of the core conflicts, especially between tradition and modernity, that the novel examines? How in their lives do we see emotions at work such as pride and shame that get connected to class, ethnicity, and nationality? How do these emotions blind the characters to their real interests or to what would make them happy?

Poor Mutt. First loved, then stolen, then in all likelihood abused. How is he a symbol of modernity? Why is it significant that he is stolen by people who are poor and whose relative was abused by the police? How do they fit into the novel? What do they represent? And why steal from the judge? Notice that this second theft repeats the initial theft of the guns.

Mutt's departure coincides with Biju's return. Why? What are the important elements of Biju's return? He is literally stripped of everything American by people who represent traditional ethnic affiliations and pre-modern nationalist loyalties. How does Biju's return embody a choice between an infatuation with modernity that might be flawed and a sense of cultural belonging that might entail sacrifices but that might also bring with it some good things? Why end, for example, with the joyful reunion with his father?

How does that serve as a counterpoint to Sai's epiphany, her insight into her own place in the universe?

Exercise 10.5 *Hyenas, The Fellowship of the Ring, Life and Debt,* and *Paradise Now*

I will not say much about *Life and Debt* other than to note that it is a good examination of the effects of economic globalization on formerly colonized countries.

These films are oddly matched, but so are the different parts of the modern world. Some are white, wealthy, and well fed; others are dark-skinned, poor, and undernourished. Some enjoy the "freedom" of a modern capitalist global economy; others – usually inhabitants of countries in Asia, South America, and Africa – are comparatively less free and often work for a pittance in a factory under fairly stern discipline to make clothes and consumer goods for the first group. In many respects, the modern global economy, which consists largely of extracting value from underpaid labor in Asia, Africa, and South America, is a kind of soft colonialism. No armies are needed now, no civil servants. Just investment bankers and the compulsion of what euphemistically is called the "market," that set of pay ratios and price differentials that ensures that a small minority benefits enormously from the under-rewarded labors of the many. The economic process itself guarantees that large sectors of the world population are subordinated to the will of a modern global neocolonial investment class.

The most powerful economic countries also get to make the movies watched all over the world. Oftentimes in those movies, people with dark skins are portrayed as evil or monstrous. They seem to deserve their economic subordination in the modern global economy. Occasionally, people with dark skins get to make movies of their own. Many of them take issue with the way commerce rules the world and with the way the rulers of commerce rule them. As in African film-maker Diop Mambety's *Hyenas*, they suggest that wealth should not equal power and that commerce corrupts.

Hyenas is a story about how a longing for modern consumer goods corrupts the morals of a small African community. *The Lord of the Rings* is a story of how virtuous whites triumph over an army of blacks who are portrayed as animals. And *Paradise Now* is a story of how people angry at neocolonial mistreatment strike back using the informal military tactic of a terrorist bombing.

Hyenas is an adaptation into an African context of a play by Friedrich Dürrenmatt. It depicts a community that is moved to sacrifice its values and to murder one of its members by the lure of consumer goods from the metropolitan center.

How is the community first presented? How is a norm established that will later be breached? What is Draman's function in the community?

Why does everyone fall for the lure of consumer goods so easily? How does Diop remind the viewer of how vulnerable they are to the lure of "modernity"?

Finally, is what happens in the end justified? What do you make of the visual metaphors of wild animals? What is Diop suggesting about human nature?

The *Lord of the Rings* trilogy begins with a charming portrait of simple, home-loving hobbits who seem to care for nothing but their own comfort. They are a little like first-world people who are oblivious to how much their own economic comfort depends on cheap labor abroad. A few members of this comfortably homogeneous community venture out into the world and discover that there are dark-skinned monsters out there full of violent hatred of them.

Consider the rest of the first film, *The Fellowship of the Ring*, in this light. How are dark-skinned people represented? Often, racist representations are topographical in that what is upper or above is good and white, while what is lower or below is bad and black.

Are there moments of a "Nordic" flavoring in the film, where things Teutonic or north European seem to be associated with virtue? And what do you make of the discussion between Aragorn and Boromir about "my people"? Boromir means a particular race of white men. How is this significant in light of the battle going on all around them? How are the creatures who kill Boromir portrayed in contrast to the whites?

Notice the kinds of behavior each group engages in: how the whites are like a family (a community like the one that opens the film) while the blacks are an anonymous, family-less mass. Civilization arises when we engage in "civil" behavior with one another – reciprocal bonding or agreements. How does this fit in here? How are the whites characterized as more "civil" in this sense than the blacks?

Consider now an example of a film made in response to this kind of cultural racism. In recent years, people without power who feel abused by countries like the US have used violence to make their positions known. That violence – called "terrorism" – usually originates in grievances having to do with such things as the US-backed occupation of Palestine by Israel or with the maintaining of US armies in lands such as Saudi Arabia that are owned and run by corrupt family regimes.

Paradise Now is a controversial film because it makes a case for understanding the motives of Palestinian suicide bombers. What is that case?

How do the film-makers portray relations between Israelis and Palestinians? Pay attention to Suha's crossing into Palestine. The film-makers seem to go to some trouble to underscore that the guard and she resemble one another. Why?

How are the lives of young Palestinian men portrayed? How do their economic prospects appear? What is the point of the vignette in the care repair yard?

What is Suha's role in the film? She has been slightly westernized. What difference does this make? How does she contrast with the brothers, Khaled and Said? And why do the film-makers establish the possibility of a relationship between her and Said?

The vocabulary of this film is quite different from what you would expect from standard Hollywood fare. There is no star, no emphasis on a moral point, no love story. How is the film different? What point might the film-makers want to make by deliberately choosing this style of storytelling? How might it aid the portrait of life under colonial rule that they are drawing?

When Said and Khaled are driving around Israel we get a very brief glimpse of life on the other side. What do the film-makers want you to see here? Why include this piece of the story?

Finally, the film becomes more of a polemic and less of a depiction near the end. What is important about the bus on which Said sits, waiting to explode his bomb? And what do you make of the voiceover at the end?

Does the film want us to come away feeling that violence against colonial oppressors is justified? Or does it want us to simply think about the situation it has depicted?

Do you sympathize with Said by the end?

APPENDIX A

Helpful Websites

http://130.179.92.25/Arnason_DE/Backmaterials.html
http://www.press.jhu.edu/books/hopkins_guide_to_literary_theory/
http://vos.ucsb.edu/

APPENDIX B

Elizabeth Bishop
"In the Village"

A scream, the echo of a scream, hangs over that Nova Scotian village. No one hears it; it hangs there forever, a slight stain in those pure blue skies, skies that travelers compare to those of Switzerland, too dark, too blue, so that they seem to keep on darkening a little more around the horizon – or is it around the rims of the eyes? – the color of the cloud of bloom on the elm trees, the violet on the fields of oats; something darkening over the woods and waters as well as the sky. The scream hangs like that, unheard, in memory – in the past, in the present, and those years between. It was not even loud to begin with, perhaps. It just came there to live, forever – not loud, just alive forever. Its pitch would be the pitch of my village. Flick the lightning rod on top of the church steeple with your fingernail and you will hear it.

She stood in the large front bedroom with sloping walls on either side, papered in wide white and dim-gold stripes. Later, it was she who gave the scream.

The village dressmaker was fitting a new dress. It was her first in almost two years and she had decided to come out of black, so the dress was purple. She was very thin. She wasn't at all sure whether she was going to like the dress or not and she kept lifting the folds of the skirt, still unpinned and dragging on the floor around her, in her thin white hands, and looking down at the cloth.

"Is it a good shade for me? Is it too bright? I don't know. I haven't worn colors for so long now . . . How long? Should it be black? Do you think I should keep on wearing black?"

Drummers sometimes came around selling gilded red or green books, unlovely books, filled with bright new illustrations of the Bible stories. The people in the pictures wore clothes like the purple dress, or like the way it looked then.

It was a hot summer afternoon. Her mother and her two sisters were there. The older sister had brought her home, from Boston, not long before, and was staying on, to help. Because in Boston she had not got any better, in months and months – or had it been a year? In spite of the doctors, in spite of the frightening expenses, she had not got any better.

First, she had come home, with her child. Then she had gone away again, alone, and left the child. Then she had come home. Then she had gone away again, with her sister; and now she was home again.

Unaccustomed to having her back, the child stood now in the doorway, watching. The dressmaker was crawling around and around on her knees eating pins as Nebuchadnezzar had crawled eating grass. The wallpaper glinted and the elm trees outside hung heavy and green, and the straw matting smelled like the ghost of hay.

Clang.

Clang.

Oh, beautiful sounds, from the blacksmith's shop at the end of the garden! Its gray roof, with patches of moss, could be seen above the lilac bushes. Nate was there – Nate, wearing a long black leather apron over his trousers and bare chest, sweating hard, a black leather cap on top of dry, thick, black-and-gray curls, a black sooty face; iron filings, whiskers, and gold teeth, all together, and a smell of red-hot metal and horses' hoofs.

Clang.

The pure note: pure and angelic.

The dress was all wrong. She screamed.

The child vanishes.

Later they sit, the mother and the three sisters, in the shade on the back porch, sipping sour, diluted ruby: raspberry vinegar. The dressmaker refuses to join them and leaves, holding the dress to her heart. The child is visiting the blacksmith.

In the blacksmith's shop things hang up in the shadows and shadows hang up in the things, and there are black and glistening piles of dust in each corner. A tub of night-black water stands by the forge. The horseshoes sail through the dark like bloody little moons and follow each other like bloody little moons to drown in the black water, hissing, protesting.

Outside, along the matted eaves, painstakingly, sweetly, wasps go over and over a honeysuckle vine.

Inside, the bellows creak. Nate does wonders with both hands; with one hand. The attendant horse stamps his foot and nods his head as if agreeing to a peace treaty.

Nod.

And nod.

A Newfoundland dog looks up at him and they almost touch noses, but not quite, because at the last moment the horse decides against it and turns away.

Outside in the grass lie scattered big, pale granite discs, like millstones, for making wheel rims on. This afternoon they are too hot to touch.

Now it is settling down, the scream.

Now the dressmaker is at home, basting, but in tears. It is the most beautiful material she has worked on in years. It has been sent to the woman from Boston, a present from her mother-in-law, and heaven knows how much it cost.

Before my older aunt had brought her back, I had watched my grandmother and younger aunt unpacking her clothes, her "things." In trunks and barrels and boxes they had finally come, from Boston, where she and I had once lived. So many things in the village came from Boston, and even I had once come from there. But I remembered only being here, with my grandmother.

The clothes were black, or white, or black-and-white.

"Here's a mourning hat," says my grandmother, holding up something large, sheer, and black, with large black roses on it; at least I guess they are roses, even if black.

"There's that mourning coat she got the first winter," says my aunt.

But always I think they are saying "morning." Why, in the morning, did one put on black? How early in the morning did one begin? Before the sun came up?

"Oh, here are some housedresses!"

They are nicer. Clean and starched, stiffly folded. One with black polka dots. One of fine black-and-white stripes with black grosgrain bows. A third with a black velvet bow and on the bow a pin of pearls in a little wreath.

"Look. She forgot to take it off."

A white hat. A white embroidered parasol. Black shoes with buckles glistening like the dust in the blacksmith's shop. A silver mesh bag. A silver calling-card case on a little chain. Another bag of silver mesh, gathered to a tight, round neck of strips of silver that will open out, like the hatrack in the front hall. A silver-framed photograph, quickly turned over. Handkerchiefs with narrow black hems – "morning handkerchiefs." In bright sunlight, over breakfast tables, they flutter.

A bottle of perfume has leaked and made awful brown stains.

Oh, marvelous scent, from somewhere else! It doesn't smell like that here; but there, somewhere, it does, still.

A big bundle of postcards. The curdled elastic around them breaks. I gather them together on the floor.

Some people wrote with pale-blue ink, and some with brown, and some with black, but mostly blue. The stamps have been torn off many of them. Some are plain, or photographs, but some have lines of metallic crystals on them – how beautiful! – silver, gold, red, and green, or all four mixed together, crumbling off, sticking in the lines on my palms. All the cards like this I spread on the floor to study. The crystals outline the buildings on the cards in a way buildings never are outlined but should be – if there were a way of making the crystals stick. But probably not; they would fall to the ground, never to be seen again. Some cards, instead of lines around the buildings, have words written in their skies with the same stuff, crumbling, dazzling and crumbling, raining down a little on little people who sometimes stand about below: pictures of Pentecost? What are the messages? I cannot tell, but they are falling on those specks of hands, on the hats, on the toes of their shoes, in their paths – wherever it is they are.

Postcards come from another world, the world of the grandparents who send things, the world of sad brown perfume, and morning. (The gray postcards of the village for sale in the village store are so unilluminating that they scarcely count. After all, one steps outside and immediately sees the same thing: the village, where we live, full-size, and in color.)

Two barrels of china. White with a gold band. Broken bits. A thick white teacup with a small red-and-blue butterfly on it, painfully desirable. A teacup with little pale-blue windows in it.

"See the grains of rice?" says my grandmother, showing me the cup against the light.

Could you poke the grains out? No, it seems they aren't really there any more. They were put there just for a while and then they left something or other behind. What odd things people do with grains of rice, so innocent and small! My aunt says that she has heard they write the Lord's Prayer on them. And make them make those little pale-blue lights.

More broken china. My grandmother says it breaks her heart. "Why couldn't they have got it packed better? Heaven knows what it cost."

"Where'll we put it all? The china closet isn't nearly big enough."

"It'll just have to stay in the barrels."

"Mother, you might as well use it."

"*No*," says my grandmother.

"Where's the silver, Mother?"

"In the vault in Boston."

Vault. Awful word. I run the tip of my finger over the rough, jeweled lines on the postcards, over and over. They hold things up to each other and exclaim, and talk, and exclaim, over and over.

"There's that cake basket."

"Mrs. Miles . . ."

"Mrs. Miles's sponge cake . . ."

"She was very fond of her."

Another photograph – "Oh, that *Negro* girl! That friend."

"She went to be a medical missionary. She had a letter from her, last winter. From Africa."

"They were great friends."

They show me the picture. She, too, is black-and-white, with glasses on a chain. A morning friend.

And the smell, the wonderful smell of the dark-brown stains. Is it roses?

A tablecloth.

"She did beautiful work," says my grandmother.

"But look – it isn't finished."

Two pale, smooth wooden hoops are pressed together in the linen. There is a case of little ivory embroidery tools.

I abscond with a little ivory stick with a sharp point. To keep it forever I bury it under the bleeding heart by the crab-apple tree, but it is never found again.

Nate sings and pumps the bellows with one hand. I try to help, but he really does it all, from behind me, and laughs when the coals blow red and wild.

"Make me a ring! Make me a ring, Nate!"

Instantly it is made; it is mine.

It is too big and still hot, and blue and shiny. The horseshoe nail has a flat oblong head, pressing hot against my knuckle.

Two men stand watching, chewing or spitting tobacco, matches, horseshoe nails – anything, apparently, but with such presence; they are perfectly at home. The horse is the real guest, however. His harness hangs loose like a man's suspenders; they say pleasant things to him; one of his legs is doubled up in an improbable, affectedly polite way, and the bottom of his hoof is laid bare, but he doesn't seem to mind. Manure piles up behind him, suddenly, neatly. He, too, is very much at home. He is enormous. His rump is like a brown, glossy globe of the whole brown world. His ears are secret entrances to the underworld. His nose is supposed to feel like velvet and does, with ink spots under milk all over its pink. Clear bright-green bits of stiffened froth, like glass, are stuck around his mouth. He wears medals on his chest, too, and one on his forehead, and simpler decorations – red and blue celluloid rings overlapping each other on leather straps. On each temple is a clear glass bulge, like an eyeball, but in them are the heads of two other little horses (his dreams?), brightly colored, real and raised, untouchable, alas, against backgrounds of silver blue. His trophies hang around him, and the cloud of his odor is a chariot in itself.

At the end, all four feet are brushed with tar, and shine, and he expresses his satisfaction, rolling it from his nostrils like noisy smoke, as he backs into the shafts of his wagon.

The purple dress is to be fitted again this afternoon but I take a note to Miss Gurley to say the fitting will have to be postponed. Miss Gurley seems upset.

"Oh dear. And how is –" And she breaks off.

Her house is littered with scraps of cloth and tissue-paper patterns, yellow, pinked, with holes in the shapes of *A*, *B*, *C*, and *D* in them, and numbers; and threads everywhere like a fine vegetation. She has a bosom full of needles with threads ready to pull out and make nests with. She sleeps in her thimble. A gray kitten once lay on the treadle of her sewing machine, where she rocked it as she sewed, like a baby in a cradle, but it got hanged on the belt. Or did she make that up? But another gray-and-white one lies now by the arm of the machine, in imminent danger of being sewn into a turban. There is a table covered with laces and braids, embroidery silks, and cards of buttons of all colors – big ones for winter coats, small pearls, little glass ones delicious to suck.

She has made the very dress I have on, "for twenty-five cents." My grandmother said my other grandmother would certainly be surprised at that.

The purple stuff lies on a table; long white threads hang all about it. Oh, look away before it moves by itself, or makes a sound; before it echoes, echoes, what it has heard!

Mysteriously enough, poor Miss Gurley – I know she is poor – gives me a five-cent piece. She leans over and drops it in the pocket of the red-and-white dress that she has made herself. It is very tiny, very shiny. King George's beard is like a little silver flame. Because they look like herring- or maybe salmon-scales, five-cent pieces are called "fish scales." One heard of people's rings being found inside fish, or their long-lost jackknives. What if one could scrape a salmon and find a little picture of King George on every scale?

I put my five-cent piece in my mouth for greater safety on the way home, and swallowed it. Months later, as far as I know, it is still in me, transmuting all its precious metal into my growing teeth and hair.

Back home, I am not allowed to go upstairs. I hear my aunts running back and forth, and something like a tin washbasin falls bump in the carpeted upstairs hall.

My grandmother is sitting in the kitchen stirring potato mash for tomorrow's bread and crying into it. She gives me a spoonful and it tastes wonderful but wrong. In it I think I taste my grandmother's tears; then I kiss her and taste them on her cheek.

She says it is time for her to get fixed up, and I say I want to help her brush her hair. So I do, standing swaying on the lower rung of the back of her rocking chair.

The rocking chair has been painted and repainted so many times that it is as smooth as cream – blue, white, and gray all showing through. My grandmother's hair is silver and in it she keeps a great many celluloid combs, at the back and sides, streaked gray and silver to match. The one at the back has longer teeth than the others and a row of sunken silver dots across the top, beneath a row of little balls. I pretend to play a tune on it; then I pretend to play a tune on each of the others before we stick them in, so my grandmother's hair is full of music. She laughs. I am so pleased with myself that I do not feel obliged to mention the five-cent piece. I drink a rusty, icy drink out of the biggest dipper; still, nothing much happens.

We are waiting for a scream. But it is not screamed again, and the red sun sets in silence.

Every morning I take the cow to the pasture we rent from Mr. Chisolm. She, Nelly, could probably go by herself just as well, but I like marching through the village with a big stick, directing her.

This morning it is brilliant and cool. My grandmother and I are alone again in the kitchen. We are talking. She says it is cool enough to keep the oven going, to bake the bread, to roast a leg of lamb.

"Will you remember to go down to the brook? Take Nelly around by the brook and pick me a big bunch of mint. I thought I'd make some mint sauce."

"For the leg of lamb?"

"You finish your porridge."

"I think I've had enough now . . ."

"Hurry up and finish that porridge."

There is talking on the stairs.

"No, now wait," my grandmother says to me. "Wait a minute."

My two aunts come into the kitchen. She is with them, wearing the white cotton dress with black polka dots and the flat black velvet bow at the neck. She comes and feeds me the rest of the porridge herself, smiling at me.

"Stand up now and let's see how tall you are," she tells me.

"Almost to your elbow," they say. "See how much she's grown."

"Almost."

"It's her hair."

Hands are on my head, pushing me down; I slide out from under them. Nelly is waiting for me in the yard, holding her nose just under in the watering trough. My stick waits against the door frame, clad in bark.

Nelly looks up at me, drooling glass strings. She starts off around the corner of the house without a flicker of expression.

Switch. Switch. How annoying she is!

But she is a Jersey and we think she is very pretty. "From in front," my aunts sometimes add.

She stops to snatch at the long, untrimmed grass around the gatepost.

"Nelly!"

Whack! I hit her hipbone.

On she goes without even looking around. Flop, flop, down over the dirt sidewalk into the road, across the village green in front of the Presbyterian church. The grass is gray with dew; the church is dazzling. It is high-shouldered and secretive; it leans backwards a little.

Ahead, the road is lined with dark, thin old elms; grass grows long and blue in the ditches. Behind the elms the meadows run along, peacefully, greenly.

We pass Mrs. Peppard's house. We pass Mrs. McNeil's house. We pass Mrs. Geddes's house. We pass Hills' store.

The store is high, and a faded gray-blue, with tall windows, built on a long, high stoop of gray-blue cement with an iron hitching rail along it. Today, in one window there are big cardboard easels, shaped like houses – complete houses and houses with the roofs lifted off to show glimpses of the rooms inside, all in different colors – with cans of paint in pyramids in the middle. But they are an old story. In the other window is something new: shoes, single shoes, summer shoes, each sitting on top of its own box with its mate beneath it, inside, in the dark. Surprisingly, some of them appear to be exactly the colors and texture of pink and blue blackboard chalks, but I can't stop to examine them now. In one door, great overalls hang high in the air on hangers. Miss Ruth Hill looks out the other door and waves. We pass Mrs. Captain Mahon's house.

Nelly tenses and starts walking faster, making over to the right. Every morning and evening we go through this. We are approaching Miss Spencer's house. Miss Spencer is the milliner the way Miss Gurley is the dressmaker. She has a very small white house with the doorstep right on the sidewalk. One front window has lace curtains with a pale-yellow window shade pulled all the way down, inside them; the other one has a shelf across it on which are displayed four summer hats. Out of the corner of my eye I can see that there is a yellow chip straw with little wads of flamingo-colored feathers around the crown, but again there is no time to examine anything.

On each side of Miss Spencer's door is a large old lilac bush. Every time we go by, Nelly determines to brush off all her flies on these bushes – brush them off forever, in one fell swoop. Then Miss Spencer is apt to come to the door and stand there, shaking with anger, between the two bushes still shaking from Nelly's careening passage, and yell at me, sometimes waving a hat in my direction as well.

Nelly, leaning to the right, breaks into a cow trot. I run up with my stick.

Whack!

"Nelly!"

Whack!

Just this once she gives in and we rush safely by.

Then begins a long, pleasant stretch beneath the elms. The Presbyterian manse has a black iron fence with openwork four-sided pillars, like tall, thin bird cages, bird cages for storks. Dr. Gillespie, the minister, appears just as we come along, and rides slowly toward us on his bicycle.

"Good day." He even tips his hat.

"Good day."

He wears the most interesting hat in the village: a man's regular stiff straw sailor, only it is black. Is there a possibility that he paints it at home, with something like stove polish? Because once I had seen one of my aunts painting a straw-colored hat navy blue.

Nelly, oblivious, makes cow flops. Smack. Smack. Smack. Smack.

It is fascinating. I cannot take my eyes off her. Then I step around them: fine dark-green and lacy and watery at the edges.

We pass the McLeans', whom I know very well. Mr. McLean is just coming out of his new barn with the tin hip roof and with him is Jock, their old shepherd dog, long-haired, black and white and yellow. He runs up barking deep, cracked, soft barks in the quiet morning. I hesitate.

Mr. McLean bellows, "Jock! You! Come back here! Are you trying to frighten her?"

To me he says, "He's twice as old as you are."

Finally I pat the big round warm head.

We talk a little. I ask the exact number of Jock's years but Mr. McLean has forgotten.

"He hasn't hardly a tooth in his head and he's got rheumatism. I hope we'll get him through next winter. He still wants to go to the woods with me and it's hard for him in the snow. We'll be lost without him."

Mr. McLean speaks to me behind one hand, not to hurt Jock's feelings: "*Deaf as a post.*"

Like anybody deaf, Jock puts his head to one side.

"He used to be the best dog at finding cows for miles around. People used to come from away down the shore to borrow him to find their cows for them. And he'd always find them. The first year we had to leave him behind when we went up to the mountain to get the cows I thought it would kill him. Well, when his teeth started going he couldn't do much with the cows any more. Effie used to say, "I don't know how we'd run the farm without him.' "

Loaded down with too much black and yellow and white fur, Jock smiles, showing how few teeth he has. He has yellow caterpillars for eyebrows.

Nelly has gone on ahead. She is almost up the hill to Chisolms' when I catch up with her. We turn in to their steep, long drive, through a steep, bare yard crowded with unhappy apple trees. From the top, though, from the Chisolms' back yard, one always stops to look at the view.

There are the tops of all the elm tress in the village and there, beyond them, the long green marshes, so fresh, so salt. Then the Minas Basin, with the tide halfway in or out, the wet red mud glazed with sky blue until it meets the creeping lavender-red water. In the middle of the view, like one hand of a clock pointing straight up, is the steeple of the Presbyterian church. We are in the "Maritimes" but all that means is that we live by the sea.

Mrs. Chisolm's pale frantic face is watching me out the kitchen window as she washes the breakfast dishes. We wave, but I hurry by because she may come out and ask questions. But her questions are not as bad perhaps as those of her husband, Mr. Chisolm, who wears a beard. One evening he had met me in the pasture and asked me how my soul was. Then he held me firmly by both hands while he said a prayer, with his head bowed, Nelly right beside us chewing her cud all the time. I had felt a soul, heavy in my chest, all the way home.

I let Nelly through the set of bars to the pasture where the brook is, to get the mint. We both take drinks and I pick a big bunch of mint, eating a little, scratchy and powerful. Nelly looks over her shoulder and comes back to try it, thinking, as cows do, it might be something especially for her. Her face is close to mine and I hold her by one horn to admire her eyes again. Her nose is blue and as shiny as something in the rain. At such close quarters my feelings for her are mixed. She gives my bare arm a lick, scratchy and powerful, too, almost upsetting me into the brook; then she goes off to join a black-and-white friend she has here, mooing to her to wait until she catches up.

For a while I entertain the idea of not going home today at all, of staying safely here in the pasture all day, playing in the brook and climbing on the squishy, moss-covered hummocks in the swampy part. But an immense, sibilant, glistening loneliness suddenly faces me, and the cows are moving off to the shade of the fir trees, their bells chiming softly, individually.

One the way home there are the four hats in Miss Spencer's window to study, and the summer shoes in Hills'. There is the same shoe in white, in black patent leather, and in the chalky, sugary, unearthly pinks and blues. It has straps that button around the ankle and above, four of them, about an inch wide and an inch apart, reaching away up.

In those unlovely gilded red and green books, filled with illustrations of the Bible stories, the Roman centurions wear them, too, or something very like them.

Surely they are my size, Surely, this summer, pink or blue, my grandmother will buy me a pair!

Miss Ruth Hill gives me a Moirs chocolate out of the glass case. She talks to me: "How is she? We've always been friends. We played together from the time we were babies. We sat together in school. Right from primer class on. After she went away, she always wrote to me – even after she got sick the first time."

Then she tells a funny story about when they were little.

That afternoon, Miss Gurley comes and we go upstairs to watch the purple dress being fitted again. My grandmother holds me against her knees. My younger aunt is helping Miss Gurley, handing her the scissors when she asks. Miss Gurley is cheerful and talkative today.

The dress is smaller now; there are narrow, even folds down the skirt; the sleeves fit tightly, with little wrinkles over the thin white hands. Everyone is very pleased with it; everyone talks and laughs.

"There. You see? It's so becoming."

"I've never seen you in anything more becoming."

"And it's so nice to see you in color for a change."

And the purple is real, like a flower against the gold-and-white wallpaper.

On the bureau is a present that has just come, from an uncle in Boston whom I do not remember. It is a gleaming little bundle of flat, triangular satin pillows – sachets, tied together with a white satin ribbon, with an imitation rosebud on top of the bow. Each is a different faint color; if you take them apart, each has a different faint scent. But tied together the way they came, they make one confused, powdery odor.

The mirror has been lifted off the bureau and put on the floor against the wall.

She walks slowly up and down and looks at the skirt in it.

"I think that's about right," says Miss Gurley, down on her knees and looking into the mirror, too, but as if the skirt were miles and miles away.

But, twitching the purple skirt with her thin white hands, she says desperately, "I don't know what they're wearing any more. I have no *idea*!" It turns to a sort of wail.

"Now, now," soothes Miss Gurley. "I do think that's about right. Don't you?" She appeals to my grandmother and me.

Light, musical, constant sounds are coming from Nate's shop. It sounds as though he were making a wheel rim.

She sees me in the mirror and turns on me: "Stop sucking your thumb!"

Then in a moment she turns to me again and demands, "Do you know what I want?"

"No."

"I want some humbugs. I'm dying for some humbugs. I don't think I've had any humbugs for years and years and years. If I give you some pennies, will you go to Mealy's and buy me a bag?"

To be sent on an errand! Everything is all right.

Humbugs are a kind of candy, although not a kind I am particularly fond of. They are brown, like brook water, but hard, and shaped like little twisted pillows. They last a long time, but lack the spit-producing brilliance of cherry or strawberry.

Mealy runs a little shop where she sells candy and bananas and oranges and all kinds of things she crochets. At Christmas, she sells toys, but only at Christmas. Her real name is Amelia. She also takes care of the telephone switchboard for the village, in her dining room.

Somebody finds a black pocketbook in the bureau. She counts out five big pennies into my hand, in a column, then one more.

"That one's for you. So you won't eat up all my humbugs on the way home."

Further instructions:

"Don't run all the way."

"Don't stop on the bridge."

I do run, by Nate's shop, glimpsing him inside, pumping away with one hand. We wave. The beautiful big Newfoundland dog is there again and comes out, bounding along with me a ways.

I do not stop on the bridge but slow down long enough to find out the years on the pennies. King George is much bigger than on a five-cent piece, brown as an Indian in copper, but he wears the same clothes; on a penny, one can make out the little ermine trimmings on his coat.

Mealy has a bell that rings when you go in so that she'll hear you if she's at the switchboard. The shop is a step down, dark, with a counter along one side. The ceiling is low and the floor has settled well over to the counter side. Mealy is broad and fat and it looks as though she and the counter and the showcase, stuffed dimly with things every which way, were settling down together out of sight.

Five pennies buys a great many humbugs. I must not take too long to decide what I want for myself. I must get back quickly, quickly, while Miss Gurley is there and everyone is upstairs and the dress is still on. Without taking time to think, quickly I point at the brightest thing. It is a ball, glistening solidly with crystals of pink and yellow sugar, hung, impractically, on an elastic, like a real elastic ball. I know I don't even care for the inside of it, which is soft, but I wind most of the elastic

around my arm, to keep the ball off the ground, at least, and start hope-
fully back.

But one night, in the middle of the night, there is a fire. The church
bell wakes me up. It is in the room with me; red flames are burning the
wallpaper beside the bed. I suppose I shriek.

The door opens. My younger aunt comes in. There is a lamp lit in
the hall and everyone is talking at once.

"Don't cry!" my aunt almost shouts to me. It's just a fire. Way up
the road. It isn't going to hurt you. Don't *cry!*"

"Will! Will!" My grandmother is calling my grandfather. "Do you
have to go?"

"No, don't go, Dad!"

"It looks like McLean's place." My grandfather sounds muffled.

"Oh, not their new barn!" My grandmother.

"You can't tell from here." He must have his head out the window.

"*She's* calling for you, Mother." My older aunt: "I'll go."

"No, *I'll* go." My younger aunt.

"Light that other lamp, girl."

My older aunt comes to my door. "It's way off. Its nowhere near us.
The men will take care of it. Now you go to sleep." But she leaves my
door open.

"Leave her door open," calls my grandmother just then. "Oh, why
do they have to ring the bell like that?" It's enough to terrify anybody.
Will, be *careful.*"

Sitting up in bed, I see my grandfather starting down the stairs,
tucking his nightshirt into his trousers as he goes.

"Don't make so much noise!" My older aunt and my grandmother
seem to be quarreling.

"Noise! I can't hear myself think, with that bell!"

"I bet Spurgeon's ringing it!" They both laugh.

"It must have been heat lightning," says my grandmother, now apparently in her bedroom, as if it were all over.

"*She's* all right, Mother." My younger aunt comes back. "I don't
think she's scared. You can't see the glare so much on that side of the
house."

Then my younger aunt comes into my room and gets in bed with me.
She says to go to sleep, it's way up the road. The men have to go; my
grandfather has gone. It's probably somebody's barn full of hay, from
heat lightning. It's been such a hot summer there's been a lot of it. The
church bell stops and her voice is suddenly loud in my ear over my
shoulder. The last echo of the bell lasts for a long time.

Wagons rattle by.

"Now they're going down to the river to fill the barrels," my aunt is murmuring against my back.

The red flame dies down on the wall, then flares again.

Wagons rattle by in the dark. Men are swearing at the horses.

"Now they're coming back with the water. Go to sleep."

More wagons; men's voices. I suppose I go to sleep.

I wake up and it is the same night, the night of the fire. My aunt is getting out of bed, hurrying away. It is still dark and silent now, after the fire. No, not silent; my grandmother is crying somewhere, not in her room. It is getting gray. I hear one wagon, rumbling far off, perhaps crossing the bridge.

But now I am caught in a skein of voices, my aunts' and my grandmother's, saying the same things over and over, sometimes loudly, sometimes in whispers:

"Hurry. For heaven's sake, *shut the door!*"

"Sh!"

"Oh, we can't go on like this, we ..."

"It's too dangerous. Remember that ..."

"Sh! Don't let her ..."

A door slams.

A door opens. The voices begin again.

I am struggling to free myself.

Wait. Wait. No one is going to scream.

Slowly, slowly it gets daylight. A different red reddens the wallpaper. Now the house is silent. I get up and dress by myself and go downstairs. My grandfather is in the kitchen alone, drinking his tea. He has made the oatmeal himself, too. He gives me some and tells me about the fire very cheerfully.

It had not been the McLeans' new barn after all, but someone else's barn, off the road. All the hay was lost but they had managed somehow to save part of the barn.

But neither of us is really listening to what he is saying; we are listening for sounds from upstairs. But everything is quiet.

On the way home from taking Nelly to the pasture I go to see where the barn was. There are people still standing around, some of them the men who got up in the night to go to the river. Everyone seems quite cheerful there, too, but the smell of burned hay is awful, sickening.

Now the front bedroom is empty. My older aunt has gone back to Boston and my other aunt is making plans to go there after a while, too.

There has been a new pig. he was very cute to begin with, and skidded across the kitchen linoleum while everyone laughed. He grew and grew. Perhaps it is all the same summer, because it is unusually hot and something unusual for a pig happens to him: he gets sunburned. He really gets sunburned, bright pink, but the strangest thing of all, the curled-up end of his tail gets so sunburned it is brown and scorched. My grandmother trims it with the scissors and it doesn't hurt him.

Sometime later this pig is butchered. My grandmother, my aunt, and I shut ourselves in the parlor. My aunt plays a piece on the piano called "Out in the Fields." She plays it and plays it; then she switches to Mendelssohn's "War March of the Priests."

The front room is empty. Nobody sleeps there. Clothes are hung there.

Every week my grandmother sends off a package. In it she puts cake and fruit, a jar of preserves, Moirs chocolates.

Monday afternoon every week.

Fruit, cake, Jordan almonds, a handkerchief with a tatted edge.

Fruit. Cake. Wild-strawberry jam. A New Testament.

A little bottle of scent from Hills' store, with a purple silk tassel fastened to the stopper.

Fruit. Cake. "Selections from Tennyson."

A calendar, with a quotation from Longfellow for every day.

Fruit. Cake. Moirs chocolates.

I watch her pack them in the pantry. Sometimes she sends me to the store to get things at the last minute.

The address of the sanatorium is in my grandmother's handwriting, in purple indelible pencil, on smoothed-out wrapping paper. It will never come off.

I take the package to the post office. Going by Nate's, I walk far out in the road and hold the package on the side away from him.

He calls to me. "Come here! I want to show you something."

But I pretend I don't hear him. But at any other time I still go there just the same.

The post office is very small. It sits on the side of the road like a package once delivered by the post office. The government has painted its clapboards tan, with a red trim. The earth in front of it is worn hard. Its face is scarred and scribbled on, carved with initials. In the evening, when the Canadian Pacific mail is due, a row of big boys leans against it, but in the daytime there is nothing to be afraid of. There is no one in front, and inside it is empty. There is no one except the postmaster, Mr. Johnson, to look at my grandmother's purple handwriting.

The post office tilts a little, like Mealy's shop, and inside it looks as chewed as a horse's manger. Mr. Johnson looks out through the little window in the middle of the bank of glass-fronted boxes, like an animal looking out over its manger. But he is dignified by the thick, beveled-edged glass boxes with their solemn, upright gold-and-black-shaded numbers.

Ours is 21. Although there is nothing in it, Mr. Johnson automatically cocks his eye at it from behind when he sees me.

21.

"Well, well. Here we are again. Good day, good day," he says.

"Good day, Mr. Johnson."

I have to go outside again to hand him the package through the ordinary window, into his part of the post office, because it is too big for the little official one. He is very old, and nice. He has two fingers missing on his right hand where they were caught in a threshing machine. He wears a navy-blue cap with a black leather visor, like a ship's officer, and a shirt with feathery brown stripes, and a big gold collar button.

"Let me see. Let me see. Let me see. Hm," he says to himself, weighing the package on the scales, jiggling the bar with the two remaining fingers and thumb.

"Yes. Yes. Your grandmother is very faithful."

Every Monday afternoon I go past the blacksmith's shop with the package under my arm, hiding the address of the sanatorium with my arm and my other hand.

Going over the bridge, I stop and stare down into the river. All the little trout that have been too smart to get caught – for how long now? – are there, rushing in flank movements, foolish assaults and retreats, against and away from the old sunken fender of Malcolm McNeil's Ford. It has lain there for ages and is supposed to be a disgrace to us all. So are the tin cans that glint there, brown and gold.

From above, the trout look as transparent as the water, but if one did catch one, it would be opaque enough, with a little slick moon-white belly with a pair of tiny, pleated, rose-pink fins on it. The leaning willows soak their narrow yellowed leaves.

Clang.

Clang.

Nate is shaping a horseshoe.

Oh, beautiful pure sound!

It turns everything else to silence.

But still, once in a while, the river gives an unexpected gurgle. "*Slp*," it says, out of glassy-ridged brown knots sliding along the surface.

Clang.

And everything except the river holds its breath.

Now there is no scream. Once there was one and it settled slowly down to earth one hot summer afternoon; or did it float up, into that dark, too dark, blue sky? But surely it has gone away, forever.

It sounds like a bell buoy out at sea.

It is the elements speaking: earth, air, fire, water.

All those other things – clothes, crumbling postcards, broken china; things damaged and lost, sickened or destroyed; even the frail almost-lost scream – are they too frail for us to hear their voices long, too mortal?

Nate!

Oh, beautiful sound, strike again!

Index